THE BEST INTERESTS
OF THE CHILD

The Least Detrimental Alternative

JOSEPH GOLDSTEIN

Law School, Yale University

ALBERT J. SOLNIT

Child Study Center, Yale University

SONJA GOLDSTEIN

Eric I. B. Beller, P.C., New Haven

and the late ANNA FREUD

Hampstead Child-Therapy Clinic

THE FREE PRESS

NEW YORK   LONDON   TORONTO   SYDNEY   SINGAPORE

THE FREE PRESS
A Division of Simon & Schuster Inc.
1230 Avenue of the Americas
New York, NY 10020

THE FREE PRESS and colophon are trademarks
of Simon & Schuster Inc.

Designed by Michael Mendelsohn at MM Design 2000, Inc.

Manufactured in the United States of America

10   9   8   7   6   5   4   3   2   1

Library of Congress Cataloging-in-Publication Data

The best interests of the child : the least detrimental alternative /
    Joseph Goldstein . . . [et al.].
       p.   cm.
    "The landmark trilogy of Beyond the best interests of the child,
    Before the best interests of the child, and In the best interests of the child now in one revised
updated volume."
       Includes index.
       ISBN 0-684-82337-3
       1. Custody of children—United States.   2. Parent and child (Law)—United States.
3. Foster home care—Law and legislation—United States.   4. Children—Legal status, laws,
etc.—United States.
    I. Goldstein, Joseph.
    KF547.B47   1996
    346.7301'7—dc20   96-19923
    [347.30617]   CIP

For Our Children
and
Their Spouses

CONTENTS

PREFACE

I n the twenty-three years since publication of *Beyond the Best Interests of the Child*—the first book in the trilogy that included *Before the Best Interests of the Child* and *In the Best Interests of the Child*—the principles contained in the books have become the standard for assessing child placement decision-making in this country. Indeed, it would be difficult to imagine an expert working in the field of child custody or family law in the United States—or in Canada, England, or many other nations—who has not been influenced by these books. The authors' ideas, universally cited in these and related fields, have significantly affected our nation's efforts to deal with child placement conflicts. Now the three present authors have provided an updated and consolidated edition of the original works in this single revised volume.

Readers will benefit from the new format, which no longer requires them to consult separate volumes in putting together the relationship of invocation, adjudication, and disposition in the decision-making process. In addition, the authors now offer an introductory compendium of the central issues raised in the three volumes, providing an integrated discussion of these subjects while also explicating the authors' mode of thought, their knowledge base, and their personal value preferences where relevant. This collaboration involves the ability of the authors to vigorously promote the knowledge of their different disciplines while pointing out the limitations of that knowledge.

The intent of this new volume is to provide a cohesive approach to placement issues that affect children and their families. Decisions made now for such children impact their future and our future as a society. More than 1 million children each year experience the separation or divorce of their parents; more than 1.9 million children are reported to suffer neglect and abuse. This book provides a framework for understanding the chaotic and often disturbing human passions and experiences found in placement conflict cases. The framework consists of presumptions, based on psychoanalytic child development and legal knowledge, that are meant to guide the decision-making process in individual cases. The authors emphasize their intent that the book serve as a guide for organizing the complex data that must be taken into account—whether in the judge's legal decision-making, in the child expert's clinical recommendations, in legislative statutes, in state agencies, or in balancing the freedom in family life that is guaranteed by the Constitution with the needs of children for protection. Such guiding assumptions assist in implementing our society's value preference for the predominance of discretion over rule in placement issues. This book will reduce the temptation to convert guidelines into an instruction manual to be mechanically adhered to and espoused, or opposed and discarded—a temptation that attests to the degree of difficulty often encountered in this area of work.

Written in its present form at the close of the twentieth century, the book can be thought of as providing its own continuity from the beginning of the century, when Sigmund Freud's revolutionary work on the psychology and development of children, *Three Essays on Sexuality,* was published in 1903. That book in turn had a germinal influence on Anna Freud, whose contribution to this volume is memorialized in its authorship.

The new title, and especially the subtitle, convey the authors' belief in the pivotal importance of accepting and understanding that for children who are the subject of placement conflicts, "best" is no longer an option. Realism requires that we look instead to the *least detrimental* placement, defined as "in accord with the child's sense of time and on the basis of short-term predictions . . . that *specific placement* and *procedure for placement* which maximize her opportunity for being wanted and for maintaining, on a continuous, unconditional, and permanent basis, a relationship with at least one adult who is in fact, or is capable of becoming, her psychological parent."

The reader will recognize other key principles associated with the least detrimental alternative: the child's telescoped sense of time, which implies that the younger the child, the greater the urgency for permanent placement; continuity of care as the bedrock of secure parent-child relationships; and the child's need to be wanted. Timely new material is provided in the case selections. In the Baby Richard case, the powerful dynamic tableau created by conflicting interests—the child's, the biological parents', the adoptive parents', and the state's—can be seen as the authors untangle Richard's interests from all other interests. In so doing they point out the corrosive passage of time—especially for such a young child—and the state's diversion away from Richard toward its consideration of parental "fitness" issues; and they trace the searching but ultimately unsatisfactory legal options that resulted in Richard's removal from the only family he had known in the four years of his life.

For a quarter of a century Joseph and Sonja Goldstein together with Anna

Freud and Albert Solnit have offered leadership in developing wider applications of their ideas. Dr. Sally Provence, herself a leading contributor to our knowledge of child development until her death in 1993, noted in her preface to *In* the progressive relief of Yale Child Study Center professionals, led by the authors, as they shifted from feeling overwhelmed in tackling these cases to a stage in their professional growth when they experienced the situations and feelings engendered by the cases as signals that alerted them to problems they could analyze systematically without being overwhelmed. That advance in knowledge, the result of the authors' groundbreaking work, serves as a foundation for continuing progress in the field. Exposure to child placement evaluations now forms part of the clinical training experience of child psychiatrists, psychologists, and social workers at the Child Study Center. It can be observed repeatedly that without the guidelines provided by the authors, trainees would not be able to navigate the stormy seas they experience in child placement cases.

This new synthesis of the classic trilogy will thus serve as a legacy for future generations of practitioners and teachers and for the children who are the ultimate beneficiaries of its wisdom. It is an essential companion for all who work in this and related fields.

—BARBARA F. NORDHAUS

ACKNOWLEDGMENTS

M any individuals and several institutions have encouraged and facilitated our writing of this book. We wish to acknowledge our appreciation for their support.

For providing the space, resources, and intellectual climate that supported our work: Yale Law School's Guido Calabresi and Anthony Kronman, and Yale Child Study Center's Donald J. Cohen and John E. Schowalter.

For his valuable insights, careful research, demanding criticism, and imaginative contributions to both substance and style in two years of working with us, and above all for his unstinting commitment to the integrity of this book: Rick St. John.

For her sophisticated research assistance: Anne Adelman.

For organizing and inviting our participation in clinical child conflict placement conferences: Barbara Nordhaus and her colleagues and students.

For maintaining a user-friendly library: Morris L. Cohen and S. Blair Kauffman; and for meeting our almost daily requests: Gene Coakley.

For her extraordinarily skillful and good-humored supervision and preparation of numerous manuscript drafts: Pat Blackmon; for her astute secretarial and administrative assistance: Dolores Gee; for her able assistance in last-minute arrangements: Chris Souders.

For their generous and valuable comments on the complete text: Paul Schwartz, Jonathan Weiss, and Akhil Amar; for their thoughtful suggestions: Jean Koh Peters, Kathleen Sullivan, and Jean Adnopoz.

For their uninhibited, thought-provoking, and helpful critique: the students in the "Child, Family and the State" seminar taught in Spring 1996 by Akhil Amar and the Goldsteins.

For their publishing help and encouragement: Robert Wallace, Arthur Rosenthal, Dewey Brinkley, Edith Lewis, Chris Kelly, Susan Monahan, and, above all, the late Jeremiah Kaplan, who introduced Joseph Goldstein to The Free Press of Glencoe, Illinois, more than forty years ago.

For her personal encouragement and support: Martha Solnit.

For sustaining the voice of Anna Freud in our overall work: Alice Colonna.

For generously allowing the authors and Rick St. John to spread themselves out in their conference rooms: Arthur S. Sachs and Eric I.B. Beller.

And of course we continue to acknowledge all those who assisted us with *Beyond, Before,* and *In.*

INTRODUCTION

Anna Freud, Albert, J. Solnit, and Joseph Goldstein began in 1968, together with students at the Yale Law School, to explore the role of law in child placement. That effort led to the writing of a trilogy: *Beyond the Best Interests of the Child* (1973), *Before the Best Interests of the Child* (1979), and *In the Best Interests of the Child* (with Sonja Goldstein, 1986).

In this volume we revise, update, and combine the trilogy. Even though Anna Freud died in 1982, she remains a coauthor—not only because we retain much of the text on which she worked, but also because her ideas permeated our deliberations as we prepared this new edition.

As you read this volume we urge you to imagine that you are the child whose placement is the subject of state concern. Anna Freud would remind you to "put yourself in a child's skin"—the infant, the toddler, the preschooler, the schoolchild, or the teenager—as you consider what ought to be the guiding principles for deciding:

When parents separate, which of them should have primary responsibility for the care of their child or children;

Whether and under what conditions a noncustodial parent or grandparent should be entitled or obligated to visit a child; and

Whether an award of joint custody should be made if either parent objects to such an arrangement.

Put yourself in a child's skin as you try to decide what guiding principles would best serve the child's interest:

When long-term foster parents seek to retain custody over the objection of a biological parent;

When a child care agency seeks to move a child from one foster family to another in order to prevent the development of a relationship that might threaten the chances of the biological parent regaining custody; and

Whether brothers and sisters should be kept together in adoption, foster care, and divorce placements.

These are some of the problems confronted in Book One, *Beyond.* There we focus on children already caught up in the legal system—on contested placements arising in proceedings variously labeled as *abandonment, abuse, adoption, divorce, foster care, neglect,* and *separation.* We set forth guidelines based on psychoanalytic knowledge and common sense for resolving such disputes.

In Book Two, *Before,* we ask why and under what circumstances a child's relationship to her parents or other primary caregivers should become a matter of state concern. Once again, we ask that you put yourself in the skin of a child as you evaluate the guiding principles we propose for responding to such questions as:

Should there be a presumption in law that parents are free to determine what is "best" for their children?

What should justify state intrusion on the privacy of family relationships? What must happen to or in the life of a child before the state should be authorized to investigate, modify, or terminate a child's relationship to her parents—a child's membership in her family?

More specifically:

Should the separation of parents (whether married or unmarried) be sufficient justification for state intervention, or should intervention be limited to situations in which parents bring to the court their disagreement about how and by whom their children are to be cared for in the future?

When and under what circumstances should a court appoint legal counsel to represent a child, or authorize a physician to treat a child, without regard to or against the wishes of her parents?

Should neglect and/or abuse as grounds for state intervention be defined loosely or with specificity—to enlarge or restrict the discretion of those authorized to intrude upon ongoing parent-child relationships?

Book Three, *In,* focuses on the work of the professional participant in the child placement process—on the work of judges, lawyers, social workers, psychiatrists, psychologists, and other experts. Its purpose is to help professionals recognize and be sensitive to the boundaries of their knowledge and of their authority to act, the boundaries between their personal and professional beliefs, and the boundaries between the professional and parental roles. With this in mind, we urge the professionals (as well as those who engage or are exposed to them) to consider such questions as these:

When do professional participants undertake tasks that are beyond their expertise?

When do judges act as clinicians by making their own psychological assessments of parents or children?

When do clinicians act as judges by withholding information because they are afraid the judges may "misuse" their professionally informed findings or because they believe that they know what decision is "right"?

When may or should professionals consciously and openly cross boundaries?

Does playing two roles in relation to the same family or child place a professional beyond her competence even though she may be qualified to perform either role alone?

Do professional participants act beyond their own authority or professional knowledge by assuming a parental role?

In addressing these questions we emphasize that good professional work combines humanity and expertise—softheartedness coupled with hardheadedness.

The first two books in this trilogy stress the importance to a child of minimizing intrusions by the law on a child's relationships to her primary caregivers—of leaving well enough alone in the service of safeguarding the continuity of psychological parent-child relationships. These legal intrusions should be minimized whether the underlying relationships are long-standing or newly formed. The third book, again guided by the principle of protecting primary care relationships, stresses that it is in the child's interest for all professional participants to keep in mind that they are not the child's parents—that they are specialists, not the parents who, as generalists, serve the child's needs on a day-to-day, all-day basis. Together or separately, all the professional participants do not one good parent make.

Coming from different backgrounds, with training and experiences from different disciplines, we found a common tongue in our collaboration. We learned to speak in one voice about whether and how the law may safeguard and avoid disturbing a child's growth and development toward adulthood. At the same time we recognized that guidelines to state intervention—to making placement decisions—must rest on a theory that interconnects the wide array of child-rearing practices in which children may thrive. From psychoanalytic theory, as well as from the common experience all of us have had as children (and some of us have had as parents), we have identified continuity of care— that is, continuity of a child's relationship with her adult caregivers—as a universal essential to her well-being. Continuity is a fundamental characteristic, a common denominator, of healthy growth and development. Though the illustrative cases presented can be described as culture-bound, the guidelines and underlying principles are not. We draw upon a body of generally applicable knowledge about child development which recognizes that the law must be respectful of what families of different social and economic classes, of different religions and races, of different colors and cultures, and of different lifestyles, believe to be best for their children.

With this in mind, we invite you to consider how and to what extent the law, through its power to shape a child's external environment, can protect her physical growth and emotional development.

BOOK ONE

BEYOND THE BEST INTERESTS OF THE CHILD

PART ONE

The Problem and Our Premises

CHAPTER 1

Child Placement in Perspective

T he child is singled out by law, as by custom, for special attention. The
law distinguishes between adult and child in physical, psychological,
and societal terms. Adults are presumed to be responsible for themselves and
capable of deciding what is in their own interests. Therefore the law is by and
large designed to safeguard their right to order their personal affairs free of
government intrusion. Children, on the other hand, are presumed to be dependent beings who are not fully competent to determine and safeguard their
own interests. They are seen to be in need of direct, intimate, and continuous
care by the adults who are personally committed to assume such responsibility. Thus the state seeks to assure for each child membership in a family with
at least one such adult whom the law designates "parent."

Child placement laws are designed to ensure for all children an environment that adequately serves their needs. The degree of state intervention on
the private ordering of the parent-child relationship ranges from a minimum—automatic assignment of a child by birth certificate to her biological
parents—to a maximum—court-ordered removal of a child from her "parents" because she is found to be "abused" or "delinquent," or they are found
"unfit" to be parents. The traditional goal of such interventions is to serve
"the best interests of the child." In giving meaning to this goal, decision-
makers in law must recognize the necessity of protecting a child's psychological as well as physical well-being as guides to placement. Both
well-beings are important. Any sharp distinction between them is artificial.[1]

While we do not minimize the significance of the law's efforts to safeguard
each child's bodily needs, our emphasis here is on the child's psychological
needs. To that end we have used psychoanalytic theory to develop generally
applicable guidelines to child placement. These guidelines are intended to
provide a basis for critically evaluating statutes and the procedure and substance of court decisions. The guidelines are to provide a theoretical and con-
ceptual framework to identify not only unsound practices and precedents but

5

also sound decisions—many of which law and social custom arrived at long before the advent of psychoanalysis.[2]

"Child placement," for our purposes, is a term that encompasses all legislative, judicial, and executive decisions concerned with establishing, administering, or rearranging parent-child relationships. The term covers a wide range of variously labeled legal procedures for deciding who should be assigned or expected to seize the opportunity and the task of being "parent" to a child. These procedures include birth certification, neglect, abandonment, battered child, foster care, adoption, and delinquency, as well as custody in annulment, separation, and divorce. These labels have tended to obscure for scholars, draftsmen, and practitioners one problem common to all such procedures involving a child's welfare: To what extent can and should government, through the law, manipulate a child's external environment, in order to protect her physical growth and emotional development?

Put another way, how can the law assure for each child a chance to be a member of a family where she feels wanted and where she will have the opportunity, on a continuing basis, to receive and return affection, as well as to express anger and learn to manage aggression? The law's answer is easy, automatic, and made with confidence if at birth the child is wanted by the adults who conceived her. But when—at any time between birth and adulthood—a child's placement is in dispute and subject to competing and conflicting adult interests, the law finds the answer more difficult. It must make a decision based on a prediction about who, among available alternatives, holds the most promise for meeting the child's psychological needs.

Psychoanalytic theory confirms the substantial limitations on our capacity to make such a prediction. Yet it also provides a valuable body of generally applicable knowledge about a child's needs—knowledge which may be translated into guidelines to facilitate making the decisions that inevitably must be made. It establishes, for example, as do developmental studies within other disciplines, the need of every child for unbroken continuity of affectionate and stimulating relationships with at least one adult. That knowledge casts doubt, for example, upon adoption procedures which may leave the new child-parent relationship uncertain for years. Such official invitations to discontinuity in the life of a child run contrary to the often-professed purpose of the decisions themselves—to serve the best interests of the child.

Book One focuses on the development of guidelines for making decisions about children who are already caught up in the legal process. We examine and give functional definitions to the concepts of biological, psychological, adoptive, foster, and "common-law adoptive" parent-child relationships. Alert to the limits of law and of our knowledge, we translate what we know from psychoanalysis about growth and development into procedural and substantive guidelines for deciding a child's placement.

We end this beginning by stating two value preferences. First, we believe that the law should make the child's needs paramount. Second, we have a preference for maintaining family integrity. These personal views coincide with our professional commitment to the well-being of children. To safeguard the right of parents to raise their children as they see fit—free of government intrusion except in cases of abandonment, neglect, or abuse—is to safeguard each child's need for continuity. And when the state does, as it should, intervene to break an abusive relationship, that same need for continuity demands that as soon as practicable a new family relationship be established which, in turn, will remain free of state intervention absent abandonment, neglect, or abuse. The law is, after all, incapable of effectively managing, except in a very gross sense, such delicate and complex relationships as those between parent and child and those between parent and parent.

In Book One we take it as given that the child is already caught up in the legal process—whether because the adults involved were unable to reach agreement amongst themselves and resort to the legal process for a resolution of their disputes, or because there has been state intervention on grounds of abandonment, neglect, or abuse—and we focus on what placement would provide the least detrimental available alternative.

CHAPTER 2

The Child-Parent Relationships

C hildren are presumed in law to be incomplete beings during the whole period of their development. Their inability to provide for their own basic needs, or even to maintain life without extraneous help, justifies their being automatically assigned at birth to their biological parents or, where this relationship either does not develop or fails to function, assigned by later court proceedings to parent substitutes. This intimate group of adults and their children constitutes the central core of a family. Responsibility for the child—for her survival, for her physical and mental growth, and for her eventual adaptation to community standards—thus becomes that of the designated adults or adult in a family, to whom the child in turn is responsive and accountable.

The legal status of the child is matched on the psychological side by a number of tenets. A child's emotional reliance on adults is at least as long-lived as her physical dependence. Each child develops in response to the environmental influences to which she is exposed. Her emotional, intellectual, and moral capacities unfold—not in a void, and not without conflict—within her family relationships. These capacities in turn are reflected in her social behavior.

However valuable these tenets are, if used by themselves they are misleading; they highlight one side of child development while obscuring another. The problem arises if the child is viewed as a mere adjunct to the adult world, a passive recipient of parental impact. The fact is that children interact with the environment on the basis of their individual innate characteristics. It is this interaction, not mere reaction, that accounts for the countless variations in human character and personality, including differences between siblings growing up in the same family. To see children one-sidedly, as mere mirrors of their background, blinds the observer to the uniqueness of each child. Nevertheless, whatever their individual differences, the mental makeup of children generally differs from that of adults in the following respects:

8

(1) Unlike adults, children change constantly, from one stage of growth to another. They change with regard to their understanding of events, their tolerance for frustration, and their needs for and demands on parents' care for support, stimulation, guidance, and restraint. These demands vary as the child matures and is capable of independence (that is, gradual freedom from control). Since none of the child's needs remains stable, what serves her developmental interests at one level may be detrimental to her progression at another level.

(2) Unlike adults, who measure the passing of time by clock and calendar, children have their own built-in time sense, based on the urgency of their instinctual and emotional needs and on the limits of their cognitive capacities. This results in their intolerance for postponement of gratification and their sensitivity to the length of separations.

(3) Unlike adults, young children experience events as happening solely with reference to their own persons.[1] Thus they may experience the birth of a sibling as an act of parental hostility; the emotional preoccupation or illness of a parent as rejection; or the death or involuntary absence of a parent as intentional abandonment.

(4) Unlike adults, children are governed in much of their functioning by the irrational parts of their minds—their primitive wishes and impulses. Consequently, they respond to any threat to their emotional security with reactions that do not help them to cope, but rather put them at the mercy of events.[2]

(5) Unlike adults, children have no psychological conception of blood-tie relationships until quite late in their development. For the biological parents, the experience of conceiving, carrying, and giving birth prepares them to feel close to and responsible for their child.[3] These considerations carry no weight with children, who are emotionally unaware of the events leading to their existence. What matters to them is the pattern of day-to-day interchanges with the adults who take care of them and who, on the strength of such interactions, become the parent figures to whom they are attached.

Children, then, are not adults in miniature. They differ from their elders in their mental nature, their functioning, their understanding of events, and their reactions to them. This, however, should not obscure the enormous variations in the quality and degree of such differences not only among different children but also in each individual child during the fluctuating course of her growth and development.

Families, too, may change through time and differ among cultures, both in function and membership. Yet the "family" is generally seen as the fundamental unit responsible for and capable of providing a child on a continuing basis with an environment that serves her numerous physical, mental, and emotional needs.[4] The child needs her body to be tended, nourished, and protected. She needs her intellect to be stimulated and alerted to the happenings in her environment. She needs help in understanding and organizing her feelings and perceptions. She needs people whom she can love, who love her, and who can serve as safe targets for her anger and aggression. She needs assistance from the adults in curbing and modifying her primitive drives of sex and aggression. She needs parents who, by example and guidance, will enable her to develop and heed her inner voice of right and wrong. As much as anything else, she needs to be accepted, valued, and wanted as a member of her family—single-parent, two-parent, or however extended.

In meeting these needs, parents play a fundamental part in the socializing of their child. They represent a set of demands, prohibitions, and attitudes toward work and community with which the child can identify,

- The parent who feeds the infant and puts her to bed thereby introduces a first compliance with a time schedule; the parent who grants but also withholds bodily and mental satisfactions helps the child to realize that not all wishes can be fulfilled at all times. This increases the child's capacity to tolerate postponement of gratification and inevitable frustration.
- The parent who enables the child to play, to use toys, and to listen to stories helps her to wait and find distractions and other partial gratifications to replace the original wish.
- The parent who reacts to the child's behavior with appropriate praise and encouragement (or criticism and discouragement) lays the first foundations for the child's own control of her drives and impulses, the lessening of her selfishness, and the beginning of consideration for others.
- Experiences with other children in the family provide the child with additional opportunities to form her conceptions of sharing, fair play, and justice.

This picture of the family is an ideal one, not always matched by reality. Adults may fail to meet the child's needs, or indeed may be abusive. Furthermore, children do not always develop according to their parents' expectations. There may be delays, deviations, and arrests in every aspect of the child's development, and each of these affects her response to environmental influences. Involvement with other children may be so minimal that the child does not learn to balance her own wishes against those of others.

When families malfunction, the consequences for the child's social adaptation may be many:

- Physical care of the infant and toddler in the family may be given by rote and insensitively or, conversely, may be exaggerated and exceed the child's needs.
- Parental involvement may be so minimal, even in a "complete" family, that the child's emotional demands remain unfulfilled.
- Parents may provide the child with unsuitable models for identification.
- The prolonged absence or death of a parent who has been important to the child may set back her developmental progress.

But where the family exerts its influence for the most part benevolently, with consideration, understanding, and compassion for each individual child member, the balanced opportunities for a unique development and for social adaptation are maximized. In such families—whether they develop out of biological, adoptive, foster, or common-law adoptive ties—the adults are the psychological parents, and the children are wanted. It is on the meaning of these terms and concepts that we now focus.

The Biological Parent-Child Relationship

For the parents who bring the child into the world, the physical facts of having begotten a child or given birth to her have far-reaching psychological meanings. These range from a sense of accomplishment when the child is born to the gradual enhancement of self-worth as the child thrives in their care. For the infant, on the other hand, attachment to her parents results from their day-to-day attention to her needs for physical care, nourishment, comfort, affection, and stimulation. A parent who satisfies these needs builds a psychological relationship with the child on the basis of the biological one and will become her "psychological parent" in whose care the child can feel secure, valued, and "wanted."

The Psychological Parent-Child Relationship

The child's psychological tie to her parents is not an uncomplicated relationship. While it is rooted inevitably in the infant's inability to ensure her own survival, it varies according to the manner in which protection is given and her physical needs fulfilled. Where this is done impersonally and routinely, as happens in some institutions, the infant may not take an alert interest in her surroundings.[5] Where her parents are emotionally involved and provide bodily care with affection, a mutually satisfactory relationship can develop. Then the child's interest will be drawn for the first time to her parents—to someone outside herself.

Such primitive and tenuous first attachments form the base from which further relationships develop. What the child brings to them are no longer only her needs for bodily comfort and gratification but her emotional demands for affection, companionship, and stimulating intimacy. Where these are answered reliably, the child-parent relationship becomes firm, with immensely productive effects on the child's emotional and social development.

Where parental care is inadequate, on the other hand, this may be associated with deficits in the child's mental growth. Where there are hurtful interruptions, such as a prolonged or permanent absence of a parent, the child's vulnerability and the fragility of the relationship become evident. Then the child tends to regress along the line of her affections, skills, achievements, and social adaptation. As the child matures, the emotional ties to the parent become less fragile. The first relief in this respect is the formation of internal mental images of the parents that remain available to her even if the parents are absent. The next step is to identify with parental attitudes. Once these have become the child's own, she can see herself as a person in her own right.

Like all human relationships, the psychological parent-child relationship is not wholly positive. Both parents and child bring to it the combination of loving and resentful feelings that characterizes the emotional life of all human beings. The balance between positive and negative feelings fluctuates during the years. For children, this culminates in the inevitable and potentially constructive struggle with their parents during adolescence.

Where the tie is to persons who are "unfit" as parents, unbroken closeness to them, and especially identification with them, may cease to be a benefit and become a threat. In extreme cases this necessitates state intervention.* Nevertheless, so far as the child's emotions are concerned, interference with the tie, whether to a "fit" or "unfit" psychological parent, is extremely painful.

Whether a person becomes the psychological parent of a child is based on day-to-day interaction, companionship, and shared experiences. This can be

---

*Justifications for state intervention are examined in Book Two.

done by an adoptive parent, or by any other caring person*—but never by a physically or psychologically absent person, whatever that person's biological or legal relationship to the child may be.

The Wanted Child

A child who has at least one psychological parent whom she can love, and who also feels loved, valued, and wanted by that person, will develop a healthy self-esteem. That child is a wanted child.† She can then become confident of her own chances of achievement in life and convinced of her own human value. Where the child does not experience this love in infancy, she may in her later life lack interest in her well-being, in her physical appearance, in her clothing, and in the image she presents to her fellow beings. What is damaged is her love and regard for herself, and consequently her capacity to love and care for others, including her own children.

To be a wanted child may cease to be beneficial if the parents' valuation of the child is excessive and if no or too little return from her side is expected. In such situations, a child may become ineducable since she may not sense the need to earn her parents' approval by curbing her own impulses and wishes.

The Adoptive Parent–Child Relationship

The term *adoptive parent* designates an adult other than the biological parent to whom the state has assigned parental responsibility.[6]

Adoption is no guarantee that the adopting adults will become the psychological parents, or that the adopted child will become a wanted child. Adoption in the early weeks of an infant's life enhances the chance for the adoptive parents and child to develop a psychological parent-child relationship. Although adoptive parents are deprived of the psychological preparation that accompanies pregnancy, their capacity for parenthood may develop in response to the helplessness and dependence of the infant. This is less likely to happen if adoption occurs at a later age, because prior temporary placements are often associated with deprivation, disruption, or broken attachments. The

---

*We use the word *person* rather than *adult* advisedly to include teenage biological parents and minor siblings, who under certain circumstances may become psychological parents.

†An unwanted pregnancy does not necessarily mean that a child born of that pregnancy will not become wanted by her birth parents.

statutory requirement of a trial period before adoption is finalized may also impede bonding between parent and child.[7] Due to the uncertainty, the adoptive parents may hesitate during the waiting period to make the full commitment that allows the child to feel wanted.

A child's knowledge of her adoptive status is likely to have different meanings at different ages. The young child tends to ignore it, even if informed repeatedly, and to develop her attachments as a wanted child to her psychological parents. The older child uses the information to a greater or lesser extent, depending on her developmental conflicts with her legal parents. Whenever she is disappointed in them, or as she learns to appraise them realistically, the adoptive parents may be compared with a fantasy image of the biological parents, however little these figured earlier in the child's mind. Adolescents frequently search for the lost and unknown parents as a step preliminary to achieving independence from parental authority and reaching maturity.[8]

The Foster Parent–Child Relationship

The term *foster parent* is used in law to designate adults with whom a state child care agency places a child pursuant to the terms of a written agreement. The stated purpose of foster care placement is to provide temporary care for the child, either while protecting her ties to the absent parent with whom she is expected to be reunited or while a search is on for adoptive parents. When the child is merely held for others, special techniques must be used, whether to keep existing attachments alive in the child or (insofar as it is possible) to prepare the way for future attachments.[9]

In situations that are short-term—in fact as well as in theory—the task is more professional than parental. The services expected from foster parents, and for which they receive compensation, may range from the physical and material (such as that the child shall be given sufficient and suitable food, the opportunity to attend school, and attend religious services, shall receive medical care, shall not be required to perform an amount of labor unsuitable for her age and strength) to the psychological (such as that the child should receive all the emotional benefits of a true member of the new family). The foster care agreement may also provide guidance with respect to visiting by the biological parents, granting of pocket money, and arrangements for day-to-day activities.

Agreements made with foster parents are generally premised on two conditions:

(1) that the child is placed on a temporary basis, and
(2) that the child care agency has the right to cancel the agreement and to re-move the child at any time from the foster home.

These conditions have unquestionable consequences for the child–foster parent relationship, particularly if it becomes long-term.

For foster parents, the agreement carries with it an implicit warning against "excessive" emotional involvement. Because of the conditional and temporary nature of their assignment, they may find themselves deprived of the kind of authority on which parental tolerance, endurance, and devotion are commonly based. What remains for them is a sense of responsibility that may be reinforced by the appeal of the child's helplessness. This can be counted on in many instances to create the semblance of a family setting; however, the appeal is likely to be greatly diminished in the case of the older child, who is both less helpless and in many respects more "troublesome."

For the foster child, efforts by foster parents to observe the terms of such agreements mean that she will, at least after early infancy has passed, react to the impermanence and insecurity of the arrangement—conditions that clash with her need for emotional stability. She will feel herself to be in the care of parents who are by no means all-powerful, but have no more than partial abil-ity to protect her and to control her fate.

If foster parents heed the warning implicit in the agreements and go about their task with the detachment of a semi-professional, they evoke in the child a response that is too lukewarm to serve either the infant's developmental needs for emotional bonding or the older child's need to feel that she is a fully wanted member of a family. Furthermore—and this may partially explain the frequent breakdown of foster placements—the emotional ties of the adults to the children will be weak enough to be broken readily whenever external cir-cumstances make the presence of the foster child in the home inconvenient or irksome. In short, under the terms of the foster care agreement, the child–foster parent relationship is not meant to become a psychological parent–wanted child relationship.

Long-term fostering fails in a different sense when the adults transgress the role assigned to them: when, as time passes, they become fully involved with the child in their care. As the child responds to their emotional involve-ment and feels truly wanted, her foster parents become her psychological par-ents as well. Though they may be precluded from officially adopting her, they have become her parents as if by "common-law adoption"—a status that, we argue, deserves legal recognition.[10]

The Common-Law Adoptive Parent–Child Relationship

We use the term *common-law adoptive parent* to designate those psycholog-ical parent-child relationships that develop outside of placement by formal adoption or by the initial assignment of a child to her biological parents.[11] Such relationships may develop when a parent, without resort to any legal process, leaves his or her child with a friend or relative for an extended period of time.[12] Further, as already indicated, long-term foster parents in daily re-sponse to a child's demands may become the child's psychological parents and may seek to make the placement permanent.

Where the psychological interactions are present and functioning effec-tively, the relationship between child and long-term foster parents deserves legal recognition, either by legislature or court as "common-law adoption." If legal recognition is withheld and the child removed, the forcible interruption of the relationship not only causes distress to the fostering adults but, more importantly, is reacted to by the child with emotional distress and a setback of ongoing development.

We have sought in this chapter to define some basic terms and concepts out of which to construct guidelines for child placement in the contexts of adop-tion, divorce, separation, and foster care.[13] Such guidelines must not be-come shorthands that obscure how intricate and delicate are the interpersonal processes we have described.

PART TWO

Guidelines and Their Implications for the Laws of Child Placement

In this part, we propose three guidelines for making *procedural* and *substantive* decisions about the placement of a child. The guidelines are designed to ensure for all children whose placements have become the subject of controversy an opportunity to be placed with adults who are or are likely to become their psychological parents. Together these guidelines make up the *least detrimental alternative* standard.

CHAPTER 3

Placement Decisions Should Safeguard the Child's Need for Continuity of Relationships

C ontinuity of relationships is essential for a child's healthy development. Since continuity may not play as significant a role in later life, its importance may be underrated by adult decision-makers.

Growth—physical, emotional, intellectual, social, and moral—does not happen without the child experiencing internal tension. The inherent instability of mental processes during the course of development needs to be offset by a supportive environment. Smooth growth may be disrupted when upheavals and changes in the external world are added to the inevitable internal ones.[1]

Discontinuities can evoke different responses at different ages as well as among children of the same age:

For infants and toddlers, changes in routine may lead to food refusals, digestive upsets, sleeping difficulties, crying, or withdrawal states. These reactions may occur even if care is divided between parent and baby-sitter. They can be severe where infants are displaced from parent to a foster home; from foster home to foster home; from foster home to institution; or from foster home to adopting parents. Such moves bring with them changes in the way the infant is handled, fed, put to bed, and comforted. Being moved from the familiar to the unfamiliar person is often associated with discomfort and distress, and affects the infant's orientation and adaptation to her surroundings. The attachments of infants and toddlers are as upset by separations as they are promoted by the constant, unrationed, consistent presence and attention of a familiar adult. When these children feel themselves abandoned by their parent, their distress leads to weakening their next attachments. Where continuity of such relationships is interrupted more than once, as happens with multiple foster placements in the early years, the children's emotional attachments become increasingly shallow and indiscriminate. They tend to grow up as persons who lack sustained warmth in their relationships.

19

For *young children* (those under the age of five years), disruptions of continuity also affect those achievements that are rooted and develop in the intimate interchange with a caregiver who is, or is in the process of becoming, the psychological parent. After separation from the familiar parent, young children are known to have breakdowns in toilet training and to experience deterioration of their ability to communicate verbally.[2] The more recently the achievement has been acquired, the more likely it is for the child to lose it.

For *school-age children,* the breaks in their relationships with their psychological parents affect above all those cognitive and social achievements that are based significantly on their identifications with the parents' demands, prohibitions, and social ideals. Such identifications develop where attachments are stable, and they tend to be attenuated if children feel abandoned by their primary caregiver. Resentment toward the adults who have disappointed them in the past may lead them to distrust others and to make the new parent the scapegoat for the shortcomings of an earlier one. Multiple placements at these ages put many children at an educational and social disadvantage. This in turn may cause behavior that schools and the community at large experience as disorganized and disruptive.[3]

Adolescents frequently convey the idea that they desire to discontinue relationships with their parents rather than to preserve them. This impression may be misleading. Their revolt against parental authority is often developmentally normal; it may be their way of moving toward establishing independence. But for a successful outcome it is important that the breaks and disruptions of attachment come exclusively from the child's side and not be imposed on her by abandonment or rejection by the psychological parent.[4]

Thus continuity is a guideline because emotional attachments are tenuous and vulnerable in early life, and children need stability of relationships for their healthy growth and development.

Implications

Except where specifically designed for brief temporary care, child placements should be as free of further state intervention and as permanent as the assignment of a newborn to her biological parents. Here we examine the meaning of foster care, adoption, and custody in light of the continuity guideline.

FOSTER AND OTHER TEMPORARY PLACEMENTS
Except when the purpose is to "groom" the child for adoption, foster and less formal temporary placements should be administered so as to safeguard and

maintain the continuity of ties to the absent parents with whom the child is expected to be reunited.[5] This does not mean that foster parents are to remain aloof and uninvolved. Nor does this mean that foster care is to be used as a means of keeping the child from establishing positive ties with her "temporary" adult custodians by constantly shifting her from one foster setting to another in order to protect her legal parents' rights to reclaim her. Once prior ties have been substantially weakened, foster placements can no longer be considered temporary. They may begin to become psychological parent-child relationships, which once again deserve recognition and protection under the continuity guideline.

The decision to place a child in foster care must carry with it an expectation for all parties, including the court, that the child will shortly, in accord with the *child's* sense of time (discussed in Chapter 4), be restored to her family. Otherwise foster care may unwittingly become an instrument for destroying families. The period of separation must be used for keeping alive, or for helping to establish, ties that bond both child and the parents from whom she has been separated. Disturbance to the continuity of these reciprocal ties must be kept to a minimum if the reunion of parent and child is to safeguard their mutual interests. Foster parents have the difficult task of supplying the missing parental care for the child without, at the same time, undermining her ties to her absent parents. What this will mean, both in terms of temporariness and in terms of provisions for maintaining reciprocity of affectionate relationships, will depend in large measure on the child's age at the time she is placed in foster care, upon the extent and form of accessibility of child and parents to each other during the period of separation, and upon whether the biological and foster parents have a positive relationship. The younger the child, the shorter should be the duration of such a placement if it is to be temporary.

Decision-makers in each case must make a realistic evaluation of the circumstances that prompt consideration of foster care, in order to determine if the relationship between the child and her absent parents can be preserved. If the problems confronting the family are chronic, the continuity guideline would suggest the consideration of in-home support services to keep the family intact. Where this is not feasible, continuity would dictate that adoption rather than foster care be chosen to assure for the child an opportunity to become a regular member of a new but permanent family.

If the circumstances do justify foster care, the legislature or court must set in advance the maximum length of time for the placement. That period would take into account the child's capacity to sustain the relationship with her parents during the separation. To assure that such placements do not extend beyond this maximum without reconsideration by the court, each case should be tagged to resurface for review in timely fashion.[6] Such an *early warning system* would uncover those cases in which the child had not yet been restored to her family. A new determination would then be required to consider the advisability of restoration with or without supportive services and, if that is found not to be a realistic option, to arrange for the *adoption* of the child— preferably by the foster family, with whom significant ties have begun to be established.

When "temporary" placements become long-term, for whatever reason, familial bonds that are developing between the foster child and her caregivers should be protected. If foster families do not wish to adopt but wish to continue indefinitely the now long-term foster relationship, they should be encouraged to do so. Such relationships might be reclassified as *foster care with tenure*. Like adoptive families, tenured foster families would be insulated from the threat of interruption by the long-absent biological parents or by the child care agency whose policy may have been offended.

ADOPTION

The continuity guideline would require that adoption be as final, as permanent, and as unconditional as the child's placement by birth certificate. Statutes that provide for a "waiting period" before the order of adoption becomes final promote uncertainty for both adult and child. The waiting period is a time of probation encumbered by investigative visits and the fear of interruption. It is not, as it ought to be, a full opportunity for developing secure and stable attachments.

For the state, the waiting period provides an opportunity to interrupt developing relationships for reasons that would not justify intrusion into any permanent parent-child relationship. For some adopting parents the period may be one in which they place the child on "trial," an intolerable handicap for initiating such a delicate relationship. Moreover, the knowledge that the state can take the new child away may be experienced by other children in the family as a threat to their own security. The fear that biological parents may revoke consent may also be a hindrance to immediately stabilizing the relationship.

We propose that the adoption decree be made final the moment a child is actually placed with the adopting family. We recognize that due process may require an opportunity to revoke consent or to appeal. The period allotted for making these determinations, though, should be sensitive to the need to limit the period of uncertainty.[7] This would mean that once the shortened time allotted has elapsed the adoption order would be as final as a birth certificate, not subject to special supervision or open to special challenge by state or agency.

The certainty of permanent placement should make the participants aware of the seriousness of the decision to place a child for adoption, as well as the decision to adopt a child. If adopting parents do change their minds, they could activate legal processes designed to provide the child with another opportunity to be placed, just as biological parents can.[8] Moreover, as for all permanent placements (whether by birth certificate or adoption), situations deemed to constitute "abuse," "neglect," or "abandonment," for example, could trigger state intervention. But even such placement proceedings must consider the continuity guideline in deciding whether an existing relationship should be interrupted. The advantages of continuing ongoing "unperfect" relationships must be weighed, even in neglect proceedings, against those of the alternative placements that can be made available.

CUSTODY IN DIVORCE AND SEPARATION

The placement of a child by custody decree in divorce and separation is neither final nor unconditional. The continuing jurisdiction of the court, once the decree has been issued, poses a serious threat to the child's need for continuity of caregiver. Custody decrees should be as final and free from outside interference as placements by birth certificate are and as placements by adoption ought to be.[9] Neither the noncustodial parent nor the court should be able to dictate special conditions—such as requirements to send the child to religious school, to live in a given geographical area, or to grant visitation to relatives.

Where courts impose visitation as a condition of custody, this may itself be a source of discontinuity. Children have difficulty profiting from and maintaining contact with two psychological parents who are at odds with each other—especially when the child herself is the focus of the dispute. Loyalty conflicts are common under such conditions and may have devastating consequences by destroying the child's positive relationships to both parents. A parent visiting *against or without regard to the wishes of the custodial parent* has less chance of serving as a constructive force in the life of her child. The noncustodial parent should have no legally enforceable right to visit the child, and the custodial parent should have the right to decide whether it is desirable for the child to have such visits.*[10] Similarly, grandparents ought not to have a legally enforceable right to visit.[11]

---

*Separating parents should be free to arrange voluntarily and mutually any custody or visitation plan they see fit.

Our conclusion that noncustodial parents should have "no legally enforceable right to visit" their children has proved to be the most misunderstood, most controversial, and most resisted aspect of our suggestion in *Beyond the Best Interests of the Child* (1973) that all but emergency and other truly temporary placements should be unconditional. It has been misread to mean that we oppose the continuation of contact between a child and her noncustodial parent. It has been challenged with the argument that our position (a) conflicts with the continuity guideline; (b) deprives a child of her basic right to maintain her ties to the noncustodial parent; and (c) places an instrument of revenge in the hands of the custodial parent (usually pictured as an angry mother) who will use it to spite the noncustodial parent (usually pictured as a thwarted and well-motivated father).[12]

We reasoned, always from the child's point of view, that custodial parents—not courts or noncustodial parents—should determine when and if it is desirable to arrange visits. We continue to take this position because it is beyond the capacity of courts to help a child establish or maintain positive relationships to two people who are at cross-purposes with each other; because, by forcing visits, courts are more likely to prevent the child from developing a reliable tie to either parent; and because children who are shaken, disoriented, and confused by the breakup of their family need an opportunity to settle down in the privacy of their reorganized family, with one person in authority upon whom they can rely for answers to their questions and for protection from external interference. After all, the goal of every placement decision, whether made at birth by certificate or later by more direct state intervention, should be to provide each child with an opportunity—unbroken by further intrusion—to establish or reestablish and maintain psychological bonds with those to whom she is entrusted.*

A child develops best if she can trust the adults who are responsible for her to be the arbiters of her care and control as she moves toward the full independence of adulthood, and gradually comes to rely upon herself as her own caregiver. A court undermines that trust when it subjects her custodial parent to special rules about raising her by ordering (even scheduling) visits with the noncustodial parent.[13] In the child's eyes, the court, by directing her to visit against the express wishes of her custodial parent, casts doubt on that parent's authority and capacity to parent. Particularly for the younger child, this undermines her confidence in her parent's omnipotence. It invites the older child to pit one parent against the other rather than to learn to work things

*Temporary placements pending appeal in a custody dispute must assure that both competing adults have access to the child.

out with her custodial parent. The continuity guideline means that the already-stressed relationship between child and custodial parent should not be plagued with the never-ending threat of disruption by the impersonal authority of the court.

We did not and do not oppose visits. We oppose only *forced* visits—court-ordered visits. Indeed, other things being equal, courts, in order to accord with the continuity guideline, could award custody to the parent who is most willing to provide opportunities for the child to see the other parent. And—even though we do not believe that a noncustodial parent can play the same significant role in a child's life as a parent in an intact family—we encourage custodial parents who seek our advice to facilitate the maintenance of the relationship between the child and her noncustodial parent.* It might even be desirable for courts to attach to their unconditional custody decrees this warning: "Denial of visits may be detrimental to your child and to her relationship with you."

But such advice can and should be nothing more. Custodial parents should remain free to accept or reject other people's notions about the importance of continuity.[14] The continuity guideline cannot be pressed any further in favor of the child's now-secondary relationship with the noncustodial parent without putting at risk her relationship to her custodial parent. Visits that are meaningful for the child can occur only if both the custodial and the noncustodial parents are of a mind to make them work.[15] If parents agree, a court order is both unnecessary and undesirable; if they do not agree, such an order and the threat or actual attempt to enforce it can do the child no good.[16] The child needs a parent who can help her to resolve her wishes to see and not to see the other parent and who can help her to deal with her joys and sorrows following visits, and her hurts when the noncustodial parent refuses to maintain contact or fails to show up.

Our reasons for objecting to court-enforceable visits sometimes seem to be recognized more easily when courts resolve disputes about visitation that are camouflaged under the labels of "joint" or "split" custody. Yet, from a child's point of view, court-ordered "joint" or "split" custody is but another form of court-ordered visitation. In *Braiman v. Braiman,* Chief Judge Breitel of the New York Court of Appeals reversed a joint custody order for reasons that apply to all other types of visitation orders. The lower court had "awarded to the

---

*Visits under favorable circumstances are, at best, a poor substitute for a parent in the family. Weekend visits do not compensate the child for parental absence at crucial moments in her life. Prolonged visits during summer vacation only too often arouse unwillingness to return to the custodial parent or, at least, increase the loyalty conflict.

parents jointly [two sons aged six and seven] to spend weekdays with the mother and weekends with the father." Judge Breitel said:

> Entrusting the custody of young children to their [divorced] parents jointly, especially where the shared responsibility and control includes alternating physical custody, is insupportable when parents are severely antagonistic and embattled. . . . [I]t can only enhance family chaos. . . . It would, moreover, take more than reasonable self restraint to shield the children as they go from house to house, from the ill feelings, hatred, and disrespect each parent harbors towards the other.[17]

After observing that the court must "recognize the division in fact of the family" and that "there are no painless solutions," Judge Breitel said:

> In the rare case, joint custody may approximate the former family relationships more closely than other custodial arrangements. It may not, however, be indiscriminately substituted for an award of sole custody to one parent.[18]*

What the court fails to recognize is that no parent has sole custody so long as he or she is subject to rules of visitation, and that courts are as powerless to forge affection by a visitation order as they are by decreeing any other form of "joint," "divided," or "split" custody.†

Finally, courts and commentators, blinded by the specter of the spiteful custodial parent denying visits at the child's expense, have rejected our position with the misleading assertion that visitation or access is a right of the child, not of the parents. In fact, by subjecting an award of custody to an order imposing visits, the court does not protect the child's "basic right" to see her noncustodial parent. It merely shifts the power to deprive the child of that "right" *from* the custodial parent to the noncustodial parent. Visitation orders make the noncustodial parent—rather than the parent who is responsible for the child's day-to-day care—the final authority for deciding whether to visit. Even if the court orders visits because it believes they will serve the child's best interest, the noncustodial parent remains free not to visit, to "reverse" the court without risk of being held in contempt. The court is powerless, as it

---

*Of course, if both parents agree to joint custody, the court should have no power to forbid it even if the court does not believe the arrangement to be appropriate. But neither should it have the power to enforce the agreement.

†These terms are often used to describe the same arrangement. From a child's point of view, custody is likely to be "split" or "divided" rather than "joint" so long as her separated parents are in conflict.[19]

should be, to order noncustodial parents to visit their "waiting" children.[20] But the court has the corrosive power to have a child forcibly removed from a custodial parent who refuses to allow visits, or to imprison that parent for contempt. When it exercises such power, the court demonstrates for the child that her custodial parent cannot be trusted and is powerless to protect her. Courts obscure the real issues when they say what they cannot mean—that visitation is "a basic right of the child."

When Visitation Is Mandated—Two Interpretations: The Cases of Joanna Pierce (1974) and Vanessa Richards (1995)

The opinions that follow dramatically illustrate how two different perceptions of the noncustodial parent's right to visit can affect the life of a child:

JOANNA PIERCE

PIERCE V. YERKOVICH
363 N.Y.S.2d 403 (1974)

Hugh R. Elwyn, Judge:
    The petitioner, Franklin Pierce, the acknowledged father of an illegitimate child, seeks to have defined and enforced his asserted right of visitation with his five year old daughter, [Joanna], which right the mother has, for the past year and a half, adamantly refused to recognize.
    Custody of the child is not at issue. What is at issue is whether through de-emphasis of parental rights . . . and strict adherence to the "best interests of the child" criterion as conceived and defined by the mother alone, the court should permit the mother as custodial parent the prerogative of making the determination as to when and under what circumstances, if at all, the child may see her father, as is urged upon the court by her expert witness, or whether the court should exercise its authority as *parens patriae* to temper the "best interests of the child" maxim with a recognition that the father of a child, even though illegitimate, has a right to association with his child which . . . must be recognized by the courts.

             *   *   *

From the history of the relationship of these parents it is obvious that the child was not born of a casual relationship, but of one which endured for over two and a half years, and one in which, even after separation and up until shortly before her marriage [in July 1973], contact between father and daughter was actively encouraged by the mother. It is equally apparent that up until the time of the mother's marriage when the child's attitude toward her father completely changed that father and child enjoyed a mutually rewarding warm, loving father and daughter relationship.

Twice during the course of this lengthy proceeding which was begun in October 1973, the Court on application of the petitioner permitted him to take his daughter for visits to his home in Florida, the first time for two weeks in April 1974 and the second time for a month in July and August, upon condition that he post a cash bond in the amount of $10,000 to insure the return of the child to the mother's home and the jurisdiction of the Court. In each instance the petitioner readily complied with the condition and the child was returned to the mother's home at the appointed time.

At no time has there been any suggestion that the father is not a fit and capable custodian of his daughter or that when she has been temporarily in his custody is anything but well cared for. Indeed, the photographic evidence in this case shows that when the child has been in the father's custody she has been pampered with every luxury and attention a doting father can bestow.

The Court is completely satisfied that the petitioner is in all respects a wholly suitable and proper person to have the temporary care and custody of his daughter, even for an extended period of time. He has, through the creation of substantial trusts for the benefit of [his] daughter, demonstrated his concern for her financial security and he has on two separate occasions demonstrated to the Court his financial responsibility. More importantly, he has also demonstrated his complete trustworthiness.

Thus, a decision in this case does not turn upon the fitness of either parent to be permanent or temporary custodian of the child, but rather upon whether in "the best interests of the child" she should be permitted some periodic association with her father or whether, as the mother would have it, she should be shielded from all further contact. To assist in resolving this issue both parties presented the testimony of psychiatrists.

Dr. Bernard F. Kalina, a psychiatrist, of Liberty, New York was called as a witness on behalf of the petitioner. Dr. Kalina who had examined the child at his office on March 12, 1974, pursuant to Court order, testified that he found the child to be very intelligent and bright with no mental disorders whatever. He expressed the opinion that the child loves her father; he thought that the child's negative feeling toward the father had developed because of the negative things the mother had said about the father and explained the child's change in attitude toward father by saying: "I feel her reactions would have to be negative since she loves Mommy and wants to please Mommy. . . ."

Dr. Kalina further expressed the opinion that substantial visitation rights for the father "would be beneficial to the child. . . ."

*　　　*　　　*

Professor Solnit [a psychoanalyst, on behalf of the respondent] conducted a clinical examination of Joanna on two occasions at the Yale University Child Study Center.

[T]he Professor said he found the child apprehensive and anxious and that it was his impression that she is under extraordinary tension. "She is anxious and she is insecure because of the experience she's had in which the visits with Mr. Pierce are felt as a threat to her and are not comfortable for her especially because she had to leave home to visit Mr. Pierce soon after a new baby arrived in her family. I think that made her very uncomfortable and uncertain and insecure."

Based upon these clinical observations, the Professor then stated that "in (his) opinion, Joanna's best interest would be served if she could feel that Mr. and Mrs. Yerkovich were her parents . . . [having] all the rights and privileges of parents. . . . In other words I believe that she should not have the feeling that they lack the authority or the ability to give her this security, of feeling wanted and permanent in her family. . . ."

*　　　*　　　*

. . . I do not believe that the law of this State would tolerate this Court, charged as it is with a responsibility for the welfare of children, so supinely and abjectly abdicating its function to any parent, however well intentioned. The danger and folly of such a course is aptly illustrated by the circumstances of this case wherein a mother, who once permitted and actively encouraged free association between father and child, has, upon the contraction of a marriage, arbitrarily reversed her field and is now unwilling to permit any contact whatever between her daughter and the man who is the father of her child. . . .

. . . . Experience and common sense teach that, given the imperfections of human nature from which flow the bitterness and resentment which all too often accompany a marital or illicit love affair breakup, no one parent can, under such circumstances, be safely entrusted with a power so susceptible of abuse. . . .

Thus, we approach the central vital issue in this case. Is it in this child's best interest to be shielded by the mother from all future contact with her father, except through the mother's sufferance or do her best interests require that she should through her formative and growing up years have some continuing association with a father who has amply demonstrated his love and concern for his daughter? . . .

Any analysis of this situation brings one back to a fundamental truth which the psychiatrists, with all their talk of the psychological parent, have a tendency to overlook. Joanna, as is everyone, was born of two parents and, in my judgment, neither one has any God given exclusive right to control her destiny.

The concept of psychological parenthood should never be permitted to obscure the truth that the natural father, as well as the natural mother, remains a parent no matter how estranged parent and child may become. . . .

In spite of the circumstances of her birth, Joanna will one day have to come to grips with the fact that she does indeed have a father. As Dr. Kalina said, "Joanna will have to understand that father really exists as she grows older and learns to decide for herself." In the interim, he said, "it would be harmful if she wasn't allowed to see both parents."

The Special Guardian in her report to the court makes essentially the same point when she says that the mother's refusal of all visitation rights to the father "raises the question, not touched upon by the litigants, herein, of whether a child has a right to get to know and appreciate who her father is."

*   *   *

The Court is aware that when visitation is renewed by the father such visits may cause the child some temporary emotional upset and perhaps some disruption of the Yerkovich household, but this is a price that must be paid if the child's larger long term interests are to be best served. Any emotional upset to this child occasioned by the presence of her father could be minimized if the mother would recognize the reality of the child's origins and be supportive of the tie that binds father and child together.

The willingness of the Court to afford this father an opportunity to permit Joanna to come once again to know, love and respect him as her father should not be regarded as novel. In fact, it but reflects the ancient wisdom of God's law as given to Moses on Mount Sinai wherein as the Fifth Commandment of the Decalogue it is written: "Honor thy father and thy mother: that thy days may be long upon the land which the Lord thy God giveth thee."

Consequently, in the exercise of discretion, the father is hereby accorded the right and privilege of visiting with his daughter Joanna on alternate weekends, a weekend being defined as from Friday evening at 5 P.M. to the following Sunday evening at 7 P.M., such visitation to take place away from the Yerkovich household and within the State of New York. In addition, the petitioner may have the temporary care and custody of his daughter for one month during the period from June 30 to September 1st of each year, with travel unrestricted.

Franklin Pierce took Joanna for a visit on December 20, 1974. Her mother had no choice but to comply with the court's order. She described herself as

stripped of all power to protect my daughter. At 5:30 that afternoon, Franklin Pierce came to our door with a "witness" from the . . . law firm. Tears were streaming down Joanna's little face. She kept begging me to do something. I assured her that it was just for a couple of days and that before she knew it she would be home with us for Christmas. As I buttoned her coat, she repeated, "Please, Mommy, tell him to just leave me alone. I just want to stay with my family." Ray [Mrs. Yerkovich's husband, who wanted to adopt Joanna] stood outside our apartment door, and I persuaded Joanna to go with Franklin Pierce because she must obey the law. Outside the door she clung to her "Raymie's" leg for protection. Franklin Pierce seeing that Joanna would not go on her own physically pulled her away, flung her over his shoulder as she kicked and screamed in outrage. He carried my little daughter to his waiting Toyota station wagon, stuffed her into it and drove away.[21]

Franklin Pierce did not return Joanna on December 22, 1974, as the court order required.[22] Not until 1984, when Joanna was fifteen years old, did Mrs. Yerkovich (who, in 1980, had cofounded Child Find Inc. to search for her daughter and other missing children) succeed in locating Joanna's whereabouts. Mother and daughter had a three-day reunion, after which Joanna decided to stay with her father in Florida.[23]*

These were the consequences of a system of justice that makes the child a pawn of the court, a victim of the simplistic notion that as *parens patriae* it has the capacity to manage and monitor a child's growing up better than a flesh-and-blood parent.

A child's need for continuity requires the state to recognize that a new family has been established the moment it has been determined who shall be the custodial parent. The new family deserves, therefore, to be as free of state intervention as any other "intact" family. Chancery Judge Pressler of the New Jersey Superior Court captured the essence of what we have in mind when he wrote in 1976 concerning visitation:

> Even under the best of circumstances and where the custodial parent is supportive of a continuing relationship between the child and the noncustodial parent, the nature of a parental relationship sustainable by way of visitation is necessarily and inevitably of a different character than that which is possible where the parents and children reside together as a single-family unit. . . . The children, after the parents' divorce or separation, belong to a different family unit than they did when the parents lived together. The *new family unit* consists only of the children and the custodial parent, and what is advantageous to that unit as a whole, to each of its members individually and to the way they relate to each other and function together is obviously in the best interests of the children.[25]

Unlike Judge Elwyn in Joanna Pierce's case, Justice Abella in Vanessa Richards' case recognized the *new family unit* and made it the cornerstone of her opinion. Like state courts in the United States, the Ontario, Canada, courts are generally obligated to provide visits ("access") to noncustodial parents. However, stressing the importance for the child of the *new family,* Justice Abella explains why the child's best interests require that the wishes of the custodial parent must be accorded greater deference than the wishes of the noncustodial parent.

---

*In 1989 a federal jury ordered Franklin Pierce to pay Mrs. Yerkovich $856,000 in compensatory damages for the severe mental anguish she had suffered as a result of his abducting Joanna and keeping her hidden from her mother for a decade, plus $725,000 in punitive damages. At the hearing Joanna told the jury that she hated her mother and considered her boring.[24]

VANESSA RICHARDS

MACGYVER V. RICHARDS
22 O.R. (3d)481, 482–495.
Court of Appeals for Ontario
March 23, 1995

Abella J.A. (Grange J.A. concurring):
The issue in this appeal is whether a custodial parent can change where he or she lives when the effect of that change is to prevent the other parent from continuing an established pattern of access [visits] with a child.

Both parents were 30 at the time of trial. They had met in 1983 when they were students at Memorial University in Newfoundland. The father, Lee MacGyver, left university to work in Ontario. The mother, Mary Richards, soon followed. They eventually moved to North Bay, where these proceedings took place. In early 1989, when she was four months pregnant, Mary Richards moved back to Newfoundland to live with her mother. The relationship with Lee MacGyver had ended by then. . . .

*   *   *

On June 20, 1991, pursuant to minutes of settlement dated June 19, 1991, Judge Duchesneau-McLachlan of the Ontario court (Provincial Division) ordered that the mother be given custody of Vanessa and that the father be given access on alternate weekends, from noon on Saturday until noon on Sunday, in addition to two hours during the week. . . .

Early in 1992, the mother became involved with Ron White, a Master Corporal with the Department of National Defense. In July 1993, White was transferred for four years to Tacoma, Washington. The couple made plans to marry on December 17, 1993, [and for] Vanessa and her mother [to move] to Washington to form a new family unit.

In January 1993, the father applied to vary the June 20, 1991 consent order . . . to prevent either parent being able to remove the child from the jurisdiction . . . without the other parent's consent. . . .

On December 7, 1993, after a two-day trial, Judge Duchesneau-McLachlan, who had made all the previous orders in connection with the child, ordered that the mother retain sole custody of Vanessa, who was by then almost four years old. . . .

The most contentious part of Judge Duchesneau-McLachlan's decision was an order that the child "shall reside in the City of North Bay until further order of the court."

*   *   *

[I] think the question of whether Vanessa should be required to remain in North Bay should be analyzed based on the father's current warm relationship with his daughter, and on an assumption of the father's sincerity in declaring his commitment to sobriety. The issue in this appeal, therefore, is not the scope of the right to move when one parent is abusive, but the scope of that right even when he or she is not.

*   *   *

The trial judge concluded:

Had I not been faced with this evidence [of the mother's intended marriage and move to Washington] *I am convinced that the proper order would have been, without doubt, the retention of sole custody by the mother,* with generous specific access to the father. (Emphasis added.)

There is nothing in the trial judge's reasons to indicate why the mother's intended marriage and move were detrimental to an award of sole custody. Several times in her reasons, the judge accepted that the only reasonable order in the circumstances was that there be no variation in the custody arrangement. Unequivocally, she tied the child's best interests exclusively to the mother. . . . For reasons that remain unclear from her reasons, however, the trial judge added: "I also feel that the child must remain in the North Bay area."

The trial judge found that several factors weighed in favor of the proposed move: the mother has always cared for the child; Vanessa was happy to go to Washington with her mother and Ron White, whom the child called "her bestest friend"; the assessment concluded that the child be part of the mother's proposed *new family**; the Department of National Defense was prepared to pay for two access visits per year for Vanessa with her father; and "preventing the child from going with her mother to Tacoma, Washington, for a period of four years . . . would

*Our emphasis.

prove a difficulty for the mother because obviously she is in love with Mr. White and would like to marry him."

She balanced these against the following factors: the pre-existing affectionate relationship between Vanessa and her father; taking the child away "from an environment she knows"; taking her away from the French immersion school system the mother had chosen for her; the father's financial situation; and the child's age. . . .

Accordingly, the trial judge concluded:

> *It's not necessary to move the child;* for example, we're dealing now with a four-year period when Mr. White is to be in Tacoma, Washington. There are a lot of other situations where parents are not together because one must go to school, one must do something else; one gets postings overseas perhaps where families cannot follow. It's not the best situation, I agree. It's not. But it's not the best situation for the mother. It is the best situation for the child. (Emphasis added.)

The mother's evidence at trial was that she would not move to Washington without her child. According to Ron White's commanding officer, a request to change his posting from Tacoma, Washington would be resisted by his employers, and have "serious career implications," including the possibility of being released from the military and losing his pension. To date, the relationship between White and the mother is ongoing, but there has been no marriage.

*   *   *

The evidence in this case clearly supported the trial judge's conclusion that it is in the child's best interests that the mother have sole custody. It also supported her conclusion that the father had a warm relationship with his daughter and that both he and the child hoped it would continue.

But it is, in my view, a quantum leap from the observation that a child has a good relationship with a noncustodial parent to the conclusion that the preservation of this relationship is the determinative factor in deciding what is in the child's best interests. In a dispute over mobility, the certainty of a good relationship between the parent with access and the child is known. The decision to move, on the other hand, contains uncertainty. But this does not mean that it will not be best for the child.

*　　*　　*

The "best interests" test has to be understood in its context: it never arises when two parents live together, or agree to a decision about the child's care. Absent the kind of neglect which triggers child welfare legislation, parents are largely free to make whatever decisions they feel are best for their children. Parents who separate but can agree as to the child's care, are subject to no outside scrutiny of what they determine to be in the child's best interests. . . . [T]he only time courts scrutinize whether parental conduct is conducive to a child's best interests is when the parents are involved in the kind of fractious situation that is probably, in the inevitability of its stress and pain and ambiguity, least conducive to the child's or anyone else's best interests.

Deciding what is best for a child is uniquely delicate. The judge in a custody case is called upon to prognosticate about a child's future, and to speculate about which parenting proposal will turn out to be best for a child. Judges are left to do their best with the evidence, on the understanding that deciding what is best for a child is a judgment the accuracy of which may be unknowable until later events prove—or disprove—its wisdom.

The speculative nature of the task clearly cannot absolve judges from responsibility for exercising their judgment about what, according to the evidence, augurs best at that point for the balance of the childhood. It can, however, and should, in deciding the incidents of custody, give pause about the extent to which judges interpose themselves between the child and the parent responsible for exercising, on a daily basis, the kind of judgment a judge is called upon to make only once. The parent, not the judge, will be left to live with the daily consequences of caring for the child within the limits of that one judicial pronouncement.

This argues, it seems to me, for particular sensitivity and a presumptive deference to the needs of the responsible custodial parent who, in the final analysis, lives the reality, not the speculation, of decisions dealing with the incidents of custody. The judicial perspective should acknowledge the overwhelmingly relentless nature of the custodial responsibility, and respect its day-to-day demands.

More importantly, that perspective should incorporate an emphasis on recovery, that is, an approach that respects the rehabilitative rights and needs of every adult and child recovering from the dissolution of a former family. It is likely that no one is going to be able to have every wish or need accommodated, but there should at least be an emphasis on eliminating as much disadvantage for everyone as the circumstances reasonably permit, consistent with facilitating the possibility that every member of the former family can get on with his or her life.

In this facilitative, rehabilitative model, the custodial parent must be understood as bearing a disproportionate amount of responsibility. The reality and constancy of that responsibility cannot be said to be the same as the responsibilities imposed on the parent who exercises access and sees the child intermittently. During those days or hours when parents without custody are not with their child, they are largely free to conduct their lives in any way they choose. The same cannot be said for parents with custody, most of whose decisions and choices are restricted by their role as the only adult legally responsible for the child.

Custody is an enormous undertaking which ought to be pre-eminently recognized by the courts in deciding disputed issues incidental to that custody, including mobility. The right or wish to see a child every weekend or two may be of genuine benefit to a child; but it cannot begin to approach the benefit to a child of someone who takes care of him or her every day. The scales used to weigh a child's best interests are not evenly balanced between two parents when one is an occasional and the other a constant presence. They are both, usually, beneficial. But, prima facie, one is demonstrably more beneficial than the other. . . .

In deciding what restrictions, if any, should be placed on a parent with custody, courts should be wary about interfering with that parent's capacity to decide, daily, what is best for the child. That is the very responsibility a custody order imposes on a parent, and it obliges—and entitles—the parent to exercise judgments which range from the trivial to the dramatic. Those judgments may include whether to change neighborhoods, or provinces, or partners, or jobs, or friends, or schools, or religions. Each of those significant judgments may affect the child in some way, but that does not mean that the court has the right to prevent the change.

. . . To minimize future stresses, as opposed to more utopian and less realistic objectives, the court should be overwhelmingly respectful of the decision-making capacity of the person in whom the court or the other parent has entrusted primary responsibility for the child. We cannot design a system which shields the non-custodial parent from any change in the custodial parent's life which may affect the exercise of access. The emphasis should be, rather, on deferring to the decision-making responsibilities of the custodial parent, unless there is substantial evidence that those decisions impair the child's, not the access parent's, long-term well-being.

We must also forcefully acknowledge that the custodial parent's best interests are inextricably tied to those of the child. The young child is almost totally dependent on that parent, not on the parent seen during visits. While it would always be preferable to attempt to find a solution which protects the child's relationship with both parents, this ideal is simply not always possible. It is practically inevitable, when two parents no longer live together, that the child's relationship with each will be different. This means that the child, and each of its parents, must adjust to the new realities. The adjustments may be painful, including the adjustment of a parent seeing a child less often than anticipated. However painful, that parent's desire cannot be paramount.

The child's best interests must be assessed not from the perspective of the parent seeking to preserve access, but from that of the child entitled to the best environment possible. It is a mistake to look down at the child as a prize to be distributed, rather than from the child up to the parent as an adult to be accountable. This by no means eliminates the adult's wishes from the equation; it means that those wishes cannot always be accommodated. It is the child's right to see a parent with whom she does not live, rather than the parent's right to insist on access to that child. That access, its duration, and quality, are regulated according to what is best for the child, rather than what is best for the parent seeking access.

*   *   *

[O]nce the parties themselves or a court decide that a particular person is primarily responsible for protecting a child and promoting the environment that best facilitates adjustments to change, that responsible parent should largely be free to carry on with parental decisions and duties. Unfortunately, this may affect the parent with access, but in the long run it may not affect the child. And it is the child, after all, who is at the centre of the exercise.

When, therefore, a court has been asked to decide what is in a child's best interests, and a choice must be made between the responsible wishes and needs of the parent with custody and the parent with access, it seems to me manifestly unfair to treat these wishes and needs as being on an equal footing. When one adds to this the dimension that a court's decision ought to favor the possibility that the former partners can get on with their lives and their responsibilities, one reaches the admittedly difficult conclusion that a parent with custody, acting responsibly, should not be prevented from leaving a jurisdiction because the move would interfere with access by the other parent with the child, even if the relationship between the child and the access parent is a good one.

To conclude otherwise may render custody a unilaterally punitive order. No court could—or would—prevent a parent with access from moving anywhere or at any time he or she chose. Lee MacGyver could, for example, anytime he chose, and for whatever reason he chose, decide to leave North Bay for anywhere he chose, whether or not a court deemed the move "necessary." Whether or not the motivation was benign, and whether or not the loss of the visits was harmful to the child, it is inconceivable that a court would insist that the parent with access remain in the jurisdiction for the sake of the child's best interests. To do so would be an unwarranted intrusion into an entirely personal decision.

I have difficulty understanding why, then, courts should not feel equally constrained in interfering with the right of a custodial parent to decide where to live. In my view, it is not for a court to pass judgment on whether a move is "necessary" for the custodial parent, any more than it would be for a court to pass judgment on a similar decision by the parent with access. It is hard enough for members of a former family to adjust to separation without courts telling them where they should live.

In the case before us, the trial judge put the mother in the Solomonic position of having to choose between her child and her marriage. The mother made it clear that she would never leave North Bay without her child, and the trial judge made it clear that the mother should continue to have sole custody. By deciding that the child should remain in North Bay, the trial judge disregarded the recommendations of an expert assessment that this new family would be in the child's best interests, effectively denied the mother the opportunity to carry on with her life, and deprived the child of the opportunity to live in a new family unit. Instead, the trial judge tied the future prospects of the mother and child to the visiting parent's wishes and convenience.

. . . In suggesting that the move was "not necessary," the trial judge was imposing an idiosyncratic, inappropriate and arbitrary test. The test is not whether a judge feels subjectively that a move is "necessary," but whether there is any reason to conclude that the move would not be in the child's best interests.

*   *   *

. . . . Vanessa's long-term best interests are tied to those of the parent responsible for her day-to-day care. There is no reason why her father's visiting rights should be permitted to create an insurmountable wall around North Bay for her mother. Custodial parents are expected to conduct their lives in conformity with the needs of their children, not with those of the parent with access. Where, as here, the mother is chained to the anchor of access and she, unlike the father, is thereby prevented from choosing her future, an error has clearly been made about the parent to whom the child's best interests are predominantly attached. Without denying the mutual affection between Lee MacGyver and Vanessa, it cannot be said, based on the evidence, that the accommodation of his wish to see her every two weekends is more conducive to the child's best interests than her mother's right to get on with her life and establish a new home for the child.

Custody and access represent symmetrical relationships with a child, but not identical ones. The trial judge erred in giving priority to the imperatives of the access relationship over those of the custodial one, by requiring the child, and therefore the mother, to remain in North Bay. There was no evidence that move would impair the child's best interests, only that it would impair access. The two are not synonymous interests, and "access" must defer to "best interests" rather than the other way around. [There is an] inconsistency between the trial judge's conclusion that it was in the child's best interests to remain with her mother and her decision to deprive the mother of the right to decide where to live with her child. Accordingly, . . . the requirement that the child remain in North Bay [is deleted].

Justice Abella evidenced an understanding of the continuity guideline as well as the yet-to-be discussed guidelines—that placement decisions should reflect a child's sense of time, and should take into account the law's incapacity to make long-range predictions and to manage day-to-day family relationships.

CHAPTER 4

Placement Decisions Should Reflect
the Child's Sense of Time

A child's sense of time is an integral part of the continuity concept that merits independent consideration.

Unlike adults, who have learned—at least in theory—to anticipate the future and thus to manage delay, children have a built-in time sense based on the urgency of their instinctual and emotional needs. As an infant begins to incorporate the way in which parents satisfy wishes and needs, either directly or by distraction, as well as the experience of the reappearance of parents after their disappearance, a child gradually develops the capacity to anticipate the future and to postpone gratification. For example, an interval of separation between parent and child that would constitute a break in continuity for an infant would be of no or little significance to a school-age youngster. The time it takes to break an old attachment or to form a new one will depend upon the different meanings time has for children at each stage of their development.

Emotionally and intellectually, an infant or toddler cannot stretch her waiting more than a few days without feeling overwhelmed by the absence of her parents. She cannot take care of herself physically, and her emotional and intellectual memory has not matured sufficiently to enable her to hold on mentally to the parent she has "lost." During such an absence, the child under two years of age "quickly"* latches on to the new adult who cares for the child's needs.[1] For children under the age of five years, an absence of parents for more than two months is intolerable. For the younger school-age child, an absence of six months or more may be similarly experienced. More than a year of being without parents and without evidence that there are parental concerns and expectations is not likely to be understood by the older school-age

---

*We should be alert to the fact that time words such as *quickly* express an adult's sense of time. From an infant's point of view, the sentence in the text should read *"after a prolonged period of time* latches on . . ."

41

child and will carry with it the detrimental implications of the breaches in continuity we have already described. After adolescence is fully launched, an individual's sense of time closely approaches that of most adults.

Thus a child may experience a given time period not according to its actual duration, measured objectively by calendar and clock, but according to her subjective feelings of impatience, frustration, and loss. These feelings will affect whether the intervals set for feeding (or for the absence of the parent, or the duration of hospitalization, and so forth) will seem to the child short or long, tolerable or intolerable—and as a result, whether they will prove harmless or harmful in their consequences. The significance of parental absences depends upon their duration, their frequency, and the developmental period during which they occur. The younger the child, the shorter is the interval before a leave-taking will be experienced as a permanent loss accompanied by feelings of helplessness, abandonment, and profound deprivation. Since a child's sense of time is directly related to her capacity to cope with breaches in continuity, it becomes a factor in determining if, when, and with what urgency the law should act.

Implications

The child's-sense-of-time guideline would require decision-makers to act "quickly" (in child time) to maximize each child's opportunity either to restore stability to an existing relationship or to facilitate the establishment of new relationships. Procedural and substantive decision-making should not exceed the time that the child-to-be-placed can endure loss and uncertainty.

When the *physical* well-being of a child or adult may be endangered by delay, both administrative and judicial bodies recognize that they confront an emergency and demonstrate their capacity to make prompt determinations. When, for example, parents refuse to authorize a blood transfusion for their deathly ill child, hospitals and courts can and do move with great dispatch and flexibility by giving such cases priority. Judges may act in a matter of hours after an application for decision is made—they may even conduct their hearings at bedside in the hospital. The blood transfusion cases may be perceived as emergency child placement cases for a temporary period and a limited purpose.

Yet when the child's *psychological* well-being is involved, the child placement process does not assure prompt, final decisions. It is characterized by extended periods of uncertainty caused by overcautious and overworked administrative agencies; by overcrowded court dockets and oft-postponed judicial hearings; and by lengthy periods for appeal after trial.

In order to minimize *psychological* harm, the unresolved placement must be treated as the matter of urgency that it is for the child. Three months may not be a long time for an adult decision-maker. For a young child it may seem forever. Whatever the cause of the time-taking, the costs as well as the benefits of the delay to the child must be weighed. Our guideline would allow for no more delay than that required for reasoned judgment. We do not mean certainty of judgment. We mean no more than the most reasonable judgment that can be made within the time available—measured to accord with the child's sense of time.

As a matter of normal procedure, a child's placement must be treated by legislatures, courts, and administrative agencies as a matter of urgency that comports with the child's sense of time.

ADOPTION

For adoption agencies, the child's-sense-of-time guideline would mean pursuing a policy of earliest possible placement. Infants should, if possible, be "placed" even before birth. Expectant parents who contemplate putting their child up for adoption should receive agency assistance in reaching a firm decision before birth, either to keep or not to keep the child. Adopting families should be investigated and selected in advance of a child's availability for adoption. If anyone is to be kept waiting, it should not be the child but the adults, for whom the anticipation may be a positive factor. Once the child is born, there should be only brief periods for birth parents to change their minds or for gathering information about the child or the adopting parents in order to certify "fitness." Adopting families should be prepared to accept the child the moment she becomes available. We share the view of Littner, who observed:

> There is no question that the longer we wait, the more we will know. Yet . . . to be able to give complete assurance of normal development we would have to place adults, and not children. [A]ny program that does not place children early is running the risk of exposing the majority of their children to certain perils of late placement in order to protect the minority from the possible dangers of misplacement.[2]

Of course, the older a child is at the time of adoption, the longer may be the justifiable delay to find a placement that will maximize continuity of environment including lifestyle, relationships with siblings, and educational opportunities.

As for court procedures in adoption, initial hearings should be scheduled promptly and decisions rendered quickly. The time allowed for making an appeal should be extremely short—not more than a week or two—with a final decision rendered within days after the close of the appellate hearing. Prompt appeals and decisions safeguard not only the interests of the child but also those of aggrieved adult parties. The longer a child remains with the adult who retains custody pending appeal, the less likely, under the continuity guideline, will it be appropriate to change her placement.

SEPARATION AND DIVORCE

What has been said with regard to judicial proceedings in adoption applies as well to child custody in divorce or separation. The child's-sense-of-time guideline, as well as the continuity guideline, would require that all disputes between the parents about the placement of their children be resolved by separate and accelerated proceedings prior to and without waiting for a determination of the divorce.[3]

ABANDONMENT AND NEGLECT

The concept of abandonment or permanent neglect, to turn from procedure to substance, provides another illustration for the application of our guidelines. In determining the eligibility of a child for adoption, for example, the law of abandonment rests primarily on the intent of the parent, not the length of her absence.[4] It may even rest on how diligent a child care agency has been in its efforts "to encourage and strengthen" the relationship between a child in foster care and the absent biological parent.[5] The failure of an agency to make such an effort can preclude a court from finding that a child has been abandoned in law, even though from the child's point of view she has been abandoned in fact.[6] Moreover, abandonment has been perceived as a continuing process that may be reversed by the absent parent's express declaration of a change of mind.[7]

Application of the child's-sense-of-time guideline would require a shift of focus to the individual child's tolerance of absence and sense of abandonment, and away from the adult's intent to abandon or from an agency's failure to encourage a relationship. The time factor varies with a child's maturity at the time of separation and the extent to which the ties with the absent adults have effectively been kept alive. The process through which a new child-parent status emerges is complex and subject to many individual variations. For the purposes of declaring a child eligible for adoption or of acknowledging the existence of a common-law adoptive relationship, abandonment in law would have taken place by the time the parents' absence has caused the child to feel no longer wanted by them. It would be that time when the child, having felt helpless and abandoned, has reached out to establish a new relationship with an adult who is to become or has already become her psychological parent.

CHAPTER 5

Placement Decisions Should Take into Account the Law's Incapacity to Make Long-range Predictions and to Manage Family Relationships

Though obvious once said, when left unsaid the limitations of law often go unacknowledged in discussions about child placement. Too frequently there is attributed to the law and its agents a magical power—a power to do what is far beyond their means. While the law may claim to regulate parent-child relationships, it can at best do little more than give them recognition and provide an opportunity for them to develop.

The law, so far as specific individual relationships are concerned, is a relatively crude instrument.[1] It may be able to undermine human relationships, but it does not have the power to compel them to develop. It has neither the sensitivity nor the resources to maintain or supervise ongoing day-to-day happenings between parent and child.[2] Nor does it have the capacity to predict future events and needs that would justify or make workable over the *long run* any *specific* conditions it might impose upon the parent or parents with whom the child is placed. We share the view of Judge Wachenfeld, a view that is too easily ignored in the law and administration of child placement:

> The uncertainties of life . . . will always remain to be encountered as long as one lives. . . . Their devious forms and variations are too complicated and numerous to be susceptible of tabulation. Our inability to predict or solve them anchors us closely to nature's intendment. . . .
>
> A judicial approach does not make the future more readily foreseeable and the assurance of our decisions, whatever it be, is unfortunately circumscribed by the frailties of human judgment.[3]

The law, then, ought to and generally does prefer the private ordering of interpersonal relationships over state intrusions on them.[4] Yet the state does intrude. It is therefore important to recognize the limits of law, as well as how limited is the predictive value of the knowledge on which decision-makers rely.

Each child placement—even that by birth certificate—is based upon general assumptions and predictions about children and the adults who are designated as parents. As the continuity and the child's-sense-of-time guidelines suggest, placement decisions can and should be based on certain generally applicable presumptions. For example, properly informed decision-makers can identify who among *presently available* adults is or has the capacity to become a psychological parent and to allow a child to feel wanted. They can decide that the adult most likely suited for this role is the one (if there be one), with whom the child has already had and continues to have an affectionate bond. Further, they can predict that the younger the child and the more extended the period of uncertainty or separation, the more detrimental this will be to the child's well-being, and the more urgent it becomes—even without perfect knowledge—to place the child permanently.

No one can forecast, however, just what experiences, events, or changes a child (or, for that matter, her adult caregiver) will encounter. Nor can anyone predict in detail how the unfolding development of a child in her family will in the long run be reflected in her personality and character formation.[5] Thus the law will not act in the child's interests if it tries to do the impossible—to guess the future and to impose on the caregiver special conditions for the child's day-to-day or weekend-to-weekend care. This leads to harmful and threatening discontinuity by encouraging review and revision of placement decisions. The child's interests will be better served if the law has less confidence in long-term predictions and shows more confidence in the caregiver it selects by making placements unconditional.

New York Family Court Judge Nanette Dembitz has forcefully argued that our guidelines oversimplify the complex issues in child placement disputes. She has written that the promise to provide guidelines "is seductive but impossible; [that we] fail to devise usable scales because the amalgams of factors to be appraised in custody contests are too complex."[6] Too complex for what? Surely not too complex to prevent a court from deciding what it needs to decide, namely, *who* among the competing adults or child care agencies is to assume parental control and responsibility for the child. There is, however, an important element of truth in her observation that guidelines are "beyond any discipline's competence." That truth is that it is beyond the competence of any judge, or the competence of any discipline for that matter, to appraise the amalgam of human factors in any child placement dispute for purposes of making long-term predictions or dictating special conditions for custody.

Those judges who share the Dembitz position confuse their *authority* to do with their *capacity* to do. They fail to realize that the *who* of custody and the *how* of custody do not raise the same issues and must be treated differently and separately. It is the *who* which judges must and can decide. It is the *how* which is beyond any judge's (or legislator's) competence. Yet judges often fail to see what must be obvious once said—that the intricate character of the parent-child relationship places it beyond the constructive, though not beyond the destructive, reach of the law.

Familial bonding is too complex and too vulnerable a process to be regulated by so gross and impersonal an instrument as the law. In rejecting our simple guidelines as simplistic, legislatures and courts become the oversimplifiers. They seduce themselves into believing that they can micromanage the relationships of the adults whom they have selected to be responsible for managing the child's care. Acting like the well-intentioned, overprotective, and often destructive parent who doesn't know when to let go, they decide not only *who* is to be parent, but also *how* the child is to be parented—for example, educated, medicated, and visited. Too frequently judges behave as if the function of placement decisions is to provide a child with autonomous judges, not autonomous parents.

Courts, administrative agencies, and the experts upon whom they rely must learn to reject simplistic notions about parent-child relationships. They can no longer deny what their experience should make obvious to them: They have the time and capacity to damage, but not to nurture or manage, the healthy growth of familial bonds. In their professional roles they cannot be parents to someone else's children. At best and at most, law can provide a new opportunity for the relationship between a child and her caregiver to unfold free of coercive meddling by the state.

The guidelines of continuity, of a child's sense of time, and of the limitations of law and knowledge are simple but not simplistic. These three guidelines grow out of a recognition that the process of growing up is complex and vulnerable. They recognize how vital it is for a child to be secure in the feeling that her parents are in charge and in control. Except for institutional placements and for temporary, truly short-term foster care, judges must pull out decisively after determining who shall have custody. Their decisions must evidence their trust and expectation that the caregivers selected can be relied upon to meet the child's ever-changing needs. It is precisely because human relationships are complicated that courts and administrative agencies must have simple guidelines which will lead to an immediate and unequivocal restoration of family integrity as each child is placed. The presumptions of parental autonomy and a policy of minimum state intervention require no less. When rendering a decision about a child's placement, simplicity is the ultimate sophistication.

CHAPTER 6

Placements Should Provide the Least Detrimental Available Alternative for Safeguarding the Child's Growth and Development

A t birth the interests of a child are and should be presumed to coincide with the interests of her biological parents. Therefore the child's interests require the state to respect the integrity of that family relationship unless and until there are statutory grounds for overcoming that presumption. We share the manifest purpose of the "best interests of the child" standard, which is that if the initial presumption has been overcome the law again make paramount the needs of the child to be placed. But because the best-interests standard did not in and of itself define what it is that a child needs,[1] we propose that the placement standard should be one that provides the *least detrimental available alternative for safeguarding a child's growth and development.*

The least detrimental alternative incorporates our three guidelines: in accord with the child's sense of time and on the basis of short-term predictions, it is that *specific placement* and *procedure for placement* which maximize her opportunity for being wanted and for maintaining, on a continuous, unconditional, and permanent basis, a relationship with at least one adult who is in fact, or is capable of becoming, her psychological parent. The use of "least detrimental" rather than "best interests" is intended to enable legislatures, courts, and child care agencies to recognize the detriment that is already present in every child placement decision. A child whose placement must be determined in legal controversy has already been deprived of her "best interests"—by the loss or threat of loss of her parents; by their rejection, neglect, or abuse; or by the breaking up of her family for other reasons. It is beyond any court's power to undo the disturbances that she has already suffered. Acknowledging this fact by the words "least detrimental" is intended to remind decision-makers that their task is to salvage as much as possible out of a less-than-satisfactory situation. Acknowledging this fact should

50

reduce the likelihood of decision-makers becoming enmeshed in the hope and magic associated with the "best," which can lead them into believing that the law has greater power to do "good" than to do "bad."

The concept of "available" alternatives is intended to press into focus how circumscribed are the choices generally open to decision-makers for helping a child in the placement process, and how limited is their capacity to make valid long-term predictions. The least-detrimental-available-alternative standard is less awesome and grandiose, more realistic, and thus less prone to irrelevant, time-consuming data gathering than is the best-interests standard.

Implications: The Baby Richard Case

The tension between the function of the best-interests standard and its construction in legislative, administrative, and judicial decisions is illustrated by a series of opinions in Illinois from 1991 to 1995 involving baby boy Richard.[2] The opinions of the appellate court in this case highlight most of the problems that led us to propose the least-detrimental-available-alternative standard. At the same time, these opinions demonstrate that the guidelines which underlie that standard can be subsumed under the best-interests label. And the opinion of the Illinois supreme court in overturning the appellate court's ruling highlights the detriment to a child caught up in the placement process when statutes that are designed to protect parent-child relationships are construed and applied to destroy these very relationships because of a failure to recognize who, from the child's point of view, are in fact his parents.

THE FACTS

John and Jane Doe filed a petition to adopt a newborn baby boy, Richard. Richard's biological parents, Daniella Janikova ("Daniella"), and Otakar Kirchner ("Otakar"), were not married and were not living together at the time of his birth. Four days after Richard was born, Daniella, without identifying the father, gave formal consent to have the baby placed for adoption. Daniella told Otakar that Richard had died shortly after his birth. Otakar thought Richard might be alive but was unable to verify his belief. Not until Richard was two months old did Daniella tell Otakar that the boy was alive and had been placed for adoption. Otakar opposed the granting of the adoption petition on the basis that he did not consent. Otakar and Daniella then got married. The adoption case proceeded to trial. The trial court found that, under the Illinois Adoption Statute, Otakar was an unfit person to have a child because he had failed to demonstrate a reasonable degree of interest or responsibility as to the welfare of a newborn child during the first thirty days after birth. Under the statute his consent was therefore not required. The trial court then granted the petition of John and Jane Doe to adopt Richard. Otakar appealed from the judgment of adoption.

Table of Events

March 16, 1991	The birth of Baby Richard.
March 20, 1991 (Richard is 4 days old)	Daniella gives a "Final and Irrevocable Consent to Adoption." John and Jane Doe take custody of Richard and file a petition to adopt him.
June 6, 1991 (Richard is almost 3 months old)	Otakar files an appearance in the adoption proceeding but is denied standing.
December 9, 1991 (Richard is almost 9 months old)	Otakar is declared Richard's biological father. The Does amend their petition to adopt, alleging that Otakar is unfit to have a child and that therefore his consent is not required.
May 5, 1992 (Richard is almost 14 months old)	Adoption trial begins. The Does' petition to adopt Richard is granted. Otakar's parental rights are terminated. He files an appeal.
August 18, 1993 (Richard is almost 2½ years old)	The appellate court decides.
June 16, 1994 (Richard is almost 3½ years old)	The supreme court of Illinois decides.

THE OPINIONS

Justice Rizzi, writing for the appellate court, rejected Otakar's claim that the adoption be reversed and that Richard be turned over to live with him and Daniella. In coming to that decision Justice Rizzi applied a "best interests of the child" standard in language that distinctly resonates with the words and ideas that underlie "the least detrimental alternative" formulation:

> Richard has lived *continuously* with John and Jane Doe since March 20, 1991, four days after his birth.* He is now, August 18, 1993, two years and five months old.
>
> Fortunately, the time has long past when children in our society were considered the property of their parents. Slowly, but finally, when it comes to children even the law has rid itself of the Dred Scott mentality that a human being can be considered a piece of property "belonging" to another human being. To hold that a child is the property of his parents is to deny the humanity of the child. Thus, in the present case we start with the premise that Richard is not a piece of property with property rights belonging to either his biological or adoptive parents. Richard "belongs" to no one but himself.
>
> Of course, in any parental relationship a parent and a child both have rights, vis-a-vis, each other, which are protected under the law. In an adoption, custody or abuse case, however, the child is the real party in interest. *[I]t is his best interest and corollary rights that come before anything else, including the interests and rights of biological and adoptive parents.*
>
> Here, by inherent necessity, whether or not raised by the embroiled and warring biological and adoptive parents, *the best interest of Richard surfaces as the paramount issue in the case.* If there is a conflict between Richard's best interest and the rights and interests of his parents, *whomever they may be, the rights and interests of the parents must yield and allow the best interest of Richard to pass through and prevail.* This tenet allows no exception.
>
> *A child's best interest is not part of an equation. It is not to be balanced against any other interest.* In adoption cases, like custody and abuse cases, a child's best interest is and must remain inviolate and impregnable from all other factors, including the interests of the parents. . . . In recognition of this fact, the Adoption Act provides:

*Emphasis added throughout.

Best interest and welfare of child—Construction of Act
    The best interest and welfare of the person to be adopted shall be of paramount consideration in the construction and interpretation of this Act.

Attempting to resolve what is the best interest of an infant is obviously a wrenching ordeal. In cases like the present, however, if one focuses on the child while disregarding the tendentious arguments of the biological and adoptive parents, he is left with the unquestionable conclusion that *resolution of the issue of parentage quickly is foremost in the best interest of the child. Also, serious delay in resolving the child's parentage not only frustrates the best interest of the child, but it can cause grave harm to the child.*

                        *   *   *

The present case vividly illustrates why it would be contrary to the best interest of the child to remove him from the parents who adopted him *if he has lived with them continuously.* . . . Richard is now two years and five months old. The only parents that he has ever known are John and Jane Doe. He has not touched or seen Daniella since four days after his birth, and he has never spoken a word to her. Nor has he ever touched, seen, or communicated with Otakar. In fact, he is totally unaware of the existence of Daniella and Otakar.[3]
    The fact that we have the Adoption Act in Illinois is a recognition in the law that it takes more to being a parent than being one of the sexual partners to the physiological formation of a child. Since Richard was a newborn, John and Jane Doe have done everything with Richard that is the essence of being parents, and Richard has done everything with them that is the essence of being a son. Contrariwise, since he was a newborn, Daniella and Otakar have done nothing with Richard that is the essence of being parents, and he has done nothing with them that is the essence of being a son.
    There comes a point when we should not be ignorant as judges of what we know as men and women. . . . Plainly, it would be contrary to the best interest of Richard to "switch" parents at this stage of his life. We must therefore act accordingly. Courts are here to protect children—not to victimize them.
    Under the circumstances, we conclude that it would be contrary to the best interest of Richard to disturb the judgment of adoption. We,

therefore, affirm the judgment of adoption . . . for the reason that it would be in the best interest of Richard. . . .[4]

Everything Justice Rizzi had written to this point suggests that he carefully considered and applied a child-centered approach to Baby Richard's case (whether one chooses to call it a "best interests of the child" or a "least detrimental alternative" standard). He had recognized that Richard "'belongs' to no one but himself" and that his interests are "paramount." He had explicitly recognized the importance of continuity, stating that "it would be contrary to the best interest of the child to remove him from the parents . . . he has lived with . . . continuously for . . . two years and five months. . . . The only parents that he has ever known are John and Jane Doe." He had recognized that time did not stand still for Baby Richard while the case was under appeal. He did not, as appellate courts traditionally do, stop the clock as of the time of trial—in this case on May 5, 1992—and review the facts as if Richard were still one year and two months old. He began the substantive part of his opinion by stating that Richard "is now, August 18, 1993, two years and five months old."

Justice Rizzi closed his opinion by stressing the importance of recognizing the connection between the process and the substantive result. Sensitive to Baby Richard's sense of time as well as his need for continuity, he wrote:

> Finally, we are constrained to address another matter in this case. Richard's story is the account of a helpless child caught in the quagmire of a judicial system that in attempting to resolve his problem became part of his problem. It has taken two years and five months for this case to sluggishly move through our judicial system. In a case of this nature, where plainly time is critical, it is a sad commentary on our judiciary.
>
> It shamefully took one year and almost two months from the time that the petition for adoption was filed to the time that the judgment of adoption was entered. It has shamefully taken one year and three months from the time that the notice of appeal was filed to decide this case in the appellate court.
>
> It is surely imperative that the judiciary have enough judges and proper judicial case management in place at both the trial and appellate levels so that "time" does not become a factor in the decisional process of a case. Every effort must be made to see that we do not have any more cases in Illinois where it takes two years and five months to determine the lawful parentage of a young child.

*   *   *

Accordingly, the judgment of adoption and the orders inherent to the validity of the judgment of adoption are affirmed for the reasons stated.[5]

Had Justice Rizzi said no more in his opinion, we would be persuaded that in Illinois the best-interests-of-the-child standard had come a long way toward accepting that the child's interests are to be paramount, and are not to be balanced against the interests of competing adults; that continuity of care is essential to a child's well-being; that placement decisions must be made by a process that recognizes, in terms of a child's sense of time, the urgency of restoring or establishing stability; and that harm can result from delay in deciding who are the adults whom the child knows as parents.

But Justice Rizzi did say much more in his opinion. He affirmed and rested his decision on the trial judge's finding that Otakar's consent to Richard's adoption was not required because he was "an unfit person to have a child" since he "had failed to demonstrate a reasonable degree of interest, concern, or responsibility as to the welfare of [the] newborn child during the first 30 days after [his] birth." But even if the evidence had established that Otakar had shown a reasonable degree of interest in Richard's welfare and was therefore "fit," there would have been no justification for Justice Rizzi to order his removal from the Does. He had already concluded that they were "the only parents [Richard] has ever known."[6] Rather than examine the evidence of Otakar's fitness, Justice Rizzi should have said:

> The time has long since passed since findings of fact concerning Otakar's fitness—or lack of it—could be taken into account in deciding the adoption question. Richard has gone beyond the point of no return. He must not be used to remedy the wrong that may have been done to Otakar or to punish the Does for conspiring with Daniella to deny Otakar a say.

By resting his decision on Otakar's unfitness, Justice Rizzi strained credibility. He described the facts as "clear and convincing evidence that Otakar was an unfit person to have a child." Justice Tully, in his dissenting opinion, correctly observed that "the majority . . . patently distorted and slanted the actual facts. . . ."[7]

Perhaps Justice Rizzi turned toward the "fitness" issue—and ultimately chose to base his decision on that issue—not because of a genuine belief that this was the important question, but because of his fear as an appellate judge that not doing so would make the case vulnerable to further appeal and reversal.[8] But as a result, Justice Rizzi undermined and caused confusion where initially he had brought clarity to the real issue before the court. By turning away from the issue of Richard's needs to Otakar's fitness, Justice Rizzi muffled his own cry that "we should not be ignorant as judges of what we know as men and women"; that "it takes more to being a parent than being one of the sexual partners to the physiological formation of a child"; that the Does "have done everything with Richard that is the essence of being parents, and [that] Richard has done everything with them that is the essence of being a son;" that "Daniella and Otakar have done nothing with Richard that is the essence of being parents, and he has done nothing with them that is the essence of being a son"; that "it would be contrary to the best interest of Richard to 'switch' parents at this stage of his life"; and that "courts are here to protect children."

In turning away from what should be the central issue of the case—determining who, from Richard's point of view, were his parents—and confusing the matter with the issue of Otakar's "fitness," Justice Rizzi's opinion sent a mixed message to other courts, particularly the Illinois supreme court, which might be expected to hear an appeal. Instead of attempting to ground his decision on the "fitness" issue, Justice Rizzi should have clearly stated that he was required to protect an ongoing parent-child relationship: the one between Richard and the Does. If he had made this argument, Justice Rizzi would have been better able to assert and to reinforce society's strong preference for keeping families intact.

What Justice Rizzi should have emphasized was that Richard's biological father was the "third party" in this case. In another case, the Illinois supreme court has required a third party seeking to obtain custody of a child to demonstrate "good cause or reason to overcome the presumption that a parent has a superior right to custody and further to show that it is in the child's best interests that the third party be awarded the care, custody and control of the minor."[9] Because at the time of decision Richard had an established parent-child relationship with the Does, that family relationship deserved the same protection as the relationship between a child and his caregiving biological parents. The questions the court should have addressed are: first; who, from Richard's point of view, are his parents? and second; is there any justification, such as neglect or abuse, for removing Richard from them?

The dissenting appellate court judge, Justice Tully, as we have noted, was not convinced by the court's reasons for its judgment. He contended (correctly, we think) that the court's finding of Otakar's "unfitness" was a charade.[10] Taking into account a child's sense of time and need for continuity of care, he also observed:

First and foremost, laws are needed mandating a good-faith investigation into the identity and location of the biological father prior to the finalization of any adoption. Severe sanctions should be imposed upon parties and their counsel for concealing information regarding the whereabouts of the natural father. Secondly, the time period within which the natural father may assert his rights must be limited to a fixed period of time, for example, no more than 30 days from the birth of the child, unless he possesses an affirmative defense, but in no case should this period be extended beyond 120 days. Finally, any assertion of parental rights within this time period should mandate an emergency hearing on the best interests of the child's disposition which should encompass the rights of the biological parent who had not terminated his parental rights. Within 30 days of this hearing, an expedited appeal should be filed and scheduled for immediate hearing and an expedited ruling. The entire process should take no more than six months, unlike the instant case, where the process took two and one-half years. If this had been the law, we would now be deciding the fate of a six-month old infant and not that of a two and one-half year old toddler.[11]

Nearly a year later the appellate court's decision was reversed by the Illinois supreme court. In a terse opinion for the court, Justice Heiple defined the issue narrowly:

In the opinion below, the appellate court, wholly missing the threshold issue in this case, dwelt on the best interests of the child. Since, however, the father's parental interest was improperly terminated, there was no occasion to reach the factor of the child's best interests. That point should never have been reached and need never have been discussed.

Unfortunately, over three years have elapsed since the birth of the baby who is the subject of these proceedings. To the extent that it is relevant to assign fault in this case the fault lies initially with the mother, who fraudulently tried to deprive the father of his rights, and secondly, with the adoptive parents and their attorney, who proceeded with the adoption when they knew that a real father was out there who had been denied knowledge of his baby's existence. When the father entered his appearance in the adoption proceedings 57 days after the baby's birth and demanded his rights as a father, the petitioners should have relinquished the baby at that time. It was their decision to prolong this litigation through a lengthy, and ultimately fruitless, appeal.

The adoption laws of Illinois are neither complex nor difficult of application. Those laws intentionally place the burden of proof on the adoptive parents in establishing both the relinquishment and/or unfitness of the natural parents and, coincidentally, the fitness and the right to adopt of the adoptive parents. In addition, Illinois law requires a good-faith effort to notify the natural parents of the adoption proceedings. These laws are designed to protect natural parents in their preemptive rights to their own children wholly apart from any consideration of the so-called best interests of the child. If it were otherwise, few parents should be secure in the custody of their own children. If best interests of the child were a sufficient qualification to determine child custody, anyone with superior income, intelligence, education, etc., might challenge and deprive the parents of their right to their own children. The law is otherwise and was not complied with in this case.

Accordingly, we reverse.[12]

Was the outcome in Richard's case, and the procedure by which it was determined, the least detrimental alternative? For Richard, as for any child, the least detrimental alternative would have been that placement and procedure for placement which maximized, in accord with his sense of time, and on the basis of short-term predictions, his opportunity to be wanted by adults who had assumed or, if there were none, who would assume, responsibility for his continuous care. *Substantively,* had the trial court decided the Does' adoption petition promptly after Otakar tried to intervene, the outcome, which would have depended on how the consent question was resolved, could, from Richard's point of view, have gone either way. That is because Richard, not yet three months old, might not have been with the Does long enough for a firm psychological tie to have developed. *Substantively,* by the time the trial court actually rendered its ruling—to leave Richard with the Does—this was the least detrimental alternative for him. That is because by this time Richard had been with the Does, more than a year—long enough for a firm child-parent relationship to have developed. *Substantively,* for the same reason, the appellate court decision to leave two-and-a-half-year-old Richard with the Does was the least detrimental alternative for him. *Substantively,* again for the same reason, the decision of the Illinois supreme court almost a year later to remove Richard from the Does and award him to Otakar was *not* the least detrimental alternative for him.[13]

The supreme court, and not the appellate court, "wholly miss[ed] the threshold issue in this case." It asserted, correctly, that until parental interests in Richard were properly terminated "there was no occasion to reach . . . the child's best interests. That point should never have been reached. . . ." But the supreme court failed to identify correctly which parental interests were the ones that had to be terminated before Richard's best interests could properly become an issue. Justice Heiple failed to recognize that at the time the case came before his court the *Does* were in fact Richard's parents. Consequently the burden should have been on *Otakar* to disqualify the Does as parents, not the other way around, before the court could seek to determine what would be the best (or least detrimental) placement for him.

To make this observation is not to deny that wrongs may have been inflicted on Otakar by Daniella, by the Does, and by the entire Illinois justice system, which allowed and even fostered long delays in coming to a final decision. Otakar might well have been entitled to a judicial remedy for these wrongs. What confronted the supreme court of Illinois was a tragic choice, largely of the system's own making. But it made the wrong choice when it decided to remedy the harm done to Otakar by doing harm to Richard—what amounted to violence against him. It "awarded" a child, rather than possibly money damages, as compensation to Otakar. The supreme court should have recognized and acknowledged that Richard was a member of a functioning family—the Does—and that there was no justification for the state to violate the integrity of that family.

But even if the appellate court's decision had been upheld rather than reversed by the supreme court, this should not obscure the detriment to Richard inflicted by the system's long delays. Had the overall guidelines that we propose been followed, the three-and-one-half years of uncertainty could have been avoided.

If it were to follow our guidelines of continuity and the child's sense of time, an adoption statute would specifically prohibit withdrawal of consent, or any other motion on the part of a parent (biological or statutory or common-law adoptive) seeking to gain custody, after a psychological parent-child relationship with another adult had developed—as happened in Richard's case. The trial court might have decided, promptly after Otakar's attempt to intervene, to deny the Does' adoption petition and, had a psychological parent-child relationship then begun to develop between Richard and Otakar, the Does should not have been permitted to disturb it by seeking judicial intervention. Given the fact, however, that the trial court decided to grant the Does' adoption petition, and that a psychological parent-child relationship had begun to develop between Richard and the Does, Otakar should not have been permitted to disturb it by seeking judicial intervention. In either case our emphasis on the crucial role of a psychological parent would have given Richard the status of a wanted child.

Given the actual facts of Richard's case, the appellate court judge, rather than feeling compelled to pursue a roundabout course through the morass of "unfitness," could have upheld the trial court's adoption decision on the ground that Richard was not in need of a new placement. He should have asserted that the law, in accord with a child's need for continuity, presumes in a case such as Richard's that the present (and now long-standing) relationship ought not be disturbed.

Under an adoption statute that conformed to our guidelines, any court would place the burden to overcome the presumption—that an existing psychological parent-child relationship should not be disturbed—squarely on the adult claimant who challenged that relationship. To do otherwise would increase rather than minimize the detriment to the child.

Further, under an adoption statute that we (as well as, judging by their opinions, appellate court Justices Rizzi and Tully) would support, each child's placement would be treated as a matter of urgency to be finally resolved in days rather than years. Thus, to safeguard not only the child's needs but also the rights of all adult claimants (including the rights of biological caregiving parents who want the child) to a fair hearing, and in order to minimize the pain of what must prove for at least one of the adults to be false hopes, Richard's case should have been treated as an emergency. Had this been done, Otakar might have prevailed without causing additional harm to Richard.

We recognize that the least-detrimental-available-alternative standard can be compromised and litanized by decision-makers, just like the best-interest standard. But in this new formulation there is at least an opportunity for legislators, courts, and agencies to reexamine their task. Above all, these decision-makers must recognize that in all placement cases the development of a growing child is involved—a nonjudicial process that cannot be put on hold.

PART THREE

The Guidelines Applied

CHAPTER 7

The Rothman Decisions

We reproduce in full the actual decision about the placement of Stacey, an eight-year-old foster child, by Trial Justice Nadel of the New York Supreme Court. Following this, under the fictitious name of Judge Baltimore, we rewrite his decision in light of the guidelines incorporated in the least-detrimental-alternative formulation.

Decision 1

ROTHMAN V. JEWISH CHILD CARE ASSOCIATION
Supreme Court New York County
166 *N.Y. Law Journal*, p. 17, Col. 1
(Nov. 5, 1971)

Justice Nadel

In this proceeding, the natural mother seeks a judgment for the return of her eight-year-old daughter, Stacey. Petitioner gave her daughter to respondents for temporary care in December, 1964, when she voluntarily entered a hospital for treatment of a mental illness. Petitioner left the hospital for a period of time and then was readmitted. In December, 1969, the petitioner was released from the hospital and has not been hospitalized since. She is living with her parents, is employed as an executive secretary, and earns $140 per week.

The petitioner has never surrendered the child for adoption. The respondent, Jewish Child Care Association, opposes giving custody to the natural mother on the ground that she is unfit to care for the child by reason of her vast mental illness. However, in the trial they failed to produce any evidence upon which the court could make a finding that the petitioner is unfit to have custody of the child. The burden is upon the nonparent respondent to prove that petitioner is unfit to care for her daughter, and that the child's well-being requires separation from her mother. The Court of Appeals has ruled that absent abandonment of the child, statutory surrender of the child or the established unfitness of the mother, a court is without power to deprive the mother of custody (*Spence-Chapin Adoption Service, v. Polk, N.Y.L.J.,* Sept. 27, 1971, p. 1, col. 1). At best, respondents have shown that the relationship between mother and daughter is not as good as it should be. That this is so, is primarily the fault of the Jewish Child Care Association. Its extrajudicial determination that the child should not be returned, its hindrance of visitation and its failure to encourage the parental relationship were, to a great extent, responsible for the lack of a better relationship. It has been established in the Family Court that the said Association failed to make any real efforts to encourage and strengthen the parental relationship. The petitioner had to commence court proceedings for visitation and custody of her child, which were denied her by the Association.

Not only have respondents failed to sustain their burden of proof, but the evidence submitted amply demonstrates petitioner's fitness to have custody of her child. It was in the interest of the welfare of her daughter that the petitioner gave respondents temporary custody when she was hospitalized and unable to care for the child.

In the period of nearly two years preceding this trial, petitioner has been gainfully employed and she has been active in community, charitable and religious affairs. During the trying period of her hospitalization and separation from her child, petitioner appears to have successfully rehabilitated herself. The court has observed petitioner during the course of her testimony. After hearing and observing the petitioner, the court finds that she is sincere in her desire to care for her daughter, and that she is able to do so. Petitioner is residing with her parents, and they will be able to care for their grandchild in the interim between the child's return from school and the time when the petitioner comes home from work. Their presence adds two persons to aid petitioner in the care of her daughter.

The request by the attorneys for the respondent Association to reargue the motion to refer this case to the Family Counseling Service is denied. Similar relief was denied respondent by several justices of this court. In any event, there has been a trial of the issues involved and the court finds no valid reason for any further delay in returning the child to her natural mother.

The petitioner indicated that she realizes that the attitude of her daughter may require a transitional period before acquiring full custody. The parties shall, therefore, confer and shall submit in the judgment to be settled herein, a program for visitation and transfer of custody.

Should the parties fail to agree, the court will determine such provisions, giving due consideration to their suggestions.

Settle judgment. . . .

*   *   *

Our fictitious Judge Baltimore rewrites Justice Nadel's opinion in accord with our guidelines. In reaching his decision, he relies on data available to Justice Nadel.

Decision 1 Rewritten

ROTHMAN ("petitioner" in Justice Nadel's opinion) V. *JEWISH CHILD CARE ASSOCIATION* ("respondent" in Justice Nadel's opinion)

Supreme Court Hampstead-Haven County
1 *New World Law Journal,* p. 1, Col. 1

Judge Baltimore.

In this proceeding, Ms. Rothman seeks the custody and care of her eight-year-old daughter, Stacey. To support her claim, she established the following uncontested facts:

(1) In December of 1963 she gave birth to Stacey and, in accord with custom, practice, and the law, was automatically assigned parental responsibility for the custody and care of her child.

(2) When Stacey was one year old, her mother entered the hospital for treatment of a mental illness. At the same time, she gave Stacey to the Jewish Child Care Association with the intention that the child be cared for temporarily.

(3) Five years later, when Stacey was six years old, Ms. Rothman was released from the hospital and has not been hospitalized since. She is now living with her parents and is employed as an executive secretary.

(4) Ms. Rothman is sincere in her desire to care for Stacey. Her parents are prepared to take over while she is at work.

(5) The Association has refused to disturb Stacey's present relationship with her foster parents.* It has hindered Ms. Rothman's efforts to visit Stacey and to reestablish a parental relationship.

---

*Stacey's foster parents are identified as the "D.'s" in Justice Nadel's second opinion, reproduced in full starting on p. 73.

The Association, on Stacey's behalf, opposed giving custody to petitioner. Because of her prior illness, it asserts that she is unfit to care for the child, to serve as a parent. However, we need not and do not reach that question.

The real question is: Does Stacey currently have parents, or does she need to have a new parent assigned to her by the court? Ms. Rothman's fitness to be the "new parent" could have become an issue only if it had first been established that Stacey is currently an unwanted child.

What is strangely missing is any evidence in this case on Stacey's current needs. In the absence of such evidence, the law must and does presume that Stacey is a wanted child, well settled in a reciprocal relationship with her custodians. The burden is on Ms. Rothman to overcome the presumption that the adults who have been caring for Stacey are fit to remain her parents. Another facet of these presumptions is that Stacey has been psychologically abandoned by her biological mother. Seven years have elapsed since their last contact. The burden then is on Ms. Rothman to establish that there is a necessity for altering the long-standing ongoing relationship between Stacey and whoever may be her psychological parents. In short, petitioner must establish that Stacey is unwanted in her present family. If Ms. Rothman were to meet that burden, she would then have to establish that among the available alternatives, her taking custody would be the least detrimental for Stacey.

Ms. Rothman further argues that she never lost custody-in-law of Stacey. She established that she has always considered herself responsible for Stacey's care; that she had made "temporary" arrangements for her with the Association; that from the outset it was understood that they were to be temporary; and that she had always intended, once her health was restored, to care personally for Stacey. At no time during the last seven years, she asserts, has she abandoned Stacey or ceased being her "mother." If anyone is at fault, she claims, it is the Association. It has prevented her from maintaining, or at least establishing, a parental relationship with Stacey.

These arguments and the supporting facts reflect an understandable, but still mistaken, notion. Abandonment of a child by an adult, at least for the purpose of determining who is the parent, rests not on the intentions of the adult but rather on the impact such a leave-taking has on the child. Stacey, since the age of one year, has been deprived of continuous, affectionate, and otherwise nurturing contact with her mother. In the absence of specific evidence to the contrary, for purposes of custody and care Stacey must be presumed in law to have been abandoned. If nothing else, from Stacey's vantage point there has been a critical break in whatever psychological tie had begun to develop between herself and her mother. Painful as it must be for this well-meaning woman, her intentions alone are not enough to prevent such psychological abandonment. Even if those intentions had been accompanied by a carefully designed program to maintain contact with the child, over the time elapsed petitioner could hardly have been the primary adult source for Stacey of affection, stimulation, and, most importantly, a sense of continuity essential to securing healthy growth and development.

So far as Stacey's interests are concerned, it matters not that the implementation of those intentions may have actually been thwarted by the staff of the Association or by anyone else. Nor does it matter, for purposes of determining custody, whether petitioner's intentions were defeated through her misunderstanding, her illness, or her ignorance. Whatever the cause, whoever may feel responsible, the psychological fact—which the law must acknowledge—is that Stacey does not now recognize Ms. Rothman as her parent.

It would be impossible to locate precisely the moment in time when Ms. Rothman's "temporary" relinquishment became abandonment. Nor is it possible to determine if, or just when, a new psychological parent-child relationship was formed. Nevertheless, in the absence of contrary evidence, it must be presumed that such a relationship developed over the past seven years. That relationship deserves the recognition and protection of the law, and may be perceived, not unlike common-law marriage, as common-law parenthood or common-law adoption. Such an adoption carries with it all the legal protections generally available to nurture and secure healthy ties between parent and child.[1]

This decision is not and must not be read to require the assigning of fault to any person or to any child placement agency.* Their intent is not relevant to the decision. By shifting the focus of decision to the problem of meeting the needs of the child, the law moves, as it should, away from making moral judgments about fitness to be a parent; away from assigning blame; and away from looking at the child and the award or denial of custody as reward or punishment. It becomes unimportant then whether the parent-child relationship grew out of circumstances within or beyond the "control" of an adult claimant. Even if the court

---

*Of course, a child care agency may lose its license or be liable for damages if it is negligent in carrying out responsibilities it undertakes. What is important here is that the child not become the award for damages.

decreed that Stacey be returned to her biological "mother," it would be wholly beyond its power to establish a psychological parent-child relationship between them. In addition, far from being benign, such a decree would inflict damage and pain on the child as well as the adults.

Though the status of parent is not easily lost in law, it can exist only so long as it is real in terms of the health and well-being of the child. It is a relationship from birth, whether legitimate or illegitimate, or from adoption, whether statutory or common-law, which requires a continuing interaction between adult and child to survive. It can be broken by the adult parent by "chance," by the establishment of a new adult-child relationship, which we call common-law adoption, or by "choice," through a more formal legal process we have come to call adoption. It is the real tie—the reality of an ongoing relationship—that is crucial to this court's decision and that demands the protection of the state through law. The court must not, despite its sympathetic concern for Ms. Rothman, become a party to tearing Stacey away from the only affectionate parents she knows. Stacey must be presumed to be, in her present surroundings, a wanted child.

Finally, it must be observed that this decision does not constitute a break with the past. Rather, the past is future. There is in law, as psychoanalysis teaches that there is in man, a rich residue which each generation preserves from the past, modifies for the now, and in turn leaves for the future. Law is, after all, a continuous process for meeting society's need for stability by providing authority and precedent and, at the same time, meeting its need for flexibility and change by providing for each authority a counterauthority and for each precedent a counterprecedent. The living law thus seeks to secure an environment conducive to society's healthy growth and development.

That this decision is not incompatible with legal decisions of the last century will come as no surprise then, either to students of law who constructively resist sharp breaks with the past or to students of child development who have made us understand our need for continuity. In 1824, for example, the distinguished American jurist and Justice of the United States Supreme Court, Joseph Story, had no psychoanalytic theory of child development to draw upon; yet, acting as Circuit Justice, he could write in *U.S. v. Green* (3 Mason 482 Fed. Cas. No. 15256 [1824]):

As to the question of the right of the father to have the custody of his infant child, in a general sense it is true. But this is not on account of any absolute right of the father, but for the benefit of the infant, the law presuming it to be for its interests to be under the nurture and care of his natural protector, both for maintenance and education. When, therefore, the court is asked to lend its aid to put the infant into the custody of the father, and to withdraw him from other persons, it will look into all the circumstances, and ascertain whether it will be for the real, permanent interests of the infant and if the infant be of sufficient discretion, it will also consult its personal wishes.

Far less vague and in language often sounding psychoanalytic, yet written more than a decade before Freud published *The Interpretation of Dreams,* are the words of Justice Brewer speaking for the Supreme Court of Kansas in 1881 in the child placement case of *Chapsky v. Wood* (26 Kan. Reports, pp. 650-658 [1881]):

[When a] child has been left for years in the care and custody of others, who have discharged all the obligations of support and care which naturally rest upon the parent, then, whether the courts will enforce the father's right to the custody of the child, will depend mainly upon the question whether such custody will promote the welfare and interest of such child. This distinction must be recognized. If, immediately after [giving up the child] reclamation be sought, and the father is not what may be called an unfit person by reasons of immorality, etc., the courts will pay little attention to any mere speculation as to the probability of benefit to the child by leaving or returning it. In other words, they will consider that the law of nature, which declares the strength of a father's love is more to be considered than any mere speculation whatever as to the advantages which possible wealth and social position might otherwise bestow. But, on the other hand, when reclamation is not sought until a lapse of years, when new ties have been formed and a certain current given to the child's life and thought, much attention should be paid to the probabilities of a benefit to the child from the change. *It is an obvious fact that ties of blood weaken, and ties of companionship strengthen, by lapse of time; and the prosperity and welfare of the child depend on the number and strength of these ties, as well as on the ability to do all which the promptings of these ties compel* [my emphasis].
[T]hey who have for years filled the place of the parent, have discharged all the obligations of care and support, and especially when they have discharged these duties during those years of infancy when the burden is especially heavy, when the labor and care are of a kind

whose value cannot be expressed in money—when all these labors have been performed and the child has bloomed into bright and happy girl-hood, it is but fair and proper that their previous faithfulness, and the in-terest and affection which these labors have created in them, should be respected. Above all things, the paramount consideration is, what will promote the welfare of the child? These, I think, are about all the rules of law applicable to a case of this kind.

. . . What the future of the child will be is a question of probability. No one is wise enough to forecast or determine absolutely what would or what would not be best for it; yet we have to act upon these proba-bilities from the testimony before us, guided by the ordinary laws of hu-man experience. . . .

[T]he child has had, and has today, all that a mother's love and care can give. The affection which a mother may have and does have, spring-ing from the fact that a child is her offspring, is an affection which per-haps no other one can really possess; but so far as it is possible, springing from years of patient care of a little, helpless babe, from as-sociation, and as an outgrowth from those little cares and motherly at-tentions bestowed upon it, an affection for the child is seen in Mrs. Wood that can be found nowhere else. And it is apparent, that so far as a mother's love can be equaled, its foster-mother has that love, and will continue to have it.

On the other hand, if she goes to the house of her father's family, the female inmates are an aunt, just ripening into womanhood, and a grand-mother; they have never seen the child; they have no affection for it springing from years of companionship. . . . Human impulses are such that doubtless they would form an affection for the child—it is hardly possible to believe otherwise; but to that deep, strong, patient love which springs from either motherhood, or from a patient care during years of helpless babyhood, they will be strangers.

In acknowledging Stacey's adoption by affirming the Association's assertion of the right to remain with her psychological parents of the past eight years, the court takes the position of Justice Brewer in the *Chapsky* case:

It is a serious question, always to be considered, whether a change should be advised. "Let well enough alone" is an axiom founded on abundant experience [at p. 656].

So ordered.

Almost one year after the Nadel and Baltimore opinions were written, Justice Nadel was asked to reconsider his first decision on the placement of Stacey. Here follows his second opinion in full, which invites comment.

Decision 2

ROTHMAN V. JEWISH CHILD CARE ASSOCIATION
Supreme Court New York County
N.Y. Law Journal, p. 17, Col. 2-4
(Nov. 1, 1972)

Justice Nadel:
In this *habeas corpus* proceeding, brought by the mother against the Jewish Child Care Association, the court, after a hearing, directed the return of the then eight and one-half-year-old girl to her mother. The petitioner [Ms. Rothman] never surrendered the child for adoption, but had placed the child with respondents [the Association] for temporary care in December, 1964, when she voluntarily entered a hospital for treatment of a mental ailment. Petitioner left the hospital and then was readmitted. In December, 1969, she was released from the hospital and since then has not been hospitalized. She lives with her parents and is gainfully employed. The court found that the respondents failed to sustain their burden of proof as to the unfitness of the mother to have custody of her child.

The mother realized that the antagonistic attitude of her daughter towards her required a transitional period before she regained full custody. The decision of the court provided for such transitional period.

In a collateral proceeding, affidavits of doctors and a medical report were submitted, based upon examination of the child subsequent to the custody hearing, which indicated that it would be detrimental to the child's mental health if she were turned over to the mother at the time. The court, on its own motion, modified the judgment of February 16, 1972, which directed the return of the child to the mother on a specific date, and by amended order and judgment dated March 2, 1972, ordered that the physical custody of the child be returned to respondent Jewish Child Care Association to enable said Agency to place the child in a facility operated by it, which would offer the specialized care and therapy which she needed, and where she would be examined by an impartial child psychiatrist, and thereafter hearings would be held at which all parties would submit competent medical proof on the issue of when and under what circumstances the said child may be returned to the mother. The hearings were scheduled for June.

However, Chapters 645 and 646 of the Laws of 1972, effective May 30, 1972, added a provision to section 383, subdivision 3 of the Social Services Law, which was tailored to specifically fit the case at bar. It provided that foster parents having had continuous care of a child for more than twenty-four months through an authorized agency, shall be permitted as a matter of right, as an interested party to intervene in any proceeding involving the custody of the child. A motion made by the foster parents to intervene in this proceeding was granted by another Justice of this court by order dated June 27, 1972. This court had denied a motion seeking a similar relief on March 1, 1972, prior to enactment of Chapters 645 and 646 of Laws of 1972, under authority of *Scarpetta v. Spence-Chapin Adoption Service,* 28 N. Y. 2d 185. In order to afford the intervenors [the D.'s, Stacey's foster parents] an opportunity to have their psychiatrist examine the child and then participate in the hearings, it was agreed to postpone the hearings to September.

The impartial psychiatrist Dr. D'Arc was selected by counsel for the petitioner and counsel for respondents from a panel submitted by the President of the Council of Child Psychiatry. Each of the parties, including the intervenors, had an opportunity to examine the child by a psychiatrist of its own choosing. Dr. D'Arc examined the child on four separate occasions.

Five psychiatrists have testified and they are unanimous in their opinion that the child is depressed and that the mere mention of the possibility of returning her to the natural mother evokes depression, sadness and tears. It is significant that not even Dr. Cohen, the psychiatrist called by the petitioner, recommends that the child be returned to her natural mother. To do so would be detrimental to the child's well-being.

Dr. Cohen felt that if the child must be turned over to the mother it should be done in a gradual way so that there would not be any undue pressure on either of the participants. He suggested a plan whereby initially the visits by the mother would be at Pleasantville for an hour or two at a time to develop a rapport, then for several hours to visit local places, and if this proceeded well, then perhaps for a day at the mother's home, and if this worked well, then for periods of a weekend, and if this plan continued to work well, for periods of a week or longer.

This plan is somewhat similar to the gradual transition recommended originally by this court. The record indicates that the visits pursuant to the court's recommended gradual transition did not work out well in its initial stages, and that the visits in Pleasantville during July through September were a complete failure.

In answer to the question, "What if the visits do not proceed well?" Dr. Cohen stated:

"Well, what I'm saying, I guess, is this: that if visits would not work out on a regular basis well, if there was a consistent pattern of total lack of rapport, if there was no progress being made, then certainly one would have to question whether that will work out."

And in answer to the question, "Assuming the initial visits at Pleasantville did not work out okay?" he stated:

"Well, I think if the initial visits did not work out all right and one was not able to determine what was it that might be interfering with them working out, then it might indeed be that further visits would not be in order."

He also testified that the child had adverse feelings to the possibility of being united with her mother, that she felt dejected, upset and tearful.

Dr. Feldman and Dr. Damino, the psychiatrists called by the intervenors, indicated that the child was depressed and was likely to develop some very dangerous propensities if forced to return to her mother. They felt strongly that the child should not be returned to the mother at the present time. Dr. Damino testified that he had a plan whereby she could possibly develop a pleasant relationship with her child. He stated:

"I concluded, from examination of the girl, that there is one probable way, and this is my opinion, and that is that if the natural mother is not a threat to the girl for several years, which I would estimate to be about—I'd say about five years, in my opinion, that if the natural mother is not a threat to the girl in regard to taking away the girl from the D.'s, then there is a substantial probability that the girl could develop some affectionate relationship to the natural mother if, seeing the natural mother, say on a regular basis, every two weeks for a day or two, but the main thing there would be that the natural mother would not be a threat to taking the girl away from the D.'s."

He further testified that at the present time there is no reliable possibility that Stacey can be returned to her mother without being a destroyed human being.

Dr. Pelner, called by the respondents, testified that the return of the child to the mother would result in mental deterioration of the child. He also testified that it was conceivable that some time in the distant future Stacey may want to consider being returned to her mother, perhaps even being curious of her mother and wanting to establish some contact with her. On cross-examination he stated that the quickest and surest way "for a child like Stacey to be able to reach the point, to reach out to her mother, I think would be actually via the D.'s."

Mr. Arest, the Resident Unit Administrator at Pleasantville Cottage School, testified as to the complete failure of the petitioner to establish any kind of rapport with the child on any of the visits. Although he made several efforts to help her during these visits, it was to no avail. The child came back after these visits crying hysterically, was very upset, was shaking. The child rejected all offers of affection by the mother. The mother then became frustrated, yelled at the child and threatened her. The visits were short and always ended on an unpleasant note; uncontradicted evidence is that the hostility of the child towards the mother has persisted, that the mother overreacted to the unyielding attitude of the child and could not win her affection or trust. The mother felt frustrated with her child. From all the testimony the court concludes that it would be against the best interests of the child and it would be detrimental and dangerous to the child's mental and emotional well-being to return her to the petitioner at this time.

The petitioner contends that since the court has heretofore found that the petitioner is not an unfit mother, the court is without option and must return Stacey forthwith because without a finding of unfitness the court cannot consider the child's well-being and cites as authority (*People ex rel. Kropp v. Shepsky,* 305 N. Y. 465; *People ex rel. Scarpetta v. Spence-Chapin Adoption Service,* 28 N. Y. 2d 185, 321 N. Y. S. 2d 65; *Spence-Chapin Adoption Service v. Polk,* 29 N. Y. 2d 196, 324 N. Y. S. 2d 937).

This court does not believe that these cases hold absent a finding of unfitness of the mother, consideration of the child's well-being is prohibited, and the child must be ordered returned forthwith to the mother.

In *Spence-Chapin Adoption Service v. Polk* (supra), the Court of Appeals reviews the leading cases on the subject, reaffirms that the primacy of parental rights may not be ignored and that a contest between a parent and a nonparent may not resolve itself into a simple factual issue as to who can provide or afford the better surroundings or as to which party is better equipped to raise the child. Then the court states, at page 204:

"'In other words, the burden rests, not, for instance, upon the mother to show that the child's welfare would be advanced by being returned to her. But rather upon the nonparents to prove that the mother is unfit to have her child and that the latter's well-being requires its separation from its mother.' (305 N.Y. at 469). Of course, this does not mean the child's rights and interests are subordinated. The principle rests on the generally accepted view that a child's best interest is that it be raised by its parent unless the parent is disqualified by gross misconduct. That the generalization has myriads of exceptions is equally true, but the exceptions do not contradict the verity of the principle."

Although the court repeats the language of the *Shepsky* case, supra, that the non-parents have the burden of proving "that the mother is unfit to have her child *and* that the latter's well-being required a separation from its mother" (emphasis ours), it immediately follows with qualifications (1) that the child's rights and interests are not subordinated and (2) that the generalization has myriads of exceptions.

General principles by themselves are not the only guide to action in specific cases. Sometimes the exceptions prove the rule. In none of the cases cited by the petitioner is there competent medical evidence that the transfer of custody to the mother would endanger the well-being of the child.

If the court failed to consider the child's mental and emotional well-being in this case it would indeed constitute a subordination of the child's rights and interests. The child is now a nine and one-half year old girl. The tragic experience during the first two years of her life, the continued absence of the mother during the next six and one-half years, the persistent rejection of the mother by the child during the past year, the mother's inability to develop any rapport or to cope with the child, regardless of who was at fault, and the comprehensive medical testimony that the child's mental and emotional well-being would be endangered, warrant a finding that this case comes within the myriads of exceptions to the general principles of the primacy of parental custody.

On the evidence, the court concludes that to return the child to the mother at this time would endanger the child's mental and emotional well-being, and would be against the best interests of the child. The petition is therefore dismissed.

Settle judgment, providing for visitation as discussed at conference with attorneys.

Decision 2 Evaluated

In contrast to Justice Nadel, our fictitious Judge Baltimore was spared the necessity to reverse his order on the placement of Stacey. Neither did he need to treat her case as one of the exceptions and to rely on medical evidence to justify his decision not to return her to her biological mother. On the basis of knowledge extrapolated from our guidelines, he was prepared for Stacey to be firmly tied to the adults who had become her psychological parents, and to answer with dismay to any intrusion into this relationship.

In accord with our guideline on the child's sense of time, Judge Baltimore would not have expected any attachment to the biological mother left in Stacey after seven years of separation, even though petitioner had been the child's first caregiver, and even though a psychological relationship may have begun to develop between them at that time.

He would have presumed that Stacey was a healthy child at the time Ms. Rothman sought to regain her custody, and he would not have thought that she was in need of "therapy." A child's attachment to her psychological parent is normal and therefore not subject to therapeutic efforts designed to affect pathological manifestations. Stacey cannot be "cured" of her love for her foster parents.

In accord with the principle of making the child's interests paramount, Judge Baltimore would not have awarded visitation rights to the biological mother, since the child rejected her and therefore was unlikely to profit from her presence or influence. He would at the same time be protecting the rights and interests of the psychological parents—who would remain free to arrange visits if they thought it good for Stacey. Certainly, he would have wondered why the psychiatric experts had accepted the initial effort to remove Stacey from her long-term foster parents, her psychological parents.* He would have recognized that to protect Stacey's relationship with the D.'s was the least detrimental alternative.

---

*Stacey was adopted by her foster parents on March 1, 1974.

PART FOUR

Examining Our Premises

CHAPTER 8

Why Should the Child's Interests Be Paramount?

Some may assert that the views presented thus far—that the placement of a child already enmeshed in the process should rest on consideration of her developmental needs—neglects the needs and rights of adults. In fact, there is nothing single-sided about making the child's interests the paramount consideration. The other side is that the law, in accord with the continuity guideline, must safeguard the autonomy of adults who serve as parents to raise their children as they see fit, free of violations of their family's integrity by the state or by disappointed adult claimants. To say that a child's relationship with her psychological parents, or with those assigned to become her psychological parents, must not be interrupted is also to say that the rights and needs of those adults as parents are to be protected.

Nevertheless, judges may find it difficult to make a child's interests determinative. They may in effect make placement decisions to reward or punish the competing adults. For example, out of an adult-centered sense of justice, judges may readily find against a biological mother who claims possession of a child whom she has deliberately abandoned, or concerning whose adoption she has changed her mind belatedly.[1] But where abandonment by the biological parent is involuntary, judges, also out of an adult-centered sense of justice and notwithstanding the child's need, may respond differently. They may use the child's placement as restitution to parents who are innocent victims of war, illness, poverty, deception, or any other circumstance "beyond their control." In such tragic instances judges must choose between causing further hardship to the innocent child who, having already been separated from her biological parents, is now torn away from her psychological parents, or causing further hardship to already-victimized innocent adults.

Our fictitious Judge Baltimore, an unwavering supporter of the child's interests, reveals how difficult and painful the choice is in these kinds of situations. He writes:

Whatever the court decides, inevitably there will be hardship. It may be the biological parents, already victimized by poverty, poor education, ill health, prejudice, or other circumstances, who are denied their child. It may be the child, who is torn away from her psychological parents. It may be the psychological parents, who are deprived of the child for whom they have long and faithfully cared. It may be all of them.

If I am to implement the state's preference for serving the child's interests—for treating her well-being as paramount—my task, though not easy, is clear: I must decide not to disturb the child's relationship with her psychological parents. I must deny the biological parents even the opportunity to call into question the existing placement of "their" child unless they can introduce evidence that "their" child is now neglected, abused, or abandoned. Harsh as it is and as it must seem to the biological parents, their standing in court may be no greater than that of a stranger.

As a judge, I have to recognize as irrelevant feelings that have been aroused in me because of my own concerns about being a parent. These feelings would often compel me to place the child with the biological parents, as compensation for their suffering, were it not for my obligation under the Code, which stresses the child's need for continuity. I emphasize that the placement of a child must never be used as reward or punishment.

Arguments have been made that the winning adult will suffer guilt for depriving the losing adult of the child, or that the child herself will feel betrayed by one set of parents or the other. But to attribute to the judicial process the capacity to work out and to weigh the significance of such imponderables in its decision-making is unrealistic.

But even if a policy of making the adult's and not the child's interests paramount were to be adopted, the court would be hard-pressed in most cases to determine, for example, whether the biological or the adoptive parent or who of the divorcing parents would be most hurt by the denial of custody.

The state might, of course, assert a special policy to be applied to cases of extreme hardship. Parents who have been forced to relinquish their children against their wishes (as was the case in the Holocaust, for example) might be granted a primary and overriding right to regain custody.[2] It might be argued that any other policy would violate a fundamental ethic of a civilized society, regardless of the individual child's needs.

But after reviewing these arguments I remain convinced that the child's interests must be paramount, and I return to the child-centered guidelines that have governed my decisions.

BOOK TWO

BEFORE THE BEST
INTERESTS OF THE CHILD

The Problem, Our Convictions, and a Framework for Examining State Decisions to Intrude on Parent-Child Relationships

CHAPTER 9

The Problem and Our Convictions

When and why should a child's relationship to her parents become a matter of state concern? What must have happened in a child's life before the state should be authorized to investigate and modify her relationship with her parents, with her family? What grounds for placing a family under state scrutiny are reasonable, considering what a child loses when her care passes—even temporarily—from the personal authority of parents to the impersonal authority of the law? What can justify overcoming the presumption in law that parents are free to determine what is best for their children in accord with their own beliefs, preferences, and lifestyles?

We did not address these questions in Book One. There we restricted our inquiry to problems involving children already caught up in the legal system. We focused on contested child placements where adults and institutions resort to the legal process for a resolution of their disputes. We did not critically examine existing *grounds* for state intrusion on parent-child relationships, but generally took them as given. We did not consider, for example, whether the divorce of parents or the separation of unmarried parents should in themselves be grounds for the state to intervene—to decide who should have custody of their children. Nor did we question the underlying justifications for invoking state authority to make placement decisions in proceedings variously labeled "neglect," "abandonment," "abuse," "delinquency," "adoption," "separation," and "divorce." We sought merely to establish guidelines, based on psychoanalytic knowledge and reinforced by common sense, for assuring that the least intrusive placement would be selected by the least detrimental procedure for each child whose custody had become a matter of state concern.

The guidelines that we developed in Book One rest on two convictions. First, we believe that a child's need for continuity of care requires acknowledging that parents should generally be entitled to raise their children as they think best, free of state interference. This conviction finds expression in our preference for *minimum state intervention*. It prompts restraint in defining justifications for intruding on family relationships. Second, we believe that, once justification for state intervention has been established, the child's well-being—not the parents', the family's, or the child care agency's—must be determinative. Whether the protective shell of the family has already been broken before the state intrudes, or breaks as a result of it, the goal of intervention must be to establish or reestablish a family for the child as quickly as possible. That conviction is expressed in our preference for *making a child's interests paramount* once her care has become a legitimate matter for the state to decide.

So long as a child is a member of a functioning family, the preservation of that family serves her developmental needs. Thus our preference for making a child's interests paramount is not to be construed as a justification in and of itself for intrusion. Such a reading would ignore the advantages that accrue to children from a policy of minimum state intervention. The goal of every child placement, whether it is made automatically by birth certificate or more deliberately following direct intervention by administrative or court order, is the same. With the possible exception of the placement of violent juveniles, the goal is to assure for each child membership in a family with at least one parent who wants her.* It is to assure for each child and her parents an opportunity to maintain, establish, or reestablish psychological ties to each other free of further interruption by the state.

The guidelines that we proposed in Book One for making placements in the best interests of the child also have substantial implications for defining justifications for state intrusion on family relationships. They call for decisions that

- safeguard the child's need for continuity of nurturing relationships†
- reflect the child's sense of time
- take into account the limits of knowledge to make long-range predictions, and the limited capacity of law to monitor interpersonal relationships.

---

*The phrase *at least one parent* is not meant to exclude family constellations that extend beyond the nuclear family.

In juvenile delinquency proceedings involving violent conduct, even if the law were to make society's immediate safety the primary goal, we would argue that within that ambit the least detrimental alternative placement should be selected for the child.

†Urie Bronfenbrenner writes:

"In order to develop—intellectually, emotionally, socially, and morally—a child requires participation in progressively more complex reciprocal activity, on a regular basis over an extended period in the child's life, with one or more persons with whom the child develops a strong, mutual, irrational, emotional attachment and who is committed to the child's well-being and development, preferably for life."[1]

Keeping these propositions in mind, we ask: Why and under what circumstances should the state be authorized to breach family integrity and to overcome the presumption of parental autonomy?

Before addressing this question, we focus on the meaning of and reasons for favoring a policy of minimum state intervention. In the eyes of the law, to be a *child* is to be at risk, dependent, and without capacity or authority to decide free of parental control what is "best" for oneself. To be an *adult* is in law to be perceived as free to take risks, with the independent capacity and authority to decide what is "best" for oneself without regard to parental wishes.[2] To be an *adult who is a parent* is therefore to be presumed by law to have the capacity, authority, and responsibility to determine and to do what is "good" for one's children, what is "best" for the entire family.

As long ago as 1840 Jeremy Bentham observed:

> The feebleness of infancy demands a continual protection. Everything must be done for an imperfect being, which as yet does nothing for itself. The complete development of its physical powers takes many years; that of its intellectual faculties is still slower. At a certain age, it has already strength and passions, without experience enough to regulate them. Too sensitive to present impulses, too negligent of the future, such a being must be kept under an authority more immediate than that of the laws. . . .[3]

That "more immediate" authority is the authority of parents. They offer children protection and nurture, and introduce them to the demands and prohibitions as well as to the promises and opportunities of society. Charged with the duty of initiating the relationships of their children to the adult world and to its institutions, parents shelter their children from direct contact with the law by being their representatives before it.

By 1926 Freud brought a psychological dimension to Bentham's societal view of the "feebleness of infancy." He refers to "the long period of time during which the young of the human species is in a condition of helplessness and dependence," that "in comparison with . . . most animals, . . . it is sent into the world in a less finished state," and "the dangers of the external world have a greater importance for it."[4] He explains how this "biological factor" on the one hand burdens the parents with the full weight of responsibility for the survival and well-being of their offspring, and on the other hand assures that the day-to-day ministering to the child's multiple requirements will turn the physical tie between them into a mutual psychological attachment.

Such constantly ongoing interactions between parents and children become for each child the starting point for a developmental line that leads toward adult functioning. What begins as the experience of physical contentment or pleasure that accompanies bodily care develops into a primary attachment to the persons who provide it. This again changes into the wish for a parent's constant presence irrespective of physical wants. Helplessness requires total care and over time is transformed into the need or wish for approval and love. It fosters the desire to please by compliance with a parent's wishes. It provides a developmental base upon which the child's responsiveness to educational efforts rests. Love for the parents leads to identification with them, without which impulse control and socialization could be deficient. Finally, after the years of childhood comes the prolonged and in many ways painful adolescent struggle to attain a separate identity with physical, emotional, and moral self-reliance.[5]

These complex and vital developments thrive in the protective enclave of family life under guardianship by parents who are autonomous. The younger the child, the greater is her need for them. When family integrity is broken or weakened by state intrusion, her needs are thwarted, and her belief that her parents are omniscient and all-powerful is shaken prematurely. The effect on the child's developmental progress is likely to be detrimental.[6] The child's need for security within the confines of the family must be met by law through its recognition of family privacy as the barrier to state intrusion upon parental autonomy.[7] These rights—parental autonomy, a child's entitlement to autonomous parents, and privacy—are essential ingredients of family integrity. "And the integrity of that life is something so fundamental that it has been found to draw to its protection the principles of more than one explicitly granted Constitutional right."[8] We use the phrase "family integrity" rather than family autonomy to encompass these rights in order to avoid the confusion caused by using interchangeably "family autonomy" and "parental autonomy."

Two purposes underlie the parents' right within the family to be free of state intrusion. The first is to provide parents with an uninterrupted *opportunity* to meet the developing physical and emotional needs of their child in establishing the familial bonds critical to every child's healthy growth and development. The second purpose, and the one on which the parental right must ultimately rest, is to safeguard the continuing *maintenance* of these family ties—of psychological parent-child relationships—once they have been established. Both of these purposes are usually fulfilled when the parental right is assigned at a child's birth simply on the basis of her biological tie to those who produce her. Likewise, for the adopted child, these purposes are usually met when the parental right is assigned simply on the basis of her legal tie to those who adopt her.

But the assignment and recognition of parental rights do not guarantee that biological or adoptive parents will exercise them, or that these parents will establish significant psychological ties to their child. Indeed, when parents abandon a child or when parents and children are separated "too long," their legal entitlement cannot and does not prevent the establishment of familial ties—psychological bonds—between their child and her long-term substitute caregivers. Such foster family relationships may, as time goes on, merit the same protection from state intervention as that accorded to the relationships in functioning biological and adoptive families.[9]

Beyond these biological and psychological justifications for protecting parent-child relationships and promoting each child's entitlement to a secure place in a family of her own, there is a further justification for a policy of minimum state intervention. It is that the law does not have the capacity to supervise the fragile, complex interpersonal bonds between child and parent.[10] As *parens patriae* the state is too crude an instrument to become an adequate substitute for flesh-and-blood parents. The legal system has neither the resources nor the sensitivity to respond to a growing child's ever-changing needs and demands. It does not have the capacity to deal on an individual basis with the consequences of its decisions, or to act with the speed that is required by a child's sense of time. Similarly, the child lacks the capacity to respond to the rulings of an impersonal court or social service agency as she responds to the demands of personal parental figures. Parental expectations, implicit and explicit, become the child's own. However, the process by which a child converts external expectations, guidance, commands, and prohibitions into the capacity for self-regulation and self-direction does not function adequately in the absence of emotional ties to her caregivers.

A policy of minimum intervention by the state thus accords not only with our firm belief as citizens in individual freedom and human dignity, but also with our professional understanding of the intricate developmental processes of childhood.

To recognize how critical are the developmental stages and how essential are autonomous parents for the protection of their children is also to recognize that parents may fail. Not all parents are able or willing to safeguard their child against the succession of risks that bedevil development from dependent infancy to independent adulthood. The family enclave may become a cover for exploiting the inherent inequality between adult and child. It may prevent detection of parental abuse or neglect. Family privacy then ceases to benefit the child and becomes a threat to her well-being, to her safety, and sometimes to her life.

Yet to acknowledge that some parents—whether biological, adoptive, or long-term foster—may threaten the well-being of their children is not to suggest that state legislatures, courts, or administrative agencies can always offer such children something better, and can compensate them for what they have missed in their own homes. By its intrusion the state may make a bad situation worse; indeed, it may turn a tolerable or even a good situation into a bad one. The intact family offers the child a rare and continuing combination of nutriments to further her growth: reciprocal affection between the child and at least one caregiving adult; the feeling of being wanted and therefore valued; and the stimulation of inborn capacities. Available alternatives too often fail to offer the whole series, and accordingly they leave one or the other part of the child's personality without developmental support.[11] Recognition of these shortcomings should alert decision-makers to ask in every case whether removal from an unsatisfactory home is a beneficial measure.

Identifying children whose placement should be called into question requires more than vague and subjective statutory language. For example, phrases like *change of conditions of custody* in divorce statutes and *denial of proper care* in neglect and abuse statutes do not give administrative agencies and courts adequate guidance. Such statutes must be revised to protect all families: poor and well-to-do; single- and two-parent; married and unmarried; minority and majority; gay and straight; biological, adoptive, and long-term foster.[12] They must provide these ongoing relationships with safeguards from unwarranted state-sponsored interruptions. They must prevent judges, lawyers, social workers, and others from imposing their personal views upon unwilling parents. To that end we ask and seek to answer:

> What ought to be established and by what procedure *before* the "best interests of the child" can be invoked over the right of parents to autonomy, the right of children to autonomous parents, and the right of both parents and children to family privacy?

CHAPTER 10

The Framework

W hat should be the role of law in protecting children from parental exploitation and protecting parents and their children from exploitation by the state? Under a policy of minimum intervention, what should the law require *before* the best interest of a specific child becomes a matter for the state to determine? What justifies invading the right of parents and their children to feel at home with one another[1] and to be secure in their persons and dwellings?[2]

Fair Warning and Power Restraint

The law has taken two distinct forms in response to the question, "What should justify substituting the state's judgment for that of parents with regard to the care of their child?" The first has been to impose relatively precise obligations on parents concerning matters about which there is a societal consensus. For example, statutes concerned with child labor, compulsory education, and immunization give parents fair warning of what would constitute a breach of their child care responsibilities and provide advance notice of the extent of the state's power to intervene.[3]

The second form which legislation takes, on which we focus, sets relatively vague and imprecise limits upon state authority to intrude, and thus fails to give fair warning. These statutes concern *standards* of child care, about which there is no clear societal consensus. They give state agencies and judges "the authority of *ad hoc* decision, which is in its nature difficult if not impossible to hold to account."[4] All agree that the "best interests" of children should be served and that they ought not to be "neglected" or "abused." But little agreement exists about the meaning of these terms. For example, laws that simply make "denial of proper care" the standard for investigating or determining "neglect" provide neither meaningful warning to parents nor adequate guidance for courts or administrative agencies. The same is true for

93

laws that make "significant change of circumstances" the standard for modifying custody set at the time of divorce.

This second form of legislation, unlike the first form, invests judges and state agency personnel as *parens patriae,* with almost limitless discretion to act in accord with their own child-rearing preferences in areas generally under the exclusive control of parents. It invites the abuse of parents and children by state officials and has led to discrimination against poor, minority, nontraditional, and other disfavored families.[5]

To reduce unwarranted intrusions on family integrity, the laws of child placement should be recast to provide fair warning for parents and to restrict the power of state officials. Legislatures should define prospectively and with greater precision their responses to the threshold question, which is: "What must be established to overcome the strong presumptions in law (a) that parents have the right, the capacity, and the obligation to care for their children in accord with their own notions of child rearing, and (b) that children need and have the right to uninterrupted and permanent membership in a family with such parents?"

But even specificity of statutory language will never be enough to preclude unjustifiable invasions of family privacy or the unnecessary rupturing of familial bonds. Nor will rules be enough to assure that those who unjustifiably violate family integrity will be held accountable for their abuse of power. Rules are only a first and necessary condition for realizing the goals of fair warning and power restraint. Another necessary condition is that those who are empowered to intrude must understand—as well as share—the philosophy that underlies a policy of minimum coercive state intervention. A tradition in the administration of child placement laws that is sensitive to the notion of family integrity must be fostered.

Further, we must recognize and work to avoid the consequences of a fantasy too often shared by those who formulate and enact justifications and procedures for intrusion. The fantasy is that only the most competent, most skilled, and most sensitive lawyers, judges, doctors, social workers, foster parents, family helpers, and other personnel will implement the grounds for intrusion under the laws of child placement. There will always be a substantial number in authority who will prevent this fantasy from becoming a realistic expectation. For that reason it is important to place a heavy burden of proof upon those who are empowered to intrude. It is equally important to establish procedures for intrusion which make highly visible the function, nature, and degree of intrusion that is justified at each point of decision.

Questions for Decision

Guided by the doctrine of minimum state intervention and the requirements of fair warning and power restraint, we focus on three questions.

1. What Constitutes Probable Cause for Inquiry into a Parent-Child Relationship, and What Must Be Found Before the State Is Authorized to Seek Modification of That Relationship?

What events provide reasonable bases for authorizing an investigation by a child protective services agency or by a court in order to determine whether an action should be brought to establish the need to modify or terminate a parent-child relationship? Should, for example, the imprisonment, hospitalization, or death of a parent; the divorce of parents; or a child's poor performance at school be treated as triggering events?

What must an inquiry uncover before parents can be forced to defend their entitlement to care for and represent their child? For example, should "physical neglect," "emotional neglect," spanking for discipline, a parent's continued absence from a child, or a parent's express wish to give up a child be considered sufficient for authorizing an agency to initiate an action and a court to determine who will be the child's caregivers or parents?

Whatever constitutes a ground for modification or termination would, of course, also constitute a ground for investigation. However, not all grounds for inquiry would necessarily constitute a sufficient cause for seeking to modify or terminate a relationship. For example, the imprisonment or death of a parent might be justification for an inquiry only to determine whether the child has another parent or whether provision has been made for her care.

Further, even if a ground for modification or termination could be established, there would be no justification for initiating an action if the state knew beforehand that it could not offer a less detrimental alternative.

2. What Should Constitute Sufficient Cause for the State to Modify a Parent-Child Relationship?

How heavy an evidentiary burden must be met before the court can find that a ground has been established for modifying a particular parent-child relationship? On whom should the burden of persuasion rest? "This burden is said to have both a location and a weight: the location specifies the party that loses if the burden is not met, and the weight specifies how persuasive the evidence must be in order to carry the burden."[6]

3. If There Is Sufficient Cause for Modification, Which of the Available Alternatives Is the Least Detrimental?

The guidelines that we developed in Book One are designed to pour content into the meaning of "least detrimental available alternative" and to enable a court or agency to answer this question. If the state finds that it cannot provide something better, the least detrimental alternative would be to leave well enough alone.[7] Between the extremes of placing a child elsewhere and making no modifications, in some cases the least detrimental alternative may involve offering or requiring supportive assistance to the family.

Stages of Decision

The three questions are seldom, if ever, confronted separately in the child placement process. Yet each question is, in fact, answered in a continuous, often muddled, flow of decisions by legislators, child care agency personnel, and judges. Since the answers and the sequence in which they are reached directly affect and often undermine society's commitment to family integrity, there is a need to refine further and to identify for separate consideration the three stages of decision which correspond to our three questions. These stages are: *invocation, adjudication,* and *disposition.* Each is defined in terms of function and in terms of degree and kind of intervention.

Invocation has two functions. One is to *determine whether to investigate* a particular child's condition or circumstances. The other, if the results of the investigation warrant, is to *commence a legal action* to overcome the presumption of parental autonomy and to seek a court order to modify the parent-child relationship.

Adjudication has three functions. First, it is to *require the state* to disclose, particularly to the parents concerned, the statutory ground and the facts that would justify modifying the parent-child relationship. Second, it is to give parents an opportunity to respond for themselves and as representatives of their child. Third, it is to determine whether those seeking modification have met the statutory burden for establishing the ground for supervening parental autonomy.

The functions of *disposition* depend upon what is determined at adjudication. If the court finds that no ground has been established, the action would be dismissed. However, if the court finds that a statutory ground has been established, that the presumption of parental autonomy has been overcome by the state or waived by parents (for example, by failing to agree on custody in a divorce proceeding), the child's interest becomes the paramount consideration.* Then *disposition* has three functions. The first is to *recognize the child's status* as a *party* and to assure her of an opportunity for an independent representation of her interests. The second is to give parties the opportunity to tell the court which available alternatives would, in their view, best meet the needs of the child. The third is for the court to decide what is the least detrimental available arrangement for the child.

An *adjudication* which does not lead directly to dismissal is in effect a *suspended judgment*—to be acted upon only after a hearing in which the child has party status and at which the court decides what *disposition* is the least detrimental.[8]

Degrees of Intrusion

Intrusion may vary in kind and degree at each decision-making stage. In abuse and neglect cases when child protective services *invoke* an inquiry about a particular child or family, the state is intruding. It intrudes further when state agents initiate an action claiming that a ground for intervention exists. Such intrusions breach family privacy. Except in emergencies, parents should be allowed to continue to care for their child and to represent her interests pending *adjudication*. Only during the *disposition* phase—after a ground has been established—should independent counsel be appointed to represent the child. In divorce cases it would be the parents who *invoke* the state's intervention when, following their inability to decide on their own, they ask the court to make a custody *disposition*.

The degree of intrusion on family integrity at each stage of decision should be no greater than that which is necessary to fulfill the function of the decision. Any invasion of family privacy alters the relationships between family members and undermines the effectiveness of parental authority. Children, on their part, react with anxiety even to temporary infringements of parental autonomy. The younger the child and the greater her own helplessness and dependence, the stronger is her need to experience her parents as her lawgivers—safe, reliable, all-powerful, and independent. Therefore, no state intrusion ought to be authorized unless probable and sufficient cause has been established in accord with limits prospectively and carefully defined by the legislature.

We propose that three corollaries to our policy of minimum state intervention become guiding principles in the laws of child placement. They are the

---

*Until the presumption of parental autonomy has been overcome, the parents remain qualified to represent the interests of the entire family.

principles of *least intrusive invocation, least intrusive adjudication,* and *least intrusive disposition.*

In Book One we examined decision-making at the disposition stage. We now focus on decision-making in the invocation and adjudication phases, as we seek to determine and define grounds that would justify modification of a parent-child relationship.

PART SIX

Grounds for Intervention

We do not suggest that the grounds we are about to propose are the only or the best justifications for state intervention. But we do maintain that whatever grounds
are established should comport with guiding principles
sensitive to the needs of family integrity—fair warning
and power restraint.

CHAPTER 11

Parental Requests to Determine Placement

Ground 1: A Request by Separating Parents for the Court to Determine Custody

I n divorce and separation, intervention is justified only when parents, married or unmarried, bring to the court their disagreement about the custody of their children.

This ground is designed, in accord with the continuity guideline, to restrain the state from forcing parents who separate to abdicate their role as exclusive representatives of their child.[1] It leaves parents free to work out for themselves, if they can, the custody and care arrangements that they believe will best serve the interests of their child in the now-divided family.[2]

When parents turn to the court to resolve custody disputes, they open up the otherwise generally "private realm of family life."[3] They no longer act as a buffer between their child and the law. There is little or no likelihood that the child will identify with the attitudes and rulings of this new impersonal authority over her life; therefore, the court's power should be limited by the scope of the dispute. For example, if separating parents are in agreement about the custody arrangements for some but not all of their children, the court, under a policy of minimum state intervention, would be empowered to determine custody only of those children about whom the parents could not agree.*

Under this ground the family is *protected from state intrusion* if the parents themselves decide who is to care for their children.

---

*If possible, courts should avoid separating siblings. Children raised together have a common background and experience usually characterized by companionship, rivalry, and mutual support in times of common threat or need. Staying together enables children to support each other by buffering the traumatic family breakup. It provides children with a sense of ongoing community that strengthens them in coping with threats to future security and self-esteem.[4] But if the parents themselves have agreed to separate siblings, courts should not prevent this.

Implications

Once having declared who should have custody, the court would lack jurisdiction to entertain the noncustodial parent's petition to change custody—unless, as with any family, the petition alleged one of the other grounds for intervention. In other words, a mere "change of circumstances" would not justify further intervention.

Ground 2: A Request by Parents to Give Up Their Child

This ground is designed to provide parents with a relatively safe (for the child), stigma-free (for the parents) opportunity to invoke the child placement process to terminate their parental rights. Its purpose is to maximize for every unwanted child the timely opportunity for being placed in a family that wants her. Once parents decide that they wish to give up their child, the child by definition becomes unwanted. This ground permits parents who do not wish to raise their child—for example, who do not want or cannot obtain the abortion of an unwanted pregnancy—to see to the child's care without first being "forced" to place her at physical or psychological risk.

This ground is intended to provide only for the relinquishment of unwanted children, not of children who are really wanted. The court should determine whether the state (a) had coerced or deceived petitioning parents into surrendering their child,[5] or (b) had failed to offer available supportive services that might have made it possible for them and their child to remain together. Such an inquiry is not intended to place pressure on the parents to keep their children. Therefore, the court could not require petitioning parents to justify their decision.[6] Rather, the court's function is to determine whether the state can relieve parents of the pressures that led them to petition for termination.

This ground rests on the presumption that forcing parents to keep an unwanted child places the child at risk.

Implications

This ground provides a nonjudgmental process for parents to give up their unwanted children without first having to "abandon," "abuse," or "neglect" them. This ground should relegate "the Dickensian portrait of mothers driven to leave babes in doorways . . . to the dark recesses of the past."[7] It should reduce the occurrence of such cases as that of the agency which refused to abide by a mother's request that her son be placed for adoption. After being told by a social worker that she must reconsider her request, the mother returned home, assaulted her son, and brought him back, battered, to the worker, saying, "I really meant it. You'll believe me now. I want him adopted."[8] This ground would enable parents to rectify their mistake "at lower cost—to them, and to the child—than if they were forced to retain custody of the child until their neglect reached the point when the state would intervene. . . ."[9]

This ground provides a means of seeking to meet a child's need to love and be loved. Adoption, if available, offers to such children the best possible second chance to form the permanent relationships vital to their development.[10]

CHAPTER 12

Safeguarding Familial Bonds
Between Children and Long-term Caregivers
Who Are Not Their Parents

Ground 3: An Attempt to Interrupt a Relationship Between Long-term Caregivers and a Child

This ground is designed to promote continuity of care. It is meant to safeguard familial bonds that have developed between children and their long-term foster parents. It is intended to prevent child care agencies and long-absent parents, natural or adoptive, from either keeping children in limbo or forcing them to separate from psychological parents who wish to care for them permanently.

This ground recognizes every child's need for an unbroken relationship with at least one adult who, alone or together with others, is, and wants to be, directly responsible for her daily needs. It acknowledges that family ties need not depend upon the technicality of biological or legal relationships. When long-term foster parents return a child's affection and make her feel wanted, "looked after," and appreciated, crucial attachments usually form, which ought not to be disturbed.[1]

This ground recognizes, in terms of a child's sense of time, the significance of the duration of care by substitute parents. No child can be "put on ice" indefinitely without jeopardizing her well-being. From a child's point of view, no absence from her parents is temporary if it exceeds the period of time during which the child, always according to her age and stage of development, can preserve inner ties to them.[2] Nor are new care arrangements temporary if they extend to a time when the new relationships take the place of prior ones or, for infants placed at birth, become the primary ones.* Once

---

*This was not understood by one mother who wished to place her new-born son in long-term foster care. Insisting that she would not sign the child away for adoption, she said, "By the time he is ready to go to school, he can live with me. He would, then, be company."

new psychological relationships form, separation from the new parents becomes no less painful and no less damaging to a child than separation from natural or adoptive caregiving parents. Indeed, to the extent that such separations are repeated (as in multiple foster care placements), they make the child more vulnerable and make each subsequent opportunity for attachment less promising and less trustworthy than prior ones.

The acceptance by adult caregivers of a child who is not their own may happen much less rapidly than the child's acceptance of them. Or they may accept the child long before she herself has let go of the tie to her own parents. But when both child and caregiver have turned to and accepted one another—when the child has a psychological parent and her caregivers have a psychological child—neither absent parents nor agencies acting on their behalf should be permitted to disrupt the new relationship. The new family deserves the same protection that ongoing relationships between children and their biological or adoptive parents deserve and traditionally receive.[3]

No precise timetable can be set for the complex process of forming psychological parent-child relationships. But we recognize, as Mr. Justice Holmes stated long ago:

> When a legal distinction is determined, as no one doubts that it may be, between night and day, childhood and maturity, or any other extremes, a point has to be fixed or a line has to be drawn, or gradually picked out by successive decisions, to mark where the change takes place. Looked at by itself without regard to the necessity behind it the line or point seems arbitrary. It might as well or nearly as well be a little more to one side or the other. But when it is seen that a line or point there must be, and that there is no mathematical or logical way of fixing it precisely, the decision of the legislature must be accepted unless we can say that it is very wide of any reasonable mark.[4]

Therefore, we propose the following statutory periods *during which a child has been in the direct and continuous care of the same adult(s)* as maximum intervals beyond which it would be unreasonable to presume that a child's residual ties with her absent parents are more significant than those that have developed between her and her long-term caregivers:

(a) six months for a child up to the age of one month at the time of placement;

(b) twelve months for a child up to the age of three years at the time of placement; and

(c) twenty-four months for a child three years or older at the time of place-
     ment.

With one exception, these time spans, when coupled with the long-term
caregiver's wish to continue caring for the child on a permanent basis, are
reasonable indicators for granting legal protection to the new relationship.*
Once this ground is established, the child could be entitled to permanent
membership in the substitute family, and prior parental ties could be terminated.

For some children in the older age group, the statutory period of twenty-
four months may be an insufficient basis for not returning the child to her absent parents who wish to regain custody. Some older children may hold on to
emotional attachments to absent parents fiercely and possessively; their early,
long-standing psychological ties may interfere with the formation of new
psychological attachments to the fostering adults. In such instances, a return
to the absent parents might be appropriate. Therefore, this ground provides a
special hearing for any child over five years of age who,

(a) at the time of placement, had been in the continuous care of her parents
     for not less than the three preceding years; *and*
(b) had *not* been separated from her parents because they inflicted or at-
     tempted to inflict serious bodily injury upon her or were convicted of a
     sexual offense against her.[†]

The hearing would attempt to determine quickly whether the child's absent parents were still her primary psychological parents and whether her return to them would be the least detrimental alternative.[‡] In the event that the
evidence was inconclusive, the child's relationship to her long-term caregivers would be given legal recognition.

In all other cases, the critical factor in defining "long-term caregivers"—
which would determine a child's entitlement to remain with them—is the
length of time that a child has been in their continuous care, not the period of

*The younger a child is, the more limited are her emotional resources for managing a "long" separation
from her parents, and the more likely it is that significant psychological ties will have developed between
her and her caregivers. Children who have been in multiple foster placements may make superficial attachments but are unwilling or unable to make deep primary ones.[5]

[†]Gross failures of care are discussed as grounds for intervention in Chapter 13.

[‡]Repeated clinical evaluations and delays in making such determinations are detrimental to the child and
should be avoided.[6]

time that she has been separated from her absent parents. The statutory periods are time *with,* not time *away from.*[7]

The time spans that we propose take into account a number of factors. They provide the least intrusive mode of state intervention on parent-child relationships. By their very specificity, they satisfy the requisites of fair warning and power restraint, because they alert parents and state agencies to the consequences that are likely to follow from lengthy separations, no matter what their cause. The time spans are conservatively set in terms of a child's sense of time and the different consequences that disruptions of continuity have for children of different ages. They are sensitive to the societal preference for maintaining biological and adoptive parent-child relationships. At the same time, they are sensitive to the painful harm done to children by forcibly separating them from "temporary" caregivers in trial-and-error efforts to restore legal relationships that are almost certainly no longer tenable human relationships. Moreover, they recognize the limits of knowledge—that there is no easy way to ascertain in each case when a substitute parent has become a child's psychological parent. And finally, they become operative only if the ongoing caregivers make it clear that they are willing to assume permanent full responsibility for the child.

This ground and the dispositional guides must include a provision for discouraging agencies from pursuing a policy of moving a child from one foster home to another. Such a policy is harmful to children and is unacceptable as a technique for preserving the rights of absent parents who are not prepared or not able to resume responsibility for the regular and continuous care of their child. Therefore this ground would provide that if the foster parents want to keep the child, and she is doing well in their care, then (even if the statutory period for them to qualify as long-term caregivers has not elapsed) a child care agency can remove her only to return her permanently to her legal parents—not to place her elsewhere.

Once this ground is invoked, the continuity guideline dictates that the child remain in the custody of her caregiver until final disposition.* And the child's-sense-of-time guideline requires that disposition, including all appeals, be resolved as a matter of urgency within the shortest possible time. For the same reason, hearings concerned with terminating the relationship between foster children and their long-term caregivers must take place *before*

---

*However, counsel for the child and/or the prevailing party should consider arguing against a stay pending appeal on the ground that there is no "fair prospect" that the decision will be erroneous, and that therefore failure to vacate the stay will ulitmately harm the child by breaking the relationship with the "losing" adults established over months (or, more likely, years) during the pendency of the appeal.[8]

separating them, not after. "An erroneous wrenching of the nurturing bonds between the long-term foster child and his long-term foster family is the kind of damage that is not fully—or even substantially—recompensable even by ordering a resumption of the broken relationships. In terms of irreparable injury, an erroneous breaking up of delicate and complex long-term foster family relationships is far more serious than would be such an unthinkable action as, for example, an agency intentionally breaking a child's arm for some therapeutic purpose, recognizing that such a mistake may be 'corrected' by resetting the limb which, though scarred, may grow together again as 'strong' as it ever was."[9]

Implications

Once this ground has been established, adoption by the long-term caregivers is preferable. But when long-term caregivers who want to continue their relationship with the child do not wish to adopt, it would still be less detrimental for the child to continue in that relationship than to break it. The child must not be made the victim of a state policy that favors adoption for adoption's sake.* Nonadoptive but permanent relationships should be given recognition as *foster care with tenure*. Such children would then be insulated from intrusion by state agencies and former parents. They could expect the continuity of care and family membership usually associated with adoption.[11]

In foster care *without* tenure, the shared authority between the fostering adults and the child care agency is likely to have an adverse impact on the children. Such children are denied the security of living with autonomous parents. The lack of such security produces in some children a fearful compliance in order to avoid being "sent away." In others it may lead to rebellion in order to test the limits of acceptance. In any case, at least for the older

---

*A state's child welfare agency handed a newly hired social worker a set of files for which she was to be responsible. In the file of eight-year-old Harry she noted that he had been in foster care with the same family for six years. The agency's policy, stated in its manual of regulations, was to find adoptive parents for children who could not be reunited with their biological parents, in order to provide them with a *permanent family*. She went to Harry's school to identify herself as his new social worker and said to him: "Don't worry any more; I'm going to find you a family that will adopt you." The child was terrified at the prospect of being taken away from the people he knew as his parents. The foster family had explained to the social worker's predecessor that they were not making a request to adopt Harry, because the foster father had been advised that he might have a terminal illness and they feared that their adoption petition would be denied and they would lose their child. The new worker failed to understand that Harry's interests required her to recognize *permanent family* in its functional and not its technical sense.[10]

child, it delays or prevents the formation of stabilizing emotional ties. Legal recognition of foster care with tenure could help to meet that need.

Without discouraging essential temporary placements, this ground is meant to force a realistic evaluation of both the circumstances that prompt voluntary and involuntary separations, and the likelihood that the ties between child and absent parents can be kept alive. For example, recognition that the circumstances that force parents and child to separate are chronic and that the separation is likely to be lengthy should cause an increased use of supportive resources to keep families together. And if the circumstances do necessitate foster care, the court should set a date for returning the child. This should not exceed the applicable statutory period, beyond which the arrangement would no longer be "temporary" for that child. Each case should be tagged to resurface for review shortly before the date set. Such an *early warning* system would uncover those cases in which the child had not yet been restored to her family, and allow time to consider the possibility of her permanent return to them, with or without supportive services. If that were found not to be a reasonable option, the warning system would trigger a process that could lead to the child's relationship with her caregivers being made permanent.[12]

A need for a temporary form of foster care does exist. The goal of such foster care should be reunion of the family. A decision to place a child in such care should carry with it an expectation for all parties, including the court, that the child will shortly—in accord with the child's sense of time—be restored to her family. The younger the child, the shorter should be the duration of such a placement if it is to be temporary. During the period of separation, provision should be made for keeping alive the ties that bond child and absent parents. Disturbances to the continuity of her relationships with parents should be kept to an absolute minimum. To maintain reciprocity of affectionate relationships will require sensitivity to the child's developmental capacities and tolerances. This, in turn, should determine the extent and form of accessibility of child and parents to each other during the period of separation. Temporary foster parents have the double task of supplying for the child the missing parental care without at the same time alienating the child's feelings for the absent parents. This is a delicate and extremely difficult job.[13]

CHAPTER 13

Failures of Parental Care

Ground 4: The Death or Disappearance of Parents Who Have Failed to Designate Who Shall Care for Their Child

This ground for intervention gives the state the authority to safeguard children for whom no day-to-day care arrangements have been made by parents who die, disappear, are imprisoned, are hospitalized, or are otherwise incapacitated. Events of this kind jeopardize a child's physical and emotional well-being, and they also deprive her of representation in law and society.

Implications

This ground focuses on the plight of the child. It does not require establishing intentional abandonment by her parents. At the same time, it acknowledges that parental autonomy includes the right of parents to designate other willing adults to care for their child. The death, disappearance, or institutionalization of a parent, in and of itself, justifies no more than an inquiry. It does not justify further intrusion *unless* the parents have failed to designate another person to take care of their child, or *unless* another ground exists for intervening in the relationship between the child and that other person.*

This ground codifies the reading given to the phrase *uncared for* in *Welfare Commissioner v. Anonymous.*[1] In that case, solely on the basis of a mother's imprisonment, the commissioner charged that her children were "uncared for" and should be declared wards of the state. Before her imprisonment the mother had placed the children in the care of their great-aunt. Making obvious what apparently was not obvious—at least to the commissioner—the court observed:

---

*Arrangements for temporary care made by absent parents themselves or by the state following an adjudication may become long-term. Such caregivers, on the basis of the ground set forth in Chapter 12, could then make their relationship with the child permanent.

[I]f a child is being properly cared for by, for example, a close relative at the request of a biological parent, the commissioner's construction would require the court to say that a child is "uncared for" when, in fact the child is "cared for.". . . [T]he commissioner's construction would have the undesirable consequence of discouraging biological parents from even temporarily entrusting their children to someone who would give them better care, for, under the commissioner's construction, even temporarily entrusting children to a nonbiological parent to enable the children to be better cared for would make the children "uncared for" and subject to commitment to the commissioner.[2]

In this case, under the principle of the least intrusive invocation, the mother's imprisonment justified nothing more than an inquiry as to whether she designated someone to care for her children.[3]

The presumption is that parents know best who should care for their child. This presumption underlies one court's explanation of a statute that requires honoring the appointment of a child's guardian under her parents' will:

No person is in a position to know as well [as the parent] who should have the custody of children. . . . He has observed them throughout their lives. By daily contact he knows their temperaments and habits, and by observation he knows those who have evidenced the greatest interest in his children, and those whose moral and spiritual values are in his judgment conducive to the best interests of his children. A judge treads on sacred ground when he overrides the directions of the deceased with reference to the custody of his children.[4]

Ground 5: Serious Bodily Injury Inflicted by Parents upon Their Child, an Attempt or a Threat to Inflict Such Injury, or the Repeated Failure of Parents to Protect the Child from Exposure to Such Injury

This ground is designed to establish a minimum standard of care below which no parents may go without calling into question their right to raise their children as they see fit. It is meant to give the state the authority to identify and to provide protection to children who are kicked, beaten, raped, or otherwise brutally attacked by their parents. It is meant to safeguard children whose parents have attempted to injure them, for example, by starvation,[5] poisoning, or strangling. It is meant to safeguard children from parents who have proved to be incapable of preventing their child from repeatedly suffering serious bodily injury or from being exposed to such harm.

This ground rests upon a recognition that a young child's enjoyment of adventuresome, impulsive behavior may far outstrip her cognitive capacity to appraise the consequences. Even after listening to and appearing to understand repeated parental warnings, children are still apt to run into heavy traffic, spill boiling water on themselves, or swallow poisonous substances. The child's lack of regard for the safety of her body becomes the concern of her parents, who normally value and protect her body as they would their own. It takes years before this state of affairs changes, before the child comprehends the consequences of risk-taking behavior and becomes capable of "looking after herself."

When parents inflict (or attempt or threaten to inflict) serious bodily injury, or when they repeatedly fail to protect their child from exposure to such physical harm, the state must be authorized to intervene. To secure the child's future safety, it should provide either supportive assistance for the family or substitute parents for the child. Assistance permits families to remain together and would, if available and accepted by the parents, be preferred as the least intrusive, least detrimental disposition. In some cases, however, such dispositions would be inappropriate. Repeated serious injuries inflicted or not prevented by parents leave the child with psychological scars that endure long beyond any physical healing and preclude her from regaining the feeling of being safe, wanted, and cared for in her parents' presence—the very emotions on which her further developmental advances need to be based.[6]

The "serious-bodily-injury" standard does not include intervention for minor assaults on the child's body which go under the name of corporal punishment. Some parents regard the infliction of physical pain as a means of disciplining their child. As psychoanalysts, educators, and parents, we believe that corporal punishment is not only harmful, humiliating, and disadvantageous to the child's development, but also sets a poor example of adult behavior. However, the abolition of corporal punishment by parents may not be a matter for legislation but for the gradual enlightenment and humanizing of public attitudes.[7]

Though the serious-bodily-injury ground, like our other grounds for intervention, is concerned with emotional repercussions on the child, it is defined solely in terms of physical harm. This ground is meant to protect families from the unwarranted intrusions authorized by neglect statutes that use such undefined terms as "denial of proper care," "sexual abuse," "psychological abuse," or "serious emotional damage." These terms are too vague to restrain state authorities who have come to exercise coercive power based on a wide range of child-rearing notions about which there is neither professional nor societal consensus.* By contrast, serious damage to any part of the child's body surface, bone structure, or organs reveals itself even to an untrained observer by the child's pain, by visible signs, or by change in body function. Medical opinion is sufficiently in agreement and diagnostic skills are sufficiently advanced to determine the causes of most injuries, traumatic and toxic.

Implications

We do not propose *emotional neglect* as a separate ground. Efforts to define emotional neglect in terms of a child's "severe anxiety, depression, or withdrawal, or untoward aggressive behavior toward self or others"[8] serve to reinforce the notion that "'[e]motional neglect' is meaningless because it is so subjective and virtually impossible to disprove."[9] Observed behavior is not enough for assessing a child's mental health. What appears to be similar behavior may, for different children, be either a symptom of illness or a sign of health. And the same deep-seated emotional disturbance may lead to diverse manifestations of behavior. The causes of "severe anxiety" may range from the rational (for example, fear of extreme violence witnessed in the parental home) to the severely neurotic (for example, the child's fear of being overwhelmed by the intensity of her own feelings). Likewise, "depression or withdrawal" may be an adaptation to environmental circumstances such as the loss of a beloved person; it may stem from the lack of parental stimulation that leaves the child uninterested in the world outside and predominantly absorbed by her own body's excitation and tension discharge; or it may be the initial sign of a child's intrinsic abnormality, such as an autistic or psychotic process. Similarly, a child may betray "untoward aggressive behavior toward self and others" for a wide variety of reasons: because of biological deficits; because as an infant she was deprived of the affection which should have aroused her loving feelings and toned down her aggression; because she was treated harshly by her parents and identified with their aggressive attitudes; because she was exposed to deprivations that were intolerable and weakened her capacity to modify natural aggressive responses; or because her moral standards, once acquired, forbade aggression to be directed against the outside world and left it to be turned against her own person.

---

*The test of mental health is to be found not in any particular style of life, but in the absence of serious internal conflicts—in the harmony of inner agencies. Evaluations of a child, or for that matter of an adult, which simply equate social compliance with mental health and noncompliance with mental illness are wrong.

In the face of these uncertainties and imprecise definitions of "emotional neglect" and "serious emotional damage," neither concept should be used as a ground for modifying parent-child relationships. And even if emotional neglect could be precisely defined, little consensus exists about the "right" treatment, and this should caution against using the power of the state to intrude.*

Under our ground, the state would not have been authorized to intrude as it did in the families of the infant *Shay; Richard Wambles;* and the *Alsager* children, George, Wanda, John, Charles, Michael, and Albert.

THE INFANT SHAY

As Ms. *Shay,* an unmarried twenty-two-year-old, neared the end of an uneventful pregnancy, she decided to keep her baby. Initially she had expressed the wish to have her adopted. The hospital social worker reported to the state's protective services that there was reason to feel worried about the child's safety and well-being because of Ms. Shay's change of mind about adoption and because she was eccentric in her attire as well as in her attitude toward food and cleanliness.

The baby and mother had a normal labor and birth experience and left the hospital for their one-room apartment a few days later. The protective services worker called on Ms. Shay after neighbors reported that she was "acting in a peculiar manner." The peculiarities observed by the neighbors and confirmed by the worker's investigation included: "(1) Ms. Shay fed the baby by leaning over the crib side and breast-feeding with the baby in the supine position; (2) Ms. Shay cut a hole in the mattress with a pail below and did not use diapers on the baby when the baby was in her crib." In addition, the neighbors said that they were upset because Ms. Shay had been throwing all the knives from her apartment into the trash; they feared she would harm the baby with a knife.

Ms. Shay's "peculiar behavior" was of considerable concern to the protective services. In order to have time to discuss with the mother how babies should be cared for, the social worker "convinced" her that it would be desirable to hospitalize the child for observation on the ward for abused and neglected children—even though, in the opinion of the baby's doctor and the public health nurse, the infant girl was well nourished and behaving normally. One evening, fearful of losing her child, the mother took the baby and

*This position should not obscure the need for state-supported voluntary services for helping parents to identify and deal with their child's emotional needs.

walked out of the hospital. Unable to find public transportation, she began hitchhiking home with the baby in her arms. The police picked her up on the road.

The child care agency then placed the baby in a distant hospital and refused to tell Ms. Shay where her daughter was until it could be determined whether the baby was a "neglected child." The state's statute provided that "a child may be found 'neglected' who . . . is being denied proper care and attention, physically, educationally, emotionally or is being permitted to live under conditions, circumstances or associations injurious to his well-being. . . ."[10] Two weeks later the social worker petitioned the court to place the baby under the guardianship of the state welfare commissioner. The court granted the petition, and the two-month-old infant was placed in a foster home.[11]

Under the grounds that we propose no such intrusiveness would have been permitted. Even the initial inquiries would not have been justified.

RICHARD WAMBLES

Richard, the son of Miss Margaret Wambles, a twenty-five-year-old white woman, was born in September 1971 and lived with her continuously until June 1975, when he was seized by a Montgomery, Alabama, policeman and placed in the custody of the Welfare Department pending an adjudication of "neglected child." Following a complaint by the putative father, this emergency placement was ordered by Judge Thetford of the Family Court under the authority of a statute that defined *neglected child* as any child under sixteen years of age who "has no proper parental care . . . or whose home . . . is an unfit and improper place for such child . . . or who for any other cause is in need of the care and protection of the state" and that provided for emergency placement without a hearing "if it appears from the petition that . . . the child is in such condition that its welfare requires that custody be immediately assumed. . . ."

After obtaining a pickup order, three police officers went to Miss Wambles' home at 8:30 in the evening and announced that they had come to take Richard into custody.[12] According to the deposition of one of the police officers:

A. She picked Richard up and ran back to the back of the house.
Q. What did you do?
A. I chased after her.

* * *

Q.   And where was Richard?

A.   He was in Margaret's arms.

*   *   *

Q.   What kind of emotional state was Margaret in?

A.   She was screaming—not screaming, but she was fussing and raising a disturbance. She was—she appeared to be upset.

*   *   *

Q.   And what about the child?

A.   He was—he was upset.

Q.   Okay. By "upset," can you explain what you mean by that? Was he crying?

A.   He was more of a—it was more of a look of what's going on, you know. He was looking at his mother and he was looking at me and couldn't—it was more of a confusion type of thing.

Q.   Did he make any noise?

A.   He did when Margaret started saying, "No, you are not going to take him." He said, "No, Mama don't let him take me."

*   *   *

Q.   What happened then?

A.   I grabbed her by the arm and pulled her back into the living room where it was lighted. It was dark in the hall.

Q.   Were you holding her tightly?

A.   I was holding [her arm] so that she would not be able to pull loose and run or anything like this. I advised her that non-compliance with this pick-up order could result in her going to jail because this was a court order.

Q.   What happened then?

A.   [S]he handed the child over to me and I gave her the court order to read. . . .

Q.   What kind of state was she in at this point?

A.   Nervous; she was shaking.

*   *   *

Q. [W]hat state was Richard in after he was handed to you?
A. He was rather confused—he didn't quite—could not figure out what was going on.*

On review, Judge Rives observed:

The only facts about Margaret Wambles known to Judge Thetford before he issued the pick-up order were that she was unemployed and that she and her child are white and were living with a black man in a black neighborhood. Judge Thetford had no information as to how long Margaret Wambles had lived in Montgomery, where she had worked, or how long she had been unemployed. He had no evidence that Richard . . . was being physically abused and no information as to the condition of the Wambles' home. Judge Thetford knew nothing about the man with whom Margaret Wambles was living, other than his race and the fact that he was not married to her. Judge Thetford testified that the race of the man with whom Plaintiff Wambles was living was relevant to his decision to order Richard . . . removed from his mother's custody, particularly because they were living in a black neighborhood. Judge Thetford concluded that this habitation in a black neighborhood could be dangerous for a child because it was his belief that "it was not a healthy thing for a white child to be the only [white] child in a black neighborhood."[14]

Under the grounds for intervention that we propose, no petition for modification or termination of parental rights could have been entertained. The finding of "neglected child" and termination of Richard's right to his mother would have been precluded. Indeed, just as in the *Shay* case and in the *Alsager* case that follows, no emergency placement could have been ordered, since there was no cause for believing that the child's physical well-being was threatened.

THE ALSAGER CHILDREN: GEORGE, WANDA, JOHN, CHARLES, MICHAEL, AND ALBERT

In the spring of 1969 the probation department in Des Moines, Iowa, received a number of complaints from neighbors about the children of Charles and Darlene *Alsager.* At that time they had been married eleven years and were

*Not only from a child's point of view, but from an adult's as well, there is no rational explanation for what was going on.[13]

the parents of six children: George, age ten; Wanda, eight; John, seven; Charles Jr., six; Michael, four; and Albert, who was less than one year old.[15] Various neighbors wrote to the probation authorities: "The oldest boy . . . does nasty things with his little sister, Wanda. . . . The children cuss me and throw rocks at me and at the house and car and at my daughter. . . . [Mrs. Alsager's mother] cusses and swears and carries on something terrible over the phone if you call them about the children. . . . We appeal to you to help us to place the children and this family where they belong. We have taken care of them long enough."[16]

On the basis of such complaints and under the authority of Iowa's child neglect statute, Jane Johnston, a probation officer, was instructed by her superiors to invoke the process—to investigate the Alsager family. The statute provided for the termination of parent-child relationships if "the parents have . . . repeatedly refused to give the child necessary parental care and protection" or "if the parents are unfit by reason of . . . conduct found by the court likely to be detrimental to the physical or mental health or morals of the child." On June 20, 1969, Officer Johnston "visited" the Alsager home. She "spent approximately twenty minutes inside the Alsager residence, which at the time was occupied only by Mrs. Alsager and the baby, Albert. Based on her observations inside the house, and without seeing the other five children, Miss Johnston determined that all six children should immediately be removed to the Polk County Juvenile Home. This removal was to be temporary, pending a hearing to determine whether the children were 'neglected.'. . ."[17] As a result of the adjudication hearing, which took place within a week after the children were taken from their parents, District Judge Tidrick found the children to be neglected. The evidence revealed "that the Alsagers sometimes permitted their children to leave the house in cold weather without winter clothing on, 'allowed them' to play in traffic, to annoy neighbors, to eat mush for supper, to live in a house containing dirty dishes and laundry, and to sometimes arrive late at school. At the time of the termination, Mr. Alsager was a working man who had never been on public welfare rolls. He and his wife lived together, and shared an interest in keeping their family unit intact."[18]

In May 1970, after the Alsager children had been out of their home for almost a year, Judge Tidrick terminated the parental rights of Charles and Darlene Alsager "in and to" five of their six children. By 1974, these five children had experienced between them more than "15 separate foster home placements, and eight juvenile home placements."[19]

Under our ground, the state action that tore the Alsager family apart would have been precluded. There was not even enough evidence to justify an inquiry, let alone an emergency placement and termination of parental rights.

Had our ground been adopted at the time of their actions, the authorities in the *Shay* case, the *Wambles* case, and the *Alsager* case would not have been authorized to intrude. If "emotional neglect" or "serious emotional damage" is to be the basis of any ground for action in a child placement code, it should be used to hold the state accountable for its violations of family integrity.

As we now turn to a series of cases that illustrate circumstances that would justify state intervention under the serious-bodily-injury ground, the strange paradox that characterizes child placement law becomes evident. While the state in the preceding cases was too intrusive, it was not intrusive enough in at least two of the three cases that are discussed in the next section.

NORMAN VIGORA

The serious-bodily-injury ground would have supported intervention in the case of Norman *Vigora*. When Norman was an infant he was admitted to the hospital with "contusions on his right eye, skull, lumbar spine and both shoulders." His parents had beaten him because "he was fussy and cried too much."* Upon Norman's release from the hospital, the court ordered him placed in emergency foster care with the Wilsons, his aunt and uncle. The judge urged the Vigoras to seek counseling and encouraged them to visit Norman regularly.

Norman remained in uninterrupted care with the Wilsons for 4½ years. During this period the Vigoras visited him on an average of once every 2 weeks and tried to prepare him and themselves for his return. Shortly after the birth of another child, they brought suit to revoke the foster placement order. The court requested an evaluation of Mr. and Mrs. Vigora, Norman, and the Wilsons, who were eager to have the child become a permanent member of their family. The evaluations revealed that Norman, then age 5½, was preoccupied with being taken away from the Wilsons. When the Vigoras would tell him of their hope that he would be moving to live with them and his "new baby sister," he became confused and fearful. He resumed bed-wetting, which had stopped when he was 2½.

Nothing in the evaluation suggested that the Vigoras were unfit to take care of their second child. But the Vigoras could never be adequate parents for

---

*A young child's behavior is experienced differently by various adults or by the same adult at different times according to differing moods. For example: (1) Parents may experience their child's fussy behavior as normal; they will rock, soothe, and stay with the child patiently. (2) Parents may experience such behavior as illness in the child and call the pediatrician or discuss it with the visiting nurse. (3) Parents may experience the fussy behavior as violently and provocatively demanding, and they may react to it in terms of their own need to "survive"—by not allowing the "tyrannical" baby to destroy them. The helplessness of the infant is a magnet for nurture, for attention, and for action; it may also be a painful reminder to the adult of her own earlier helplessness and, perversely, can be a magnet for attack.

Norman—not necessarily because they might physically abuse him again, but because there was no way for him to feel safe in their care. The Vigoras argued that all they wanted was "another chance to be Norman's parents and that if they screwed up again then the courts could take him away permanently."[20] Under our ground, the Vigoras would have been denied a second chance following the initial adjudication that they had *inflicted* serious bodily injury on Norman.*

DAWN AND TODD GRAY

Under the attempt-to-inflict-serious-bodily-injury provision of this ground, the state would have had the discretion to terminate the relationships between Ruth *Gray* and her two children, Dawn and Todd, ages four and six. At the time of her divorce from their father, John Gray, she had been given custody of the children. Several months after John's remarriage, Ruth attempted to take her life and the lives of her children. She attached a plastic enclosure to the kitchen gas range to collect the fumes, then drugged herself and Dawn and Todd and placed them under the plastic. A neighbor's unanticipated visit resulted in their rescue.

When the children were released from the hospital, John and his second wife assumed responsibility for their care. Ruth was indicted for assault with intent to murder and found not guilty by reason of insanity. She was committed to a psychiatric hospital. Exercising its continuing jurisdiction over custody of the children, the court ordered liberal visitation by their mother whenever her psychiatrist felt she was well enough to benefit from visits. Upon Ruth's discharge from the hospital later that same year, the court extended the visitation order to include overnight visits.[†] Both children had extreme reactions of fear for their lives when they were told their mother would be visiting.

The night before each visit, which the father insisted should take place under his supervision, the children were extremely upset. Todd took a baseball bat to bed with him to protect himself and resumed bed-wetting. Dawn had nightmares, stomachaches, and diarrhea. They were stiff, pale, and unable to relax in Ruth's company. They repeatedly asked their father for protection, fearing that if they accepted food or drink or were alone with her, she would try to kill them. Over and over they asked their parents to keep their mother

---

*Even if there had been no history of child beating, under the long-term caregiver ground discussed in Chapter 12, Norman would have been eligible for a permanent place in the Wilson family.

†Under our Book One guidelines, the court would not have the discretion to order visits, or to reopen custody awards, unless there was a ground for intervention.

from killing them.[21] They were preoccupied with saving their lives; their fears and anxiety were anchored in reality. Despite this, the court remained convinced that the mother's blood ties to the children justified enforcing her "right" to them, and rejecting the application of John's new wife to adopt them.

Even in a legal system that generally favors visits in custody awards, our ground would prohibit the state from forcing Todd and Dawn to see their mother, and it would allow for the termination of parental rights. They would be entitled to be adopted by their stepmother and thus to feel secure in their family.

DONALD CARLSON

Under the provision of the ground that is concerned with *repeated failure* of parents *to protect* their child from suffering serious bodily injury, the relationship between Donald *Carlson* and his mother would be modified. During a routine school physical examination, Donald, aged ten, was diagnosed as having juvenile diabetes mellitus. He was immediately hospitalized, because he was dehydrated and his blood sugar level was very high. During the sixteen-day period of Donald's hospitalization his mother received instructions from hospital nurses and dieticians on how to manage his diabetes. A month later Donald was again hospitalized for hypoglycemic reaction due to his mother's inability to provide proper diet and insulin control. The hospital staff tried to help her understand what was required, but Donald soon had to be hospitalized again because of his mother's repeated failure, despite her cooperative spirit and good intentions, to manage his need for a special diet, his need for insulin shots, and his need to follow a schedule of exercise and rest. Her failure of parental care constituted a threat to Donald's physical well-being and life.

The least intrusive disposition—one that would have minimized the stress on Donald's psychological tie to his mother—would have been to provide a family helper. Assuming Mrs. Carlson could have cooperated, the helper could have managed Donald's medical care and special diet.* Unfortunately, such a service was not available. Thus, in order to protect Donald's life, the least detrimental alternative was to place him in a special foster home, where his diabetes was kept under control. He required no further hospitalization.[22]

We also do not propose "sexual abuse" as a separate ground. Our ground mandates intervention when parents, whether sexually motivated or not, in-

---

*In accord with the principle of the least intrusive intervention, the role of the family helper would be limited to meeting the specific need that was established in the adjudication of the ground for intervention.

flict (or threaten to inflict, or repeatedly fail to protect the child from) serious bodily injury on their child. The ground does not require proof of *emotional* harm. It covers the child who suffers *physical* harm at the hands of sexually abusive parents. It does not cover the child who is seduced—whose parents, without causing (or threatening) serious *physical* injury, either exploit her emotional ties to them or otherwise betray her trust by taking advantage of her sexually.

The sexual wishes and activities of an immature child are as different from those of an adult as are her bones, physical capacities, and intellectual achievements. The pattern of a child's development toward mature sex is thrown into confusion by any seducing adult who uses the child to satisfy his or her sexual appetite. Intercourse with children prematurely arouses their genital responses and intimately related erotic feelings.[23] Such children are overwhelmed emotionally. Even if their turmoil does not become immediately visible, detrimental consequences usually become manifest in adolescent and adult life in the form of unsatisfying personal and sexual relationships.

When the seducing adult is also the child's parent, the damage done to her emotional life is likely to be most severe.[24] Parental sexual advances may be met by a child's willingness to cooperate. Initial shock and surprise need not preclude pleasurable erotic excitement from the fulfillment of secret fantasies. Parents are, after all, the loved people in a child's life toward whom she first turns for satisfaction. Indeed, children regularly develop fantasies to become the partner of the parent of the opposite sex and replace the marital partner.[25] Normal as these fantasies are, the child's mental health and emotional development depend upon their not being realized.

We know enough to say, therefore, that children are hurt even by a parent's nonviolent sexual advances, but we do not know enough to be sure that state intervention can provide something less detrimental. The harm done to the child and to the family's integrity by inquiry may be greater than that caused by not intruding, especially as it may be difficult to define the difference between appropriate and inappropriate displays of affection and fondling.[26] In the absence of a sufficiently precise definition of sexual abuse and of a consensus either about proper treatment or about what disposition might be less detrimental for the child, we have been unable to formulate an independent ground that satisfies our criteria of fair warning and power restraint.*

---

*"Treatment" in childhood cannot put the prematurely simulated sexual appetite to sleep again; at best it may help the child deal with immediate psychological aftereffects. Treatment at a later age deals with pathological consequences—either inhibition or promiscuity.[27]

SARAH TENENBAUM

In September 1989, Marc and Mary *Tenenbaum* enrolled their daughter, Sarah, in kindergarten in Brooklyn. Sarah suffered from "elective mutism," meaning that she did not speak to people outside of her home. At school Sarah often fell asleep and on occasion would cry in class, according to her teacher, Mary Murphy. At first Sarah did not speak to Murphy, but over time she began to show Murphy pictures and speak one- or two-word sentences to her. On two occasions, according to Murphy, Sarah communicated in words and gestures that her father sexually abused her. On one occasion when Sarah began crying, Murphy asked her if anyone was hurting her and identified a series of people in her life to which she "shook her head no." However, when her father's name was mentioned in the litany of individuals, Sarah's eyes filled "up in tears and she shook her head, yes, and she started to really cry." Sarah pointed to the groin area of one of the dolls in the play area of her classroom when asked by Murphy where her father hurt her. Sarah drew a picture of two figures and said to Murphy that one of the figures was her father and that he "kneeled and 'hurt' her, and that she was the other figure, and then she stopped talking."

As required by New York Social Services law, Murphy reported to her superiors at the school what Sarah had done and said. An official at the school, in turn, reported the matter to the New York State Department of Social Services (DSS) Central Register of Child Abuse and Maltreatment. As required by state law, DSS forwarded the report to Nat Williams, a supervisor in the child protective unit of the New York City Child Welfare Administration (CWA). Williams immediately assigned the case to Veronica James, a newly hired caseworker.

Following Williams' instructions, James, together with coworker Thomas O'Connell, visited the Tenenbaum home and told Sarah's parents that they were there to investigate a report that Sarah had been absent from school and was developmentally delayed. They did not inform the Tenenbaums of their suspicion of sexual abuse. The Tenenbaums gave James the names of the pediatricians caring for Sarah and her younger brother, Aaron, and signed releases for their medical records. The Tenenbaums partially undressed their children so that James and O'Connell could inspect them for any bruises or marks on their chests, backs, or extremities. The case workers found no signs of maltreatment or abuse. No effort was made to inspect either child's genital area.

Three days later, James visited the school to interview Murphy and Sarah. When Murphy, with James present, asked Sarah whether her father touched her near her vagina and hurt her, however, Sarah shook her head "no." In fact, she responded to all of the questions asked of her that day by Murphy by shaking her head "no," including the question "Does your mother bathe you?" Murphy also reported to James that a gym teacher had noticed a red mark on Sarah's thigh several weeks earlier. The Tenenbaums alleged that the gym teacher could have seen the mark only by undressing Sarah, because she always wore opaque tights to school.

James reported what she had learned at the school to Williams, who instructed her to go to the school to effect an emergency removal of Sarah and to take her to Coney Island Hospital to be examined by doctors for possible sexual abuse. That same day James visited the school and gave school officials a form which indicated that she was taking Sarah into protective custody in accordance with state law. At the hospital, a pediatrician and gynecologist conducted an examination of Sarah, and found no evidence of sexual abuse. While James and Sarah were at the hospital, Williams contacted Sarah's mother by phone to advise her that the CWA had removed her daughter from school. Later that evening Williams told the Tenenbaums that the CWA would not file charges and that they could take Sarah home, because the medical examination did not find evidence that the child had been sexually abused.[28]

This case illustrates both some reasons for and the difficulties presented by having undefined "sexual abuse" as a ground for intervention. The teacher, Murphy, probably believed that Sarah had "told" her that her father had abused her. Once possessed of this "knowledge" she was required by law to report to school officials, who in turn were required by law to report to New York's Child Welfare Administration, whose agents in turn took the precipitous action of "interviewing" Sarah and removing her from the school to be examined by two doctors—all without, at any time, discussing any of this with Sarah's parents.

Murphy's dilemma was that if she had taken no action, and if it had transpired that Sarah had indeed been "sexually abused" by her father (and might continue to be subjected to such abuse), she would have blamed herself and been blamed by others. This may have made it difficult for her to recognize that the risk of doing harm by intrusion was greater than that of not intruding. Yet New York's law and the resulting actions by Murphy and the CWA, however well-meant, traumatized both Sarah and her parents.

There was no justification for the emergency removal of Sarah from school where she was safe, for taking her to the hospital, or for subjecting her to a physical examination. The state authorities had ample time to seek the permission of Sarah's parents for obtaining a physical examination. A refusal to grant permission should have precluded any further coercive intervention. Sarah's parents had never been disqualified from representing her interests, nor did the facts of the case present any justification for a court to have disqualified them.

What must be weighed in the balance is the potential damage inflicted on a child by being left in a home where she might be subject to exploitative sexual advances, as compared to damage suffered by the child and her family resulting from a state intervention that either fails to establish such advances to have taken place or is unable to provide a disposition that is less detrimental to the child than remaining in the home with her parents.

Some children may suffer either way—whether a separate ground for state intervention based on sexual abuse by a parent does or does not exist. We do not support such a separate ground—both because of the difficulty of defining what "sexual abuse" is and is not, and because of the unlikelihood of the state being able to provide a less detrimental alternative for the child if a defined sexual abuse had been proven.*

MAURICE, MARIE, AND MICHELLE VULON
In the case of the *Vulon* children—Maurice, age thirteen, Marie, ten, and Michelle, eight—New York family court Judge Dembitz wrote:[30]

> The Bureau's petition alleges that the three children are left alone and unattended from 3:30 to 5:30 P.M. on week-days; that after Michelle was admitted to Lincoln Hospital "with severe injury to the vaginal area . . . the hospital reported Michelle as an abused child whose injuries were most likely the result of rape, and the circumstances surrounding this incident were unexplained by the parents." The undisputed evidence shows that these allegations are misleading in significant respects.
>
> Both Mr. and Mrs. Vulon work to support the family, Mrs. Vulon as an IBM key punch operator. She arrives home from work at 5:30 or a few minutes before. The three children generally return from school between 3:30 and 4:30 and then stay in the apartment doing homework. It is questionable whether it would constitute "neglect" to leave habitually well-behaved children of ages 13, 10 and 8, unattended in an apparently secure apartment in the afternoon for the two hours alleged in the petition; possibly self-responsibility to this limited extent, in a family where parents show an over-all affection and concern, may not only be harmless but beneficial. In any event, Mrs. Vulon testified without contradiction that since the troubling incident here involved she had se-

---

*We have decided to eliminate "conviction, or acquittal by reason of insanity, of a sexual offense against one's child" as a ground for intervention.[29]

cured someone to stay in the apartment in the afternoons until she returns from work. . . .

The evidence showed that on the afternoon of the incident in issue—which was a partial school holiday—Maurice was in and out of the home doing errands, Marie was washing dishes, and Michelle was first using the vacuum cleaner and then taking a bath. Marie heard Michelle exclaim from the bathroom and saw she was bleeding. Mrs. Vulon came home shortly thereafter, and although the bleeding was not extreme took Michelle to Prospect Hospital. There, because no physician was available, she was referred to Lincoln Hospital. By the time of her arrival at Lincoln the bleeding was more profuse and a physician recommended a surgical procedure under anesthesia for remedial and exploratory purposes. One source of suspicion against the family appears to have been that Mrs. Vulon did not immediately consent to surgery for her daughter; she testified that she had wanted to wait for her husband to arrive from Prospect Hospital, where he had expected to meet them. (Mrs. Vulon, who emigrated from Haiti in 1958, speaks poor English). The father arrived shortly; consent was given forthwith; and the child's condition was soon remedied. The Lincoln Hospital physician called by petitioner testified that the bleeding was attributable to a laceration of the vagina of about an inch; that he could not estimate the source of the laceration with any certainty except that rape probably was *not* the cause; that the condition was probably due to "trauma" of some other type and could have been self-inflicted.

The erroneous suspicion of rape—which persisted apparently because of a failure to consult this knowledgeable physician—underlay petitioner's allegation as to the parents' failure to explain the circumstances of Michelle's bleeding. Mrs. Vulon did explain the circumstances to petitioner and other interrogators to the extent she could ascertain them from the children. There is no indication that she knew or could have known anything more than she recounted. What she failed to do was to accept the mistaken allegation of rape and to aid the Bureau in its exploration of this suspicion. According to petitioner, the parents "refused to believe that their child had been raped. They stated that they would not go into any conversation about rape with their children. They explained that in their country, a child did not learn about sex until the child was about 15 years of age; nor did the mother want me to discuss this with the child."

No doubt Mrs. Vulon's perturbation (described by petitioner) about the erroneous rape theory was due in part to the great damage that this charge would have inflicted on Maurice, the only suspect, who was an exemplary student in a Catholic school, aspiring to the priesthood. Though Mrs. Vulon apparently was herself concerned and frustrated that she was unable to ascertain the exact source of Michelle's bleeding, it was to the benefit rather than the detriment of her children that she refused to succumb to the mistaken suspicion of rape or to give it further currency.

Petitioner's attorney argued that neglect should be inferred from the parental failure to explain the basis for Michelle's bleeding. . . .

Prosecution of this petition was largely attributable, it is clear, to the parents' refusal of the Bureau's request that they consent to their children's examination by the Court psychiatrist. Such examination apparently was viewed in part by the Bureau as a possible method of determining whether Maurice committed the non-existent rape. So intent was the Bureau on its proposal that its attorney approached the Court ex parte before the hearing to ask it to order such examinations.

. . . The Vulons believe that their children's welfare will not be served by probing into the frightening episode of Michelle's bleeding by social workers or psychiatrists, and indeed indicate that the repetitive references to the incident to which the children have already been subjected were detrimental.

*   *   *

This Court believes from observation of these parents and children that they have an affectionate, mutually-respecting and beneficial relationship. A good faith appraisal by responsible and concerned parents, such as the Vulons, of the best way to handle a problem of child development on which reasonable men can differ in their value judgments, is not neglect. . . . While it was necessary and proper to conduct some investigation of whether Michelle's unusual condition indicated abuse or lack of care, the State cannot, without more justification than here appears, override the liberty of the parents, protected by the Constitution, to bring up their children as they think best. . . .

Petition dismissed.[31]

Under our ground for intervention there would not even be, as there was for Judge Dembitz, probable cause to invoke the process—to investigate the Vulon family. There would have been no report to a state agency.[32] Our ground should be seen as an inducement to parents whose children have been injured to provide them with medical care—thus eliminating a deterrent to do so because of the fear of being reported for "neglect" or "abuse."

CHAPTER 14

Refusal by Parents to Authorize Lifesaving Medical Care

Ground 6: A Parent's Refusal to Authorize Medical Care When (1) Medical Experts Agree That Treatment Is Nonexperimental and Appropriate for the Child, and (2) Denial of That Treatment Would Result in Death, and (3) the Anticipated Result of Treatment Is What Society Would Want for Every Child—a Chance for Normal, Healthy Growth or a Life Worth Living

U nder this ground, state supervention of parental judgment would be justified to provide any proven, nonexperimental medical procedure when its denial would mean death for a child who would otherwise have an opportunity for a life of relatively normal healthy growth or, at least, for a life worth living. While a life of relatively normal healthy growth is assumed to be a life worth living, it is not assumed that all lives which society views as "worth living" could be characterized as relatively normal or healthy. For example, society might view the life of a quadriplegic child, in need of a blood transfusion for reasons unrelated to that condition, as a "life worth living," though not one of normal healthy growth. Thus the state would overcome the presumption of parental autonomy if it could establish (a) that the medical profession is in agreement about what nonexperimental medical treatment is appropriate for the child; (b) that the denial of the treatment would mean death for the child; and (c) that the expected outcome of that treatment is what society agrees to be right for any child—a life worth living.*

When death is not a likely consequence of exercising a medical choice, there would be no justification for governmental intrusion. Where the ques-

---

*Nothing in this ground would preclude parents from seeking or consenting to treatment on behalf of a child who society does not think could ever have a life worth living.

tion involves not a life-or-death choice but a preference for one style of life over another, the law must restrain courts and doctors from imposing their personal preferences in the form of medical care upon nonconsenting parents and their children.

Parents normally protect their child's body as if it were their own, and they generally act responsibly in making health care choices for their children. The law cannot find in medicine (or, for that matter, in any science) the ethical, political, or social values for evaluating health care choices.*

In its commitment to family integrity, this ground does not take a simplistic view of parents, of the parent-child relationship, or of the family. Rather, it acknowledges not only human complexity but also the law's limited capacity for making more than gross distinctions about human needs, natures, and patterns of development. This ground recognizes and respects the diverse range of religious, cultural, scientific, and ethical beliefs and the overlapping and ever-changing modes of their expression within and between generations. A prime function of law is to prevent one person's truth (here about health and the good life) from becoming another person's tyranny.

This ground does not justify intrusion by the state in those life-or-death situations in which (a) there is no proven treatment; or (b) there is conflicting medical advice about which, if any, treatment to follow;† or (c) there is little chance that the nonexperimental treatment will enable the child to have either a life worth living or a life of relatively normal healthy growth, even if the medical experts agree about the treatment.[2]

In their evidentiary demands and limited scope, the requisite elements of this ground place the burden of overcoming the presumption of parental autonomy upon the state. Parents, of course, remain free to provide medical treatment that the state could not impose.

Outside a narrow central core of agreement, *a life worth living* and *a life of relatively normal healthy growth* are highly personal terms. Thus outside that core there can be no societal consensus about the "rightness" of always deciding for "life," or always preferring the predicted result of the recommended treatment over the predicted result of refusing such treatment. Those cases in which reasonable and responsible persons can and do disagree about whether the "life" after treatment will be "worth living" or "normal," and thus

---

*Courts must avoid confusing a doctor's personal preference with the scientific bases upon which the recommendation rests.[1]

†If there is a conflict about which proven treatment to follow, but failure to consent to one of the proven treatments would result in the child's death *and* denial of a life worth living or relatively normal healthy growth, the state would be authorized to order that one of the proven treatments be undertaken.

about what is "right," are precisely those in which parents must remain free of coercive state intervention in deciding whether to reject or consent to the medical program offered to their child.

No one has a greater right or responsibility, nor can anyone be presumed to be in a better position, than a child's parents to decide what course to pursue if the medical experts disagree about treatment.[3] The same is true if there is no general agreement in society that the outcome of a proven treatment is clearly preferable to the outcome of no treatment. Put somewhat more starkly, how can parents in such situations be judged to give the wrong answer when there is no way of knowing the right answer? In these circumstances, if the law's guarantee of freedom of belief is to be meaningful, parents must have the right to act on their belief within the privacy of their family. The burden must always be on the state to establish what is wrong and not on parents to establish that what may be right for them is necessarily right for others.

Unlike a ground that is concerned with the parent-child relationship *generally,* such as that concerning repeated failure to protect against serious bodily injury, this ground is concerned with unacceptable parental judgments about *specific* medical interventions. Thus, while serious bodily injury may justify changes in custody, this ground authorizes only a disposition limited to the medical intervention that is ordered. It otherwise leaves the child in the general overall care and custody of her parents and restores her to them as quickly as possible.

Implications

WHEN DEATH IS AN ISSUE

The criteria for intervention under this ground were met for Judge Murphy of the Superior Court of the District of Columbia in *In re Pogue.*[4] He authorized blood transfusions for an otherwise healthy newborn infant who would have died had his parents' decision to reject the treatment been honored. At the same time, recognizing the distinction between an adult and a child with regard to medical care choices, Judge Murphy declined to order blood transfusions for the infant's mother, who in the face of death refused to consent to such intervention. Over the objection of the "adult" parents' wishes—and, of course, without regard to the infant's "wishes"—Judge Murphy decided as a substitute parent to protect the child's right to reach the age of majority, when he will become entitled to make such life-or-death decisions for himself. The judge implicitly found the infant's parents temporarily incompetent to care for their child. Simultaneously, he acknowledged that the mother's adult status entitled her to decide to refuse blood for herself.

That death was inevitable without transfusion and that transfusion is a nonexperimental medical procedure was not in dispute. Nor was there any societal doubt about the desirability, the "rightness" of the predicted outcome of the transfusion: an opportunity for normal, healthy growth, and a life worth living. The issue was whether the judge and doctors who shared an unqualified value preference for life could use the power of the state to impose their "adult" judgment on others whose own "adult" judgment gave greater weight to another preference. On behalf of the adult, the answer was "No"; on behalf of the child, the answer was "Yes." Thus coercive intervention by the state was justified.

But this ground would let parents decide, for another example, whether their congenitally malformed newborn with an ascertainable neurological deficiency and highly predictable mental retardation should be provided with treatment that might avoid death, yet offered no chance of cure. Dr. Raymond Duff has argued persuasively:

> Families know their values, priorities and resources better than anyone else. Presumably they, with the doctor, can make the better choices as a private affair. Certainly, they, more than anyone else, must live with the consequences. . . . If they cannot cope adequately with the child and their other responsibilities and survive as a family, they may feel that the death option is a forced choice. . . . But that is not necessarily bad, and who knows of a better way?[5]

If parental autonomy is not accorded recognition and if society insists through law that children receive medical treatment rejected by their parents, the state must take upon itself the burden of providing the special financial, physical, and psychological resources essential to making real the value it prefers for the child it "saves." The state would have to demonstrate its capacity for making such "unwanted" children wanted ones.* Minimally, it should fully finance their special-care requirements. In the event parents do not wish to remain responsible for their child, the state would have to find adopting parents or other caregivers who can meet not only the child's phys-

---

*Except for meeting the child's physical needs, however, the task is beyond the limits of law, no matter how large the allocation of financial resources. The law is too crude an instrument to nurture, as only parents can, the delicate physical, psychological, and social tissues of a child's life.

ical needs but also her psychological requirements for affectionate relationships and emotional and intellectual stimulation.

No matter how limited their potential for healthy growth and development, such children demand and deserve affection and the opportunity to develop psychological ties that institutional arrangements do not provide.[6] As long as the state offers institutions that provide little more than storage space and "hay, oats, and water"[7] for these children, the law must err on the side of the strong presumption in favor of parental autonomy. The state must therefore *either assume* full responsibility for the treatment, care, and nurture of such children, *or honor* the parents' decision to consent to or refuse treatment.

The case of Karen, a teenager suffering from irreversible kidney malfunction, provides another life-or-death example in which the standard of an opportunity for a life worth living or a life of relatively normal, healthy growth toward adulthood would preclude state supervention of parental judgments. Karen's case poses the question of whether state intervention should be authorized to review the choice of an adolescent who, with her parent's permission and concurrence, decides to choose death over "life." Following an unsuccessful kidney transplant, Karen and her parents refused to consent to the continuation of "intolerable" life-support devices. The decision to proceed as if family integrity and parental autonomy were protected was described in an article by her doctors:

> [F]ollowing the transplant's failure, thrice-weekly hemodialysis was performed. Karen tolerated dialysis poorly, routinely having chills, nausea, vomiting, severe headaches and weakness. . . .
>
> [A]fter it was clear that the kidney would never function, Karen and her parents expressed the wish to stop medical treatment and let "nature take its course.". . . [S]taff members conveyed to the family that such wishes were unheard of and unacceptable, and that a decision to stop treatment could never be an alternative. The family did decide to continue dialysis, medication, and diet therapy. Karen's renal incapacity returned to pretransplant levels and she returned to her socially isolated life, diet restriction, chronic discomfort, and fatigue.
>
> On May 10, Karen was hospitalized following ten days of high fever. Three days later the transplant was removed. Its pathology resembled that of the original kidneys, and the possibility of a similar reaction forming in subsequent transplants was established.
>
> On May 21, the arteriovenous shunt placed in Karen's arm for hemodialysis was found to be infected, and part of the vein wall was ex-

cised and the shunt revised. During this portion of the hospitalization, Karen and the parents grudgingly went along with the medical recommendations, but they continued to ponder the possibility of stopping treatment. . . . On May 24, the shunt clotted closed. Karen, with her parents' agreement, refused shunt revision and any further dialysis. . . .

Karen died on June 2, with both parents at her bedside. . . .[8]

For Karen and her parents, no medical treatment offered the possibility for her to resume a life worth living. The insistence of the nursing and medical staff to continue the life-support system was based on their personal values. The rightness of forcing the consequences of their choice upon Karen, rather than honoring her and her parents' decision, could not be established. There was therefore no basis for exercising the power of the state to supervene the judgment of Karen's parents. Had Karen been an adult on the law's chronological scale, there is no question—or there ought not to be—that out of respect for her dignity as a human being, the doctors would have had to abide by her request to end treatment.

Had the situation been different, had Karen's parents insisted, over her objection, on continuing the life-support system, would the state have been justified in supervening their judgment? The answer is "No." Had Karen insisted over her parent's objection on continuing the life-support system, would the state have been justified in supervening their judgment? The answer is "Yes"—if the state provides, as it must, whatever resources are required to assure full care for the child.* But if the state will not provide such support, the answer is an uneasy "No." It is, after all, the function and responsibility of parents to evaluate and make judgments about the wishes and requests of their children. The meaning of parental autonomy is that parents make such decisions. Further, neither court nor agency is likely to be as competent as were Karen's parents to determine her capacity for choice and whether to abide by it. The law should avoid giving the discretion for such subjective judgments to its agents.

---

*Because a few parents might not follow a child's express wish to undergo treatment that might seem intolerable to them, though not to their child, the law might reinforce society's general commitment to life by respecting in life-death situations any child's express wish for treatment against the parents' wishes. Alternatively, legislatures might develop a formula for emancipation that defines the circumstances and sets an age below majority when children may become their own risk-takers for all or some specific health care decisions. Without a statutory formula, the ultimate responsibility must remain with parents, who may or may not decide to support their child's choice.[9]

WHEN DEATH IS NOT AN ISSUE

Where death is not in issue, this ground is intended to preclude a decision such as that in *In re Sampson*.[10] That case illustrates how vague neglect statutes may be invoked in the name of health care to violate a family's privacy, to undermine parental autonomy, and to foster a community's or judge's prejudice against the physically deformed. Under the Family Court Act of New York, Judge Elwyn declared fifteen-year-old Kevin Sampson "a neglected child." He made this finding in order to establish his authority to veto a decision by Kevin's mother not to force her son to undergo a series of operations that had been recommended by the Commissioner of Health and by duly qualified surgeons to correct a facial condition called neurofibromatosis. Judge Elwyn observed that Kevin had "a massive deformity of the right side of his face and neck. The outward manifestation of the disease is a large fold or flap of an overgrowth of facial tissue which causes the whole cheek, the corner of his mouth and right ear to drop down giving him an appearance which can only be described as grotesque and repulsive." Judge Elwyn went on to psychologize and predict:

> [T]he massive deformity of the entire right side of his face and neck is patently so gross and so disfiguring that it must inevitably exert a most negative effect upon his personality development, his opportunity for education and later employment and upon every phase of his relationship with his peers and others.[11]

Judge Elwyn made his assertion even though he acknowledged that "the staff psychiatrist of the County Mental Health Center reported that 'there is no evidence of any thinking disorder' and that 'in spite of marked facial disfigurement he failed to show any outstanding personality aberration.' " "Nevertheless," the judge added, "this finding hardly justifies a conclusion that he has been or will continue to be wholly unaffected by his misfortune."[12] He also noted that Kevin had been exempted from school not because he was intellectually incapable but, it may be assumed, because he appeared to his classmates and teachers (as he did to Judge Elwyn himself) "grotesque and repulsive." But the judge's speculations on behalf of the state as *parens patriae* did not lead him to consider that under the protective cloak of the family, a loving, accepting, autonomous parent had been able to nurture in Kevin a "healthy personality." Kevin, after all, had so developed in spite of state-reinforced prejudice and discrimination in school, health agency, and court against the cosmetically different.

The testimony of the doctors who recommended surgery justified not an adjudication of neglect but rather a reaffirmation of parental autonomy. The doctors admitted that "the disease poses no immediate threat to [Kevin's] life nor has it yet seriously affected his general health," and that surgery was very risky and offered no cure. Further, the doctors found in the central nervous system no brain or spinal cord involvement and concluded that delay until his majority would decrease, not increase, the risk. Yet the court replied:

> [T]o postpone the surgery merely to allow the boy to become of age so that he may make the decision himself as suggested by the surgeon and urged by both counsel for the mother and the Law Guardian . . . totally ignores the developmental and psychological factors stemming from his deformity which the Court deems to be of the utmost importance in any consideration of the boy's future welfare and begs the whole question.[13]

Without regard to the relationship of Kevin's well-being to the integrity of his family, the court added: " 'Neither by statute nor decision is the child's consent necessary or material, and we should not permit his refusal to agree, his failure to co-operate, to ruin his life and any chance for a normal, happy existence.' "[14]

Judge Elwyn, in the role of prophet, psychological expert, risk-taker, and all-knowing parent, described but ignored a powerful reason for concluding that state authority should not supervene parental judgments about the rightness for their child of a recommended medical treatment when death is not an issue. He wrote:

> It is conceded that 'there are important considerations both ways.'. . . Moreover, it must also be humbly acknowledged that under the circumstances of this case 'one cannot be certain of being right.'. . . Nevertheless, a decision must be made, and so, after much deliberation, I am persuaded that if this court is to meet its responsibilities to this boy it can neither shift the responsibility for the ultimate decision onto his shoulders nor can it permit his mother . . . to stand in the way of attaining through corrective surgery whatever chance he may have for a normal, happy existence, which . . . is difficult of attainment under the most propitious circumstances, but will unquestionably be impossible if the disfigurement is not corrected.[15]

Genuine humility would not have allowed a judge to believe that he, rather than Kevin's mother, was qualified to determine the meaning of "a normal and happy existence" for her son. In Kevin's eyes, either might be proven "wrong" retrospectively. But nothing can qualify a judge to make that prediction with equal or greater accuracy than a parent. Nor is any judge prepared or obligated, as are parents, to assume day-to-day responsibility for giving their Kevins the personal care they may require. Judges cannot be substitute parents, and courts cannot be substitute families.

In another case, a New York court refused to find 14-year-old Martin Seiferth a neglected child, even though his father would not compel him to undergo the surgery recommended for repair of a cleft palate and harelip.[16] Martin's father would have consented to surgery despite his belief that it was undesirable had Martin been willing. Despite medical evidence far less equivocal than that in Kevin's case, the court refused to be trapped by the rescue fantasies of health department doctors or by strong societal prejudices that it was being asked to reinforce in an effort to "save" the child from himself and his parents. The court refused to order surgery, not because it thought it lacked authority, but because it thought Martin's reluctance to have the surgery foretold an unwillingness to participate in the therapy following the operations. Thus it was unwilling, unlike Judge Elwyn, to substitute its or a state agency's value preferences for those of the responsible parents.

As an adult Martin chose not to have the surgery. "After attending one of the vocational high schools in the city, where he learned the trade of upholsterer and was elected president of the Student Council, he set up in business on his own and is, despite his disfigurement, active and successful."[17] Nevertheless, the county health department that originated the case reacted a decade later as if experience offered no lessons about the need to respect family integrity:

> [He] had graduated from . . . High School . . . at the head of the graduating class. It was his intention then to become an interior decorator. I have no *personal* comments to make except that . . . the operation should have been performed in order to give this young man a fuller opportunity for the development of his talents.[18]

WHEN DEATH IS THE OUTCOME
UNLESS A HEALTHY SIBLING PROVIDES A TRANSPLANT

The application of our ground is further clarified by considering what authority, if any, the state would have to investigate and review the deliberations of parents who must decide whether to let one of their children die or whether to attempt to supply a lifesaving organ for transplant by consenting to "unnecessary" surgery on one of their healthy children. Under this ground the state would not be empowered to intrude. In *Hart v. Brown,*[19] however, though the court eventually upheld the choice of the parents, it asserted the state's authority to review and supervene their judgment. The doctors had advised Mr. and Mrs. Hart that the only real prospect for saving their eight-year-old daughter Kathleen's life from a deadly kidney malfunction was to transplant a kidney from Margaret, her healthy twin sister. The doctors recommended, and the Hart parents consented to, the "unnecessary" surgery on Margaret to provide Kathleen with an opportunity to pursue a relatively normal life. But the hospital administration and the doctors refused to accept parental consent without a court review.[20] They acted out of a concern for their livelihood, not for the lives or well-being of Margaret or of Kathleen. Understandably, they feared becoming liable for money damages because the law might not accept the parents' consent as a defense to possible assault or malpractice suits.[21]

The Harts were thus forced to turn to the state to establish either their authority to decide or the rightness of their decision. There was no *probable cause* to suspect that the parents might be exploiting either of their children. The court upheld the parental choice, though not their autonomy to decide. Although the Court's decision did avoid tragic consequences for the Harts, it set a precedent for unwarranted state interference with family integrity. The Court held:

> To prohibit the natural parents and the guardians ad litem of the minor children the right to give their consent under these circumstances, *where there is supervision by this court and other persons in examining their judgment,* would be most unjust, inequitable and injudicious. Therefore, natural parents of a minor should have the right to give their consent to an isograft kidney transplantation procedure *when their motivation and reasoning are favorably reviewed by a community representation which includes a court of equity.*[22]

Had the Hart parents refused to consent to Margaret's surgery and the transplant of her kidney to Kathleen, equally unwarranted proceedings might have been brought to establish their neglect in order to obtain court authority to impose the doctors' recommendation. Because of their special training, doctors can make diagnoses and prognoses; doctors can also indicate the probable consequences for a Margaret or a Kathleen of pursuing one course or another. But in the absence of a societal consensus, nothing in their medical training—or, for that matter, in the training of judges—qualifies them to impose upon others their preferred value choices about what is good or right for such children or their families. The critical fallacy is to assume, as the Court did in its declaratory judgment (and as the legislature does in its laws of neglect and abuse), that the training and offices of doctors, legislators, and judges endow them not just with the authority but also with the capacity to determine what risks to take for someone else's child, in circumstances where no answer is right or wrong.

*   *   *

Some will object to and be uneasy about the substantial limits this ground would place upon the state's power to supervene parental decisions about health care for their children. But the absence of a substantial societal consensus about the legitimacy of state intrusion concerning these matters is the best evidence for holding in check the use of state power to impose highly personal values on those who do not share them. Further, the parameters set by the criteria of normal, healthy growth toward adulthood or a life worth living, of the life-or-death choice, and of proven medical procedures have a built-in flexibility that can respond both to new findings in medicine and to a new and changing consensus in society.

Finally, this ground's limits must be considered in the context of the scope of the already discussed ground, which concerns serious bodily injury as well as the repeated failure of parents to protect their child from suffering such harm. The two grounds overlap, in the sense that parental failure to provide for nonexperimental lifesaving treatment for their otherwise healthy child (such as the case of Donald Carlson, described in Chapter 13) could fall within the "denial of medical care" ground as well as the "serious bodily injury" ground. There is also a potential conflict between the two grounds in cases of parental failure to agree to nonexperimental treatment for their child when the absence of such treatment will lead not to imminent death, but to a lifelong structural or organic impairment serious enough to prevent the child from having a normal, healthy growth or a life worth living. Some such cases might authorize state intervention under the "serious-bodily-injury" ground, but not under the "denial-of-medical-care" ground. We decided to analyze the life-death situation as a separate ground in order to emphasize the respect that we believe must be accorded to parental judgment in such tragic circumstances when no societal consensus exists about the nature or likelihood of success of treatment and the quality of life after treatment. In any event, *neither* of these grounds would authorize intervention if the state was unable to provide a better alternative—whether it be to pay for the medical treatment or, if necessary to provide continuing care and nurturance for the child.[23]

CHAPTER 15

The Child's Need for Independent
Legal Representation

Ground 7: A Request by Parents Who Are Unable to Obtain Legal
Assistance for Their Children, an Adjudication of Any Ground
for Modifying Parent-Child Relationships, or an Emergency Placement
Pending Adjudication Should Be a Ground for the Appointment
of a Lawyer to Represent the Child

T his ground is designed to assure legal assistance in the child placement
process for the child whose parents have been disqualified as the exclusive representatives of her interests and for the child whose parents believe
she needs a lawyer and are unable to obtain one for her. Under this ground the
state could (1) *provide* legal counsel for children upon the request of parents
who cannot afford or otherwise obtain such assistance; and (2) *impose* such
services without parental consent (a) *after* an adjudication that establishes a
ground for modifying a parent-child relationship, or (b) *before* such an adjudication, during an emergency placement when a child is temporarily placed
under state care and outside parental control. This formulation accords with
our preference for the least intrusive process.

This ground recognizes that an integral part of the autonomy of parents is
their authority and presumed capacity to determine whether and how to meet
the legal care needs of their child, just as they do with regard to her medical
care needs. It acknowledges that parents, *or those whom they select,* are the
exclusive representatives of their children before the law, even though the
needs of individual family members may differ at times or even conflict.

The appointment of counsel for a child without regard to the wishes of parents is a drastic alteration of the parent-child relationship. It is, in effect, a
disposition by the state. It intrudes upon the integrity of the family and strains
the psychological bonds that hold the family together. Therefore it cannot
take place until the presumption of parental autonomy has been overcome—

139

that is, until the protective insulation from the law that parents give their children has been broken by an adjudication establishing a ground for intervention.[1]

The imposition of counsel by the state is, moreover, a disposition for a limited purpose and a limited time. Such counsel are to act as lawyers, not as parents. They are to represent a child's legal needs by safeguarding her rights during emergencies and by gathering and providing the court with information that it requires in order to determine the least detrimental placement. Like doctors who are ordered to provide medical assistance, lawyers are not to be perceived as substitutes for nurturing parents. Nurture is to be provided by the caregiving adults, either parents (natural, adoptive, or long-term foster) or state agencies, who are to retain physical custody of the child pending a final disposition.

The duration of the appointment of such counsel is limited to the period of suspended judgment between adjudication and final disposition or, in the event of emergency placements, to the period between invocation and final disposition.* Only during those phases of the placement process does a child require party status and representation by a lawyer who is independent of both child care agencies and parents. Such children must have their interests represented and protected by counsel until the least detrimental placement has been arranged. At that point, whoever is designated as the parent should be allowed to assume or resume full responsibility for all matters concerned with the child's care, including whether and for what purposes the child should have a lawyer and who that lawyer should be.

Under this ground, parents are entitled to arrange for counsel on behalf of their child at any point in the placement process. But contrary to common practice, there would be no justification for the imposition of a lawyer for a child at invocation in, for example, neglect or abuse proceedings, when no more than a *charge* of one of the grounds for modification is made. To appoint counsel for a child without parental consent is to deny both parents and child a fair process. It deprives parents of their right to represent their child through their own counsel,[†] with counsel whom they choose for their child, or even without counsel. It is to presume on the basis of an unproven charge, an unestablished ground, that parents are incompetent to represent the interests of their family and consequently the interests of their child. Also it deprives the child of her right to be represented by her parents before the law.[2]

---

*Concerning suspended judgments, see Chapter 10, p. 97.

†The same lawyer may represent both parent and child without conflict until a ground has been established because the *family's* interests are being represented.

On the other hand, not to appoint a lawyer for a child *after adjudication* establishes a ground for modifying her relationship to her parents, and *before disposition,* would be to expose her, uninsulated by an adult, to the state's authority. At that point, a child in most cases[3] will require a legal representative to assure that the process of disposition and the placement itself will make her interests paramount and provide her with the least detrimental alternative.

Likewise, a child requires representation by counsel during emergencies when there is good reason to believe that she has no adult caregiver or that she is in imminent danger of serious bodily injury. She is then taken from her parents pending adjudication and placed in the care of a state agency until final disposition. Such emergency decisions telescope invocation, adjudication, and disposition into a single transaction and not only place the child outside the care and control of her parents but also temporarily disqualify them to represent her immediate interests. To assure that the state provides the child in an emergency with adequate care until the placement process has run its course, it is necessary that she be represented by a lawyer.

In divorce and separation proceedings, the imposition of counsel under this ground is justified only if the parents are unable to decide custody on their own—that is, if they ask the court to decide. By failing to agree on a disposition, separating parents waive their claim to parental autonomy and thereby their right to be the exclusive representatives of their child's interests. The child then requires representation independent of her parents' to assure that her interests are treated as paramount in determining who shall have custody.

The continuity guideline generally requires that the same lawyer represent all of the children within a family. These children share a community of interests in maintaining their ties to one another. There may be exceptional cases when this presumption should be overcome and individual children within the same family should be accorded separate representation. Once a final disposition is made, each child is presumed to have at least one autonomous parent who is responsible for sheltering her from direct contact with the law and for generally representing her interests as a member of the family. That adult becomes responsible for determining the child's legal care needs.

Implications

To Whom Is Counsel for a Child Responsible?

Separate legal representation for children rests on recognizing both that the presumption of parental autonomy can be overcome and that state policies and practices intended to serve the best interests of children cannot be relied upon. Possibly because of its relatively recent origins, the idea of legal care for children as persons in their own right has often been perceived as an unmitigated good. Although medical care without parental consent is acknowledged to be potentially harmful, legal care for a child without parental consent is presumed to be beneficial or, at worst, harmless. Perhaps as a result of this perception, legislators, judges and commentators (including ourselves)[4] have failed to clarify how the role of the lawyer for a child client may differ from her role in relation to adult clients.* In order to clarify the lawyer-child relationship, this question must be asked: Who, if anyone is to assume responsibility for deciding to hire, to instruct, and to dismiss a lawyer for a child?

(a) When Parents Engage or Request Counsel

Charlie, a ten-year-old who tried to hire his own lawyer, helped us clarify for ourselves what it means to have a child as a "client." Charlie telephoned us long distance and asked: "Are you the people, the lawyers, who represent kids? I want you to help me. My parents are divorced. They're always fighting over visits with me and my sister, Irene."

We told Charlie that before we could give him an answer, we would have to know if the judge had already decided which of his parents had custody. He replied: "My mother has custody. But why do you have to know that? I'm asking you to represent me."

We replied that since his mother had custody, it was her responsibility to decide whether Charlie needed the assistance of a lawyer and that, if she de-

---

*In a legal action involving the common claims of many children as a class—foster children, for example—courts should assure that the children comprising the class are represented by counsel selected by or with the consent of their parents, or appoint counsel for them if their parents or long-term caregivers have been disqualified as their sole representatives. It is necessary to recognize two possibly conflicting roles for counsel representing children as a class. The goals of such counsel may be more legislative than remedial. For example, counsel may attempt to establish—in the public interest—a constitutional right to a certain procedure, in order to assure a fairer administration of the child care system in the future. But that role may require counsel to ignore or even sacrifice the particular needs of individual members of the class. In such cases, lawyers for the class must clarify for themselves the distinction between establishing what and whose rights may have been violated, and what *remedy* is most appropriate for the individual class members. New or restored placements for the particular children in the class whose rights (or whose parents' rights) may have been violated should not necessarily be the remedy. For example, children taken away from their parents by unconstitutional procedures would not be well served if they are returned to long-absent parents and separated from their long-term caregivers. Particular children in the class must not be sacrificed for the principle that counsel for a class of children may be trying to establish. Indeed, it may be that children within a class should have separate counsel if the remedy involves the possibility of new placements.[5]

cided that he needed one, she would choose the lawyer she wanted for him. We would not represent him without his mother's consent, we said. He responded: "I don't understand that. My mother may not want me to have a lawyer, and I want one."

We replied that what he wanted might not be what his mother thought best for him, and that one of the reasons for having parents is to have someone to make such decisions for their children. We explained to Charlie that just as parents decided if and when he needed to see a doctor or a dentist, it was also their responsibility to decide whether he should consult a lawyer. We told him we would not agree to his request unless his mother thought that he needed a lawyer and engaged us on his behalf.

We asked Charlie if his mother knew about the phone call. He replied: "Yes, she's right here. She'd like to talk to you." Charlie's mother then said that she wanted us to counsel Charlie and Irene: "I want the children to visit their father. I encourage them to do so. But Charlie has good reasons for not wanting to observe the schedule established by the court. More important, my lawyer and their father's lawyer confuse the children with different explanations for why they must obey the court. Charlie keeps asking: 'Why do we have to obey the court if daddy doesn't? He can cancel visits.' I want you to clarify for Charlie and Irene what is going on."

We accepted her request on the understanding that we would counsel her children, advise her as to their needs—always making clear to them that she, as their custodial parent, had final say both with regard to accepting our advice and to our continuing to provide legal assistance. What we sought to accomplish on behalf of the two children in our negotiations with counsel for each of the parents and in testimony before the court was done with the consent and at the request of their mother. We were guided by her wishes, by what she as primary parent ultimately determined would best serve the interests of her family.

One event occurred almost a year later that allowed us to define further our relationship to our clients. Toward the close of a long winter holiday visit with his father (which his mother insisted he make), Charlie called us long distance and said: "Call Mother. I don't want to go home. Tell her I'm staying with Daddy."

We told Charlie that we would try to reach his mother and tell her about the call, but that since she expected him to be home the next day, he had to return unless she called to say it was okay to stay. Charlie, obviously annoyed, said: "You call her, tell her I'm not coming back. You're my lawyers. You tell her what I want and get her to do it."

Again we reminded Charlie that what his mother decided he needed was not always the same as what he wanted, and that we would not tell his mother what she was to do. Despite our consistent efforts to respect his mother's autonomy as a parent, Charlie obviously thought that it was worth trying to maneuver us into a position that would undermine his mother's authority. When this failed, he returned home as scheduled.

What Charlie mistakenly sought to arrogate to himself was the status of an adult. He tried to choose his counsel, instruct them with regard to his wishes and intentions, and with their help fight his case with his parents. None of this is open to the child unless, of course, his parents instruct counsel to abide by their child's wishes. A child may have her wishes taken into consideration by her parents. But, like Charlie, every child before the law finds herself in the position where the adults "know best" what is good for her and decide that with or without regard to her wishes.[6]

The (largely media-created) concept that an attorney may be retained by a child to represent her in seeking to "divorce" her parents distorts, both in law and in life, the meaning of "child," of "parent," and of their relationship to each other as members of a family.[7]

(b) When the Court Imposes Counsel

Once the court has imposed counsel for a child, from whom is counsel to receive instructions? The answer is that counsel must turn to the court and to the legislature for the guidance she would normally receive from autonomous parents who engage her to represent their children.

Counsel imposed by the court may look to the parents and the child as sources of information, but not for instructions. The parents have voluntarily abdicated or have been disqualified as the exclusive representatives of their child's interests. Counsel cannot turn directly to the children whom she represents for her instructions; children are by definition persons in need of adult caregivers who determine what is best for them. But counsel may not seek to have her personal child-rearing preferences imposed upon her "client" without regard to legislative or judicial guidelines for determining what is best for children.

Like an autonomous parent, the court must advise counsel. But it must advise as the child placement statutes direct. For example, statutes might require that placements maximize the opportunity for continuity of current or, if necessary, new relationships. And counsel might be required with regard to both process and substance to press the court to take into account the child's sense of time, the inability of experts to make long-range predictions, and the inability of courts to monitor parent-child relationships. The court, like an autonomous parent, may find unconvincing, and therefore, reject evidence or recommendations of counsel for the child.* And like a parent, the court may dismiss counsel who fail to perform their duties. However, unlike the autonomous parent, the court may not dismiss counsel without good cause.[8] It does not have the final say. Counsel is empowered to appeal decisions that she believes conflict with statutory standards.

Finally, counsel appointed before adjudication for a child in an emergency placement will be responsible for monitoring the child's custody in order to assure that the state does provide the nurturing care decreed by the court. Thus the court temporarily assumes the authority of a parent to determine the legal care needs of a child during that stage of the child placement process when it must decide who is to be the parent.

In a disposition proceeding, unlike other legal proceedings, the court knows prior to the introduction of any evidence—prior to a hearing—which party will prevail. The court is obligated by statute, except in some delinquency proceedings, to make the child's interests paramount—to favor the child. Counsel for the child knows her client is supposed to win. That is another way of understanding why the court can generally be relied upon to serve as the parenting substitute in relation to counsel. In order to compensate for the loss of full parental insulation, in order to protect the now-exposed child from judicial and child care agency policies and practices that might ignore or conflict with a particular child's interests, the court is obligated to appoint "independent" counsel to represent the child pending disposition.

Once disposition is final—once the court determines who is to be the child's caregiver—the role of both the court and the child's counsel has come to an end. The child is restored to and is under the care and direction of a parental authority. In designating a custodial parent, the court expresses the state's confidence that this particular adult has the greatest capacity among those available to fulfill the child's needs, including her need to be protected from and represented before the law. To do otherwise—to impose continuing legal counsel for the child as a condition of a disposition—is to undermine that confidence. It is to threaten rather than promote family integrity.

Yet this is what the Connecticut Superior Court did in *G. v. G.* In that case Richard, age thirteen, was represented by counsel appointed at the request of the custodial parent, who wanted to prevent the noncustodial parent from resuming visits that the court had suspended. The battle over visitation had been in and out of court for more than nine years. Accepting the arguments

---

*Child care agencies and disqualified parents remain parties to such proceedings. Their lawyers represent what they believe to be the child's best interests.

made both by counsel for the custodial parent and by counsel for the child, the court denied the request for visits. But it ordered what this ground prohibits—that the lawyer continue to represent Richard after disposition. The court observed:

> The attorney for the minor child has consented to remain as counsel of record. The child should feel free to consult with his attorney at any time pertaining to matters regarding his custody. Of course without further order of this court and with the consent of the plaintiff-mother [the custodial parent] *and* the consent of the minor child through his attorney, visitation may be resumed under appropriate arrangements. . . .[9]

By interposing an attorney between Richard and his mother, the court undermined their opportunity to relate directly to one another. The court obtained only the consent of the attorney, not that of the custodial parent, for extending the appointment of Richard's counsel. Richard was thus deprived of a parent who had authority to grant or deny his wishes, to determine his needs, and to represent his interests—even to decide whether he required legal assistance. His mother could not, for example, make him visit his father or grant him permission to do so. She would first have to obtain the concurrence of Richard's counsel or permission from the court to overcome counsel's objection. And were counsel to decide over the mother's objection that visits should be resumed, he could seek judicial supervention of her judgment.

By imposing conditions of this kind, a court places itself and counsel between parent and child. It subverts rather than safeguards the child's critical need for an autonomous parent. The only continuity Richard and his parents could anticipate was the continuity of state intrusion. Occasions for court orders as intrusive and as divisive as that in *G. v. G.* would be minimized, if not eliminated, in a child placement system that observed the least detrimental alternative standard and made all placements (except for emergency, institutional, and truly temporary foster care) permanent, unconditional, and final. But whatever the state's policy with regard to visits and other conditions of custody, our ground precludes appointment of counsel for the child after disposition without the consent of the custodial parent.

Should Adolescents Be Emancipated to Determine Their Own Legal Care Needs?

Should some adolescents be given the authority, free of adult control, to engage, direct, and dismiss their own lawyers? Like adults, such children would be presumed both competent and free to determine their own placement needs. Put another way, are there circumstances which should justify the state's presuming that a child is as competent as an adult and thus entitled to be free of the care and control of her parents or some other adult authority?

Any affirmative answer to this question which would qualify a minor as an adult must provide a standard of emancipation which is as impersonal and as nonjudgmental as is chronological age for establishing adult status. To require objective criteria for emancipation is not to take a simplistic view of children. Rather it is to recognize (a) the difference between a child and an adult; (b) how varied and complex are parents and children and their ties to each other; and (c) how impersonal and thus how inadequate courts are for judging the capacity of an individual child for making and "benefiting" from her decision as to who should be her "parent," or that she does not need a "parent."[10]

For the emancipation to be real, all children in a specific category—for example, children institutionalized at their parents' request, children who are pregnant, or children over fourteen years of age—would have to be deemed qualified to refuse as well as to accept the service and advice of counsel. Emancipation would be a fiction if it covered only those children in such categories who "choose" to accept counsel or who are found to be "mature enough" on a case-by-case basis to make decisions for themselves. That would only transfer the prerogative and responsibility to decide from the parent, who has not been disqualified, to the judge, not to the child.

A genuine emancipation statute that would meet the fair-warning and power-restraint requirements of a ground for terminating parent-child relationships could be drafted.[11] For example, all children could be freed at the age of thirteen of both parental and court control in determining their legal care needs. But we do not recommend any such provisions, because we do not believe that there are or can be circumstances which justify emancipating children to meet their own legal care needs in the child placement process. Indeed, it is the purpose of the process to secure or restore for every child an uninterrupted opportunity to be represented by "parents." Because they are children, they require representation by parents or by some other adult upon the disqualification of their parents. They are persons in their own right but are not adults in their own right. Children by definition cannot be free of an adult's control in determining either their need for legal assistance or what lawyers must seek on their behalf in the process of their placement.

This ground recognizes only one situation in which a child may be treated as an adult with the authority to engage a lawyer or to instruct her as to what course to pursue. That is when her parents delegate such authority to her.

Otherwise, whether engaged by autonomous parents or by a judge, counsel for a child may be advised to take into account the child's wishes in representing her interests.[12] But such a child, because she is a child and not an adult, is without authority to engage or dismiss her counsel.

*   *   *

By applying the guidelines of Book One and by defining in objective, precise terms the justifications for state intrusion into family relationships, we hope we have provided a basis for a more balanced view of the problem and for a more just regulation of decisions and procedures that will assure as many children as possible a permanent membership in a caring family.

The fundamental right of every child is to parents who care. It is this right that must be served by grounds for state intervention. We say once again that our proposals are not necessarily the best or only grounds for justifying state intervention to protect children in jeopardy. But whatever grounds are formulated must be sensitive to the limits and limitations of law and to the need for fair warning and power restraint.

BOOK THREE

IN THE BEST INTERESTS
OF THE CHILD

PART SEVEN

The Professional and Child Placement

CHAPTER 16

The Problem and Our Questions

Parents raise their children as a labor of love and not as a professional as- signment. Unlike child development experts and other professional per- sons concerned with child care, parents are not specialists. Their responsibility is the whole child. Ordinary devoted parents[1]

> accept his love, tolerate his demands and failings, share his pain and pleasure—and get satisfaction from doing so. They may be sorely tried at times, but more than anyone else they are able to tolerate his growing pains. The child knows he is special to them, whether he is pleasing or not, well or ill, succeeding or failing. He unhesitatingly turns to them with his pleasure and miseries, confident that they will be there. He knows they are likely to see his point of view and give him the benefit of doubt before voicing critical comment. They become the brick wall he can safely kick against. Impatient or angry though they may some- times be, he recognizes that these are often signs of their concern for him. His feelings about himself reflect his parents' feeling about him. The child whose parents value him values himself. Parents usually carry these strong feelings throughout their lives—the love, the anxiety for their children's welfare and happiness.*

Acknowledging the unique place of such ordinary devoted parents, the law safeguards their obligation and authority to raise their children as they think best. That is why parental autonomy and family privacy are respected and why, for example, parents are usually relied upon to decide what is in the best interests of their child, including whether and when to seek professional as- sistance. The law also recognizes that there are situations when, on behalf of

---

*The words are those of the English child development experts James and Joyce Robertson. Perhaps we should have more accurately characterized the parents described by the Robertsons as "extraordinarily de- voted."[2]

the child, the state is justified in breaching family privacy and supervening parental autonomy. Then the child placement process is invoked, and the all-encompassing parental task is broken up and temporarily divided among specialists from law, medicine, child development, child care, social work, education, and other professions concerned with children and their families. It is in the best interests of the child that these professionals always keep in mind that they are not the child's parents. Even though each of them may assume one or more aspects of the parental task, neither alone nor together can they replace parents.

Professional persons know that the ultimate goal of the placement process is to provide children with parents who will be free from further state intrusion: free to use or refuse their help, free to accept or reject their interventions. Yet the tragic situations that they often confront in child placement cases tend to blur professionals' awareness of their own limitations and the limits of their assignments. Their personal experiences and sympathies sometimes interfere with their professional judgment. And their effort to maintain a purely professional stance carries with it the risk that they may become too distant and lose the empathy that is essential to good work with children and their families.

We did not examine this professional quandary either in Book One, where we introduced and developed the least-detrimental-alternative standard for child placement, or in Book Two, where we defined the functions of state intervention and the justifications for authorizing the state to modify parent-child relationships. We now focus on that component of the least detrimental alternative which mandates that placement decisions take into account the limits of knowledge about child development and the law's incapacity to supervise day-to-day parent-child relationships. We examine, from the vantage point of the children caught up in the placement process, the work of those professionals—legislators, lawyers, judges, social workers, child development experts, and child care agency administrators—who determine whether parents have failed or who plan, provide, order, or supervise alternative care for children. We seek to clarify their relationship to each other and to the families they serve, to identify good practices as well as situations where even the best of them are tempted to step outside of their professional roles and exceed their authority or fail to discharge their obligations.*

In Book One, we warned against attributing to judges, to lawyers, to social

*Much of the case material in this book is drawn from the clinical experiences of the authors and their review of reports prepared by colleagues. However, with the exception of matters in the public domain, the names and other identifying characteristics of individuals and the time and place of events have been changed, and statements and conversations have been combined and reconstructed.

workers, to child psychiatrists, and to other professionals in the process a magical power—the power to do what is far beyond their means. In Book Two, we stressed the importance of considering what a child loses when she passes, even temporarily, from the personal authority of parents to the impersonal authority of the law. In this book, we take as a given that the professional participants in the process accept these limits and share these concerns. We believe that they would agree that they *ought not* to exceed their authority and *ought not* to go beyond or counter to their special knowledge or training. But we do not take for granted that they always recognize when they go or are asked to go beyond these limits. Sometimes they do not recognize that they are doing what they "know" they ought not to do. This may be because the law gives them vague and ambiguous assignments; because they have a strong desire to help people in trouble; because they feel a need to justify their work; because they desire to avoid the embarrassment of acknowledging that they do not know something; because they do not pause to consider whether they are being asked to exceed their professional qualifications; or because of a combination of these and other less obvious (or, perhaps, less understandable) reasons. Though we do sometimes speculate about the *why* of professional behavior, we do not systematically explore such explanations. Our primary goal is to identify and describe situations *when, and not why,* judges, lawyers, child psychiatrists, social workers, and other nonparent participants in the child placement process stay or fail to stay within the limits of their knowledge, training, or authority.

To do this we address several questions, which we explore separately and which merit consideration by the professionals themselves, by those who engage their services, and by the families they serve:

• When do professional participants assume roles or undertake tasks that are outside their province or beyond their expertise?

For example, when does a judge act as psychiatrist by making her own psychological assessments of separating parents? When does a social worker usurp the judicial role, either by withholding relevant information because she thinks the judge will "misuse" it, or by slanting her report to ensure that the judge will reach the "right" decision? When does a child development specialist attempt to comply with a request by court or counsel rather than say, "I'm not qualified to do what you ask"? When does a court or counsel intrude upon the domain of an expert from another profession by insisting that the expert follow certain procedures which she considers unnecessary for the purpose of answering the question?

- When are professionals who have acquired knowledge from another discipline justified in acting on such knowledge without assistance from an expert in that discipline?
- When does the assumption of two roles in relation to the same child or family place a professional beyond her competence, even though she may be qualified to perform either role alone?

For example, does a social worker have the capacity to serve a child or family as *therapist* and at the same time, in relation to the same child or the same family, act as an *investigator* for a child care agency or family court?

- When do professional participants act beyond their authority or professional knowledge by assuming the role of parents?

When, for example, does a judge assume the parents' task of disciplining their child, or a lawyer assume the parents' role of deciding whether their child needs to consult a psychiatrist?

These questions do not fall into discrete units. We examine each separately in order to illustrate the many situations and multiple guises in which the problem of recognizing and respecting the boundaries of expert knowledge and the limits of professional authority may arise.

CHAPTER 17

Untangling Professional and Personal Beliefs

I t is not easy to separate personal values from professional knowledge and to distinguish both of these in turn from the societal values embedded in law. While writing Books One and Two we became aware that most of our disagreements about conclusions were based not upon our professional knowledge or our clinical experience, but upon our personal values.

This experience made us realize the importance of disclosing our personal values. Thus we have acknowledged and discussed our preferences for a policy of *minimum state intervention* in parent-child relationships and for the policy of *making the child's interest paramount* once her care has become a legitimate matter for state intervention. We recognized that it was not solely our professional knowledge but our personal values which led us to assert that the child's well-being—not the parents', the family's, or the child care agency's—must be determinative once a justification for state intervention has been established. We had to distinguish our personal commitment to children from our professional knowledge about child development and the status of children in law.[1]*

We found it particularly difficult to untangle personal values from professional knowledge when both pointed in the same direction. As citizens, for instance, we favor the right of parents generally to raise their children free from government intrusion. As experts in child development, we recognize that the continuity of a child's relationships to her parents is vital to her health and therefore deserves the protection of the law. In other words, our views of government that underlie our personal preference for a policy of *minimum state intervention* are different from, though not in conflict with, our profes-

---

*In drawing conclusions from their study of divorcing families, Maccoby and Mnookin similarly sought to distinguish personal conviction from professional knowledge: "Our conclusion is influenced by a *value judgment* that is quite independent of social science evidence. Because most divorced fathers have established a substantial relationship with their children before the breakup, we are *sympathetic* to the view that the father should ordinarily have the legal right to maintain some sort of relationship with the children after divorce."[2]

sional knowledge that a child needs to be wanted and in the uninterrupted day-to-day care of at least one adult.

Here, unlike in Books One and Two, our concern is with the practices and procedures of professional persons rather than with the substance of their recommendations or decisions. We have been careful to resist the temptation to reinforce proposals we made earlier by finding only good practices in decisions that we would support and only poor practices in decisions we would oppose. For example, though we oppose coerced visitation, we identify good as well as poor professional practices in decisions that mandate visits and poor as well as good practices in decisions that refuse to order them.

The task of untangling personal belief and professional knowledge is difficult even for a "hard" scientist. A United States Congressional Committee hearing on a bill to define when human life begins provides an example of good practice by a scientist and poor practice by the legislators. Dr. Leon Rosenberg, a geneticist, recognized that he was being pressed to answer a question outside of his scientific knowledge and said so. He drew a sharp distinction between his personal and his scientific beliefs:

> The crux . . . of the bill before you is the statement . . . "that present day scientific evidence indicates a significant likelihood that actual human life exists from conception." I must respectfully but firmly disagree with this statement for two reasons: first, because I know of no scientific evidence which bears on the question of when actual human life exists; second, because I believe that the notion embodied in the phrase "actual human life" is not a scientific one, but rather a philosophic and religious one. . . .
>
> . . . There is no reason to debate or to doubt the scientific evidence indicating that conception is a critical event in human reproduction. When the egg is fertilized by the sperm, a new cell is formed that contains all of the genetic information needed to develop ultimately into a human being. . . . But, in my view, there is an enormous difference between the *potential* for human life and, to repeat the critical phrase in Section 1 of this bill, "actual human life." To fulfill this potential, the fertilized egg must travel to the uterus, be implanted in the uterine wall, and undergo millions and millions of cell divisions leading to the development of its head, skeletal system, limbs and vital organs. To be sure, this sequence of events depends on the genetic program present in each cell of the developing embryo and fetus. As surely, however, the sequence depends on the environment offered by the mother. Without the genetic "blueprint" of the fetal cells, human development cannot be initiated; without

the protection and nutrition provided by the mother's tissues, the genetic blueprint cannot be followed to completion. This absolute dependence of fetus on mother lasts normally for nine months, after which the birth process abruptly separates mother from child.

When does this potential for human life become actual? I do not know. Moreover, I have not been able to find a single piece of *scientific* evidence which helps me with that question. . . . I have no quarrel with anyone's ideas on this matter, so long as it is clearly understood that they are personal beliefs based on personal judgments, and not scientific truths.

If such beliefs are not scientific, you might say, just why can't they be made scientific? My answer is that science, per se, doesn't deal with the complex quality called "humanness" any more than it does with such equally complex concepts as love, faith, or trust. . . . I maintain that concepts such as humanness are beyond the purview of science because no idea about them can be tested experimentally. . . . If I am correct in asserting that the question of when actual life begins is not a scientific matter, then, you may ask, why have so many scientists come here to say that it is? My answer is that scientists, like all other people, have deeply held religious feelings to which they are entitled. In their remarks at these hearings, however, I believe that those who have preceded me have failed to distinguish between their moral or religious positions and their professional, scientific judgments.

*   *   *

Let me conclude by divesting myself of all scientific or clinical credentials and speak simply as an American. I believe we all know that this bill is about abortion and about nothing but abortion. If this matter is so compelling that our society cannot continue to accept a pluralistic view which makes women and couples responsible for their own reproductive decisions, then I say [ban] abortion. . . . But, don't ask science or medicine to help justify that course because they cannot. . . .[3]

Participants in the child placement process may find it even more difficult than geneticists to separate professional knowledge from personal belief. That is because in the child development field the boundaries between fact and value are harder to define. The focus of the geneticist, for example, is on the development of the fertilized egg into a child as it is protected and nurtured, subject to the *laws of nature,* in the relatively restricted confines of the *biochemical* environment of the mother's body. The focus of professionals in child placement is on the humanizing process—on the child's development into adulthood as she is protected and nurtured by her parents under the *laws of society,* in the relatively unrestricted confines of the *social* environment of which her family is part. In addition to sharing with the geneticist an interest in the physical well-being of children, the child development expert is concerned precisely with what Dr. Rosenberg calls "humanness": with the parent-child relationship after "the birth process separates mother from child"; with human qualities and needs such as affection, security, and trust. And the nature of the evidence upon which knowledge in child development and law rests—evidence concerned with the child's humanness—makes it difficult for experts who participate in the child placement process to locate the line that divides professional knowledge from ordinary knowledge.* Further, the legal standards for intervention and disposition provide professional participants with "no exact or even nearly exact scale of measurement like grams or ounces with which to balance. Personal prejudices are likely to creep into [the judge's or counsel's] inexact measurings."[5] Another reason for the difficulty may be that all of the professional persons have been children, all have had parents, and many are themselves parents. Consequently, they have a multitude of personal beliefs and ordinary knowledge about what is good and bad for children and about what makes a satisfactory or unsatisfactory parent;[6] beliefs and knowledge which they, as adults moved by an urge to "rescue" children, are tempted to impose. The risk that actions and decisions in child placement will rest on personal values presented in the guise of professional knowledge is therefore great—and all the more important to guard against.

The knowledge of professional persons who participate in the child placement process may go, in Rosenberg's words, "beyond the purview of science." But such knowledge need not go beyond disciplined inquiry based upon clinical observations, written constitutions, statutes, and case law.[7] Experience-based wisdom is often an integral part of special competence, but professionals must be alert not to use their reputations as experts to assume roles for which they have no special competence in furtherance of their personal values or of the preferences of those who engage their services.

---

*We use *ordinary knowledge* as do Lindblom and Cohen, to "mean knowledge that does not owe its origin, testing, degree of verification, truth status, or currency to distinctive . . . professional techniques but rather to common sense, casual empiricism, or thoughtful speculation and analysis. It is highly fallible, but we shall call it knowledge even if it is false. As in the case of scientific knowledge, whether it is true or false, knowledge is knowledge to anyone who takes it as a basis for some commitment or action. . . . Everyone has ordinary knowledge—has it, uses it, offers it. It is not, however, a homogenous commodity. Some ordinary knowledge, most people would say, is more reliable, more probably true, than other. People differ from each other in the kind and quality of ordinary knowledge they possess."[4]

The coercive power of the state ought not to be used to impose the dogma of one person or group on another in the name of science or other special knowledge. "Unlike all other dogma, the dogma which underlies a secular legal system requires the state to tolerate any dogma unless its implementation would harm another who does not share it."[8] When there is no societal consensus, the law should err on the side of respecting the right of parents to follow their own beliefs.

PART EIGHT

The Ambit of Professional Competence

CHAPTER 18

Professional Boundaries

B oundaries between disciplines are not easily defined. Because professional persons bring to their work in the child placement process not
only knowledge from their own discipline but also a fund of ordinary knowledge, they sometimes make determinations that are not for them to make.
While all professionals may be fact-finders, not all facts are for them to find.
While all may be opinion givers, not all opinions are for them to give. "Am I
qualified to find this fact or to give this opinion?" is a question all professional participants should ask themselves or be pressed to confront.

A Judge Acting as a Psychologist with a Specialty in Child Development and as Expert Witness—*Jason Rose*

In *Rose v. Rose,* a divorce case, the task of the trial judge was to determine
whether it would be in the best interest of two-and-one-half-year-old Jason to
be placed in the custody of his mother, Diane, or to remain in the care of his
father, Steven.[1] When Jason was six months old, his mother had attempted
suicide by jumping from the eighth-floor window of their apartment. Since
that time Jason had been in his father's care. Following his mother's release
after a six-month hospital stay, she had started to visit him.

The trial judge found that both Diane and Steven were fit to care for Jason.
Then, after observing that each parent had a "valid and reasonable claim" to
custody, he said:

Diane is still a bit immature, and certainly tending to excessive sarcasm,
though I noticed this much less now than I did [at the hearing six
months ago, when I denied Diane custody while the divorce was pend-
ing]. Steve has progressed much faster academically than socially and
emotionally. . . .
. . . So, I come now to the part that's difficult to, for me, to really put
into words. I'm going to give my impressions, because I think it's im-

165

portant for you all to know the basis for my judgments in this particular area. I have heard a great deal about Steve Rose from him and a great many witnesses, but I've also had the opportunity to watch him on the witness stand here, and down there at counsel table, for almost sixteen days now. It appears to me that he's a very demeaning person; he's prone to criticize and quick to demonstrate some kind of intellectual superiority. I got the impression that he felt that he was smarter than a good many of the experts who testified here. And in considering the emotional makeup of the parties, the things they will pass on to their child, and in subtle ways, I have given a large preference here to Diane.

Accordingly, I find that the best interests of Jason lie in his care, custody, and control by Diane Rose. . . .[2]

The judge assumed a role for which he was not qualified. He acted as a psychologist by using his own courtroom observations to determine the emotional makeup of Steven and Diane. As a judge, he was authorized to take into account his personal observations of the witnesses' behavior on the stand for purposes of evaluating the veracity of their testimony.[3] Here, however, he used these observations not for this purpose but to assess and compare the emotional and social maturity of two adults.[4] He assumed the role of expert in child development by relating his findings about "the emotional makeup of the parties" to "the things they will pass on to their child . . . in subtle ways." Presumably deciding that Steven would "pass on" detrimental traits to Jason, he gave "a large preference" to Diane as the better parent. He reached this conclusion despite guidance from statutory and case law that "continuing an existing relationship and environment" is usually in the child's best interest, and despite uncontroverted expert evidence that Jason had thrived in Steven's custody.[5]

The statutory presumption in favor of "continuing an existing relationship and environment" equipped the judge to resolve this custody dispute between two fit parents. He did not need, nor was he competent, to compare their personalities. A West Virginia court has observed that "intelligent determination of relative degrees of fitness requires a precision of measurement which is not possible given the tools available to judges."[6] In recognizing its own limitations, that court acknowledged that the law is a relatively crude instrument and that judges need not be embarrassed by the limits of their knowledge: "Certainly it is no more reprehensible for judges to admit that they cannot measure gradations of psychological capacity between two fit parents than for a physicist to concede that it is impossible to measure the speed of an electron." Thus, except when the "facts demonstrate that care and custody were shared in an entirely equal way," the courts should determine custody in favor of whomever the facts establish as the primary caregiver. Only when there are two primary caregivers (or no primary caregiver) must the court proceed "to inquire further into relative degrees of parental competence"[7]—or perhaps to draw lots, if expert or other testimony offers no significant basis for choice.*

Had the judge in the *Rose* case realized that he was about to venture beyond what ordinary knowledge, his own training, the statutory guides, or the testimony of the experts in the case qualified him to do, he might have acted differently. He might have asked counsel for both parties to present evidence on whether Steven's personality would be harmful to Jason's development and, if so, whether that harm would be greater than the harm that would result from uprooting the child and disrupting his relationship with his father. But the judge made his finding without explicitly posing such questions.[†] He thus denied himself the opportunity to learn from experts that they cannot make subtle comparisons between two fit parents and that they are unable to assess the relevance of a parent's "arrogance" or "immaturity" to a child's future well-being. In response to such questions, child development professionals might have (or, we maintain, *should* have) said "I don't know." And they might have reinforced the statutory preference for maintaining the existing primary care relationship between a child and one of his parents by explaining that disruptions of ongoing relationships are likely to be harmful.[‡]

Even had the judge been trained to make psychological assessments, he had no authority to become a witness, particularly one who did not take the stand. By in effect receiving his own testimony—by being a covert witness—he denied Steven the opportunity to challenge his credentials as an expert. He also deprived Steven of the opportunity to introduce expert testimony that might have explained his "arrogant, overprotective, and critical behavior" as the response of an ordinary devoted parent who feared that his child's well-

*Such a situation does not justify postponing a decision for two years—as happened in a case in which one of the authors gave testimony—in the hope that enough could be learned to render a decision that would truly be in the children's best interests. The judge should have recognized the immediate threat posed to the children by this period of uncertainty.

[†]The issues we raise would be the same if the judge had decided to leave Jason in the custody of his father, not in order to safeguard "an existing relationship" but because he believed that Diane's "immaturity" would be more detrimental to Jason's interests than would Steven's "arrogance."

[‡]The judicial process is meant to preclude judges from resting their decisions on their personal opinions—even opinions about matters, such as what makes a good parent, which they might have formed in their nonprofessional daily life. "There is," as Wigmore has observed, "a real but elusive line between the judge's *personal knowledge* as a private man and these matters of which he takes judicial notice as a judge. The latter does not necessarily include the former; as a judge, indeed, he may have to ignore what he knows as a man and contrariwise."[8]

being was threatened. The judge might not have been persuaded by such testimony, but he should not have denied Steven's lawyer an opportunity to present it, or himself the obligation to consider it.

The judge was right, however, to disclose the extent to which his decision rested upon his personal observations. He said, "I think it's important for you all to know the basis for my judgments in this particular area." He made visible a problem that may often go undisclosed and undiscovered. Thus he provided a basis for an appeal to challenge his authority to be both judge and witness, his competence to make clinical psychological assessments, and the relevance of his comparison of parental fitness. Had these issues been perceived and raised, the appellate court might have reversed the trial court's judgment,* as the Connecticut Supreme Court did in another custody case:

> In effect the trial [judge], as a basis for [his] findings, made of himself a witness, and in making [these findings] availed himself of his personal knowledge; he became an unsworn witness to material facts without the [parties] having any opportunity to cross-examine, to offer countervailing evidence or to know upon what evidence the decision would be made.[9]

Four years after ordering that Jason be placed in his mother's custody, the same trial judge, on the basis of expert testimony, granted Steven's petition that Jason be returned to his care. This time the judge explicitly recognized that his task was to weigh the harm Jason might suffer while in his mother's care against the "great weight" courts generally give to the benefits of staying with "the primary custodian."[10] But though the judge's *decision* to change custody was based on uncontradicted expert testimony, his *opinion* was again permeated with his own psychological observations. He recalled having rejected Steven as custodial parent because of his "arrogant, over-protective and super-critical attitude." He then implied that it was appropriate to have done so by explaining that while the father "appeared to retain some [of these traits,] he has moderated" them and "has mellowed some in his previous poor attitudes. . . ." He then went on to suggest that Steven's improved attitude might be attributed to his remarriage. Moving further afield he observed, "I assume [that Jason's slow rate of growth] will accelerate after a decision in

---

*The judge-as-witness issue was not, at the time, perceived by one of the authors, who testified at the trial and served as a consultant to counsel for Steven in preparing his appeal. He was preoccupied with focusing appellate review on the trial court's failure to apply the continuity principle and the presumption in favor of the primary caregiver, and he never thought to raise this alternative basis for reversal. Nor did the appellate court on its own address the matter in its opinion.

this case, if it is somehow connected to something other than simply being the offspring of small parents. . . . I also assume that [Jason's] diagnosed depression, unhappiness and mood swings can be improved in time, given a better visitation schedule and more consistency in authority figures."[11] Possibly because the matter had not been addressed on the appeal from his first decision, the judge continued to act as if his law training and his appointment to the bench had qualified him to use his own observations to make psychological assessments and to determine their implications for a child's psychological and physical development.

A Judge Acting as Expert in Child Development—*Rachel Solomon*

The custodial mother in *In re Marriage of Solomon* asked the court to order her former husband to reduce his visits with their daughter Rachel.[12] In response, the father requested that all parties submit to a psychiatric evaluation and that the judge order counseling for Rachel. The judge granted the request for an evaluation; he was guided by a statute which provided that a "court shall not restrict a parent's visitation rights unless it finds that the visitation would endanger seriously the child's . . . emotional health." Following a two-month assessment that included eight sessions with the child, six with the father, two with the mother, and a consultation with a child psychologist, the psychiatrist (whose qualifications were accepted by both parties) testified that Rachel showed signs of extreme emotional tension, depression, impaired self-esteem, anxiety, and several abnormal personality traits and characteristics. He recommended that she receive treatment. In response to the judge's question, he said that it would be beneficial to alter the visitation pattern, but he testified that her problems did not arise from visitation "per se."

The judge then interviewed Rachel in chambers:

"Have you and your daddy been getting along?"

"I guess so."

"Do you like to see your daddy every week?"

"Yes."

"Do you love your daddy and mommy, do you—?"

"Yes."

In addition he asked her one question about her health, one about her participation in sports, one about her grades, and concluded: "She seems to be a
very normal, nice little girl." The mother testified that her daughter did not at
any time suffer from anxiety, nervousness, or instability.

The judge granted the mother's request for a reduction of visits and denied
the father's request that Rachel receive treatment. He did not give the basis
for either of these rulings.

Either the judge ignored the statutory mandate that emotional harm to the
child was prerequisite for restricting visits, or he overstepped his competence
when he reduced the father's visits. The statute authorized restrictions if visits would "endanger seriously the child's emotional health." Without the testimony of experts, he would have remained unqualified to restrict visits under
this provision. Therefore he had the authority—indeed, the obligation—to order psychiatric evaluations, even over the mother's objection. Having heard
the psychiatrist's uncontradicted testimony that Rachel's emotional health
was not endangered by her father's visits—even if he did not find the testimony credible—it was beyond his authority and competence to restrict visits
based on his own psychological evaluation of their impact.*

The judge may or may not have overstepped his competence when he refused to order treatment for Rachel. If he rested the denial on his conclusion,
based on his interview, that Rachel was "very normal," he overstepped professional boundaries. His training did not qualify him to conduct diagnostic
interviews or to make psychiatric assessments in order to determine whether
there was a need for therapy. It was within his competence, however, to refuse
to order treatment either because he understood judicial and legislative policy
to mean that only the mother (as custodial parent) had the right to consent to
treatment for her daughter, or because he found the psychiatric testimony un-
persuasive.[13]

The line is fine and difficult to draw between a judge who rules contrary to
uncontradicted expert testimony because he relies on his own psychological
assessments and a judge who does so because he does not believe or has not
been persuaded by the expert. No more can be asked than that judges be sensitive to this concern and—like the judge in the *Jason Rose* case, but unlike
the judge in the *Rachel Solomon* case—make visible the basis of their rulings.

---

*On appeal the trial judge's visitation order was reversed because he had not made the explicit threshold
finding of serious emotional endangerment that was required by the statute. It may be that such statutes
press experts in child development to answer questions that they cannot answer.

A Lawyer for the Child Acting as a Mental Health Expert—*Lisa Stone*

In *Stone v. Stone,* the divorced parents had agreed on a visitation schedule for their eight-year-old daughter, Lisa. The visits, however, did not go smoothly. Lisa's mother, who had custody, claimed that the child was becoming increasingly reluctant to see her father because of his verbal abuse and violent temper. Lisa's father insisted that her mind was being poisoned against him by the mother. The mother refused to allow further visits, and the father asked the court to order them. The judge was required by statute to apply the best-interest standard in adjudicating disputes about visits, and to take into account the wishes of a child who "is old enough to form an intelligent preference." He appointed a lawyer to represent Lisa.

The lawyer spoke with Lisa, her teachers, and her doctor. He also listened to complaints from each parent about the other's behavior and received several letters from Lisa describing in words and drawings her feelings of sadness and anger about having to visit her father. Her lawyer reported to the court that visits were "marked by confusion, discord, and sometimes violent and profane confrontations." Nevertheless he recommended, on Lisa's behalf, that the court order visits. And he advised: "If it is true that Lisa is having such violent overreactions to visitations with her father, then it is certainly obvious that she is in dire need of professional counseling. It might be well for the court to order that all the parties concerned submit to sessions at the Family and Child Counseling Clinic."

The task of counsel for children is to discover and to represent the interests of the specific child who is their client. There is no consensus as to the meaning of that task. Lisa's lawyer might have interpreted his assignment as limited to ascertaining and advocating her *expressed* preference; in that role, he would have had to recommend that further visits not be ordered. Or he might have perceived his role as requiring him to advocate her *real* preference, which might or might not be the same as her expressed preference; he would then have needed expert assistance because

> children of all ages have a natural tendency to deceive themselves about their motivations, to rationalize their actions, and to shy back from full awareness of their feelings, especially where conflicts of loyalty come into question. To pierce through these defenses demands more than usual skill from the investigator. Verbal and nonverbal communications (attitudes, behavior) have to be scrutinized, assessed, and translated into their underlying meaning; openings offered by the child, all unknowingly, have to be pursued and utilized. . . . The ability to make such con-

tacts is demanded from psychiatric diagnosticians or child analysts as part of their professional equipment.[14]

A third possibility is that Lisa's lawyer might have perceived his role as an advocate not of her preference, expressed or real, but of her "best interest." In that event, too, he should have recognized the need to organize expert knowledge about the impact of the visits on Lisa in order to equip the judge to make his decision. Lisa's lawyer might still have advocated that visits continue, but this time on the basis of an *informed* assessment.

No matter how Lisa's lawyer understood his appointment, he could not have viewed it as including a request to render an opinion as to whether Lisa and her family were mentally ill or in need of treatment. In fact, if he had been asked to do so, he would surely have realized that he was not qualified to make such evaluations or recommendations on his own. Yet he allowed himself to slip into the role of expert in child development as well as adult psychiatry by characterizing Lisa's responses to the visits as "violent overreactions," by finding that she was "in dire need" of professional counseling, and by suggesting that the court order parents and child to "submit to" therapy.

Lisa's lawyer failed to ask, "Am I qualified to determine on my own that visits are in the best interests of Lisa?" He did not present any expert testimony upon which the judge could rely. Nor did he recognize that as a lawyer he was not qualified to evaluate the mental health of Lisa and her parents, and that he exceeded his assignment as well as his competence when he prescribed therapy for them.*

A Social Worker Acting as Expert in Child Development— *Maria Colwell*

Social work training and experience are not as far removed from training in child development as are legal training and experience. Social workers may therefore find it even more difficult than judges and lawyers to recognize and stay within their professional boundaries when evaluating the behavior of children. The *Report of the Commission of Inquiry into the Death of Maria*

---

*Perhaps Lisa's lawyer had no resources and little time, and he might have understood that a finding of "best interest" required him to assess psychological issues. Under such circumstances he should have said to the judge who appointed him, "I'm not qualified to determine the meaning of Lisa's violent reactions. The court should appoint a mental health expert to make an evaluation and thus enable me to represent Lisa competently."

*Colwell** was critical of a social worker for relying on her own assessment of Maria's behavior (without consulting a child development expert) when Maria had been made to leave her foster parents and to visit her natural mother and stepfather:

> ... The social worker's view of Maria's distress and resistance may be summed up succinctly as (1) being due to her fear of losing [her foster parents] rather than any fear or dislike of [her natural mother and stepfather], and (2) that in any event it was within expected and well recognized limits in such circumstances. Nor was [the social worker] prepared to admit at the Inquiry that the independent views of a medical man such as a psychiatrist . . . could have added anything to the picture that would have assisted her, and presumably this was also her senior officer's opinion. . . . [The social worker] said that because of the tensions in the situation she had to make an intelligent guess as to Maria's true feelings. We were also told that . . . scenes . . . are quite common when this sort of "transfer of loyalties"—as it was described—is being attempted. While we accept that a certain amount of distress may be unavoidable, we cannot accept that in a case such as this a child should be subjected to the degree of stress shown by Maria. Nor do we consider an intelligent guess as to the cause of that stress to be sufficient in this case. We find it difficult to understand why [the social worker] took the view she did about seeking psychiatric or pediatric advice at this time. We appreciate that social work training contains an element of child psychology. Surely, however, such training should enable social workers to turn readily for specialist help when severe trauma presents, so that medical skill can supplement their own casework skill.

*   *   *

> ... To our mind, there was never at any time upon the evidence before us, any doubt at all where Maria's loyalties lay, and that was with the [foster parents]. On that ground the report can be criticized, but it is important to realize that this only arises because of the social workers' assumptions about the trauma, which we have already indicated they were not qualified to make on their own in the particular circumstance of this case. . . .

---

*Maria, a seven-year-old girl, had been beaten to death by her stepfather shortly after the court ordered her to be returned to the care of her natural mother.[15]

The Commission of Inquiry had the benefit of hindsight. Because the social worker's training included "an element of child psychology" and because in her work for the local authority she had probably observed other children who cried bitterly when they were separated from their foster parents, yet seemed to make a good adjustment to the move, she concluded that Maria's kicking and screaming was "within expected and well recognized limits in such circumstances" and decided not to oppose the natural mother's petition to have Maria returned to her permanently.

Had Maria not been murdered, it is probable that no inquiry would have occurred and that the social worker's error in not consulting an expert in child development (which led to Maria's unwarranted separation from her long-term foster parents) would not have come to light. The activities of professional participants in the child placement process are often of low visibility. This covert quality increases the importance of their recognizing the borders of their own area of expertise and remaining within them—not an easy task.

Child Development Professionals Recognizing the Limits of Their Expertise

In a Public Interest Lawsuit

At the request of two public interest lawyers, Dr. Maynard, a nationally recognized child psychoanalyst, prepared an affidavit explaining why, from a foster child's point of view, the state should establish procedures to protect long-term relationships between these children and their caregivers. The lawyers intended to use the affidavit in a class action suit to reform the state's foster care system. They later asked Dr. Maynard to prepare an additional affidavit in support of their claim that they could represent, as a single class, not only foster children but also their natural parents and their foster parents. He said:

I don't understand what you want.

They explained that in this suit all three groups had a common, nonconflicting, interest in the procedural reforms:

An affidavit from you would lend support to our view that the reforms we propose would be beneficial to all concerned. You can persuade the court that the three groups can be treated as a single class whom we can represent without conflict.

Dr. Maynard refused their request. He said:

I was qualified to say what I said in the first affidavit and to support your efforts on behalf of foster children. But I know I'm not qualified to say that what is beneficial for the children is beneficial for the competing adults.

The lawyers said:

We don't understand. You are a distinguished figure whose prestige can be used to endorse our legal strategy for achieving goals which you, as a child development expert, already support.

Dr. Maynard replied:

I don't want you to use my professional reputation to decorate your case. Let me tell you, I don't find it easy to resist the temptation to lend my name to support a cause I believe in. And I enjoy being asked for my opinion in cases that will receive nationwide attention. But I always have to ask myself, and particularly when I'm feeling flattered, "Am I being urged to lend my reputation to an opinion which I cannot substantiate on the basis of my professional knowledge and experience?"

Dr. Maynard's observation, like the testimony of Dr. Rosenberg before the Congressional Committee, illustrates how professional persons can be alert to recognize when they are being urged to answer questions on the basis of personal values rather than professional knowledge.

In an Adoption Case—Mario and Fidel Chavez

Two child development experts, Dr. Blanchard and Dr. Abel, were engaged by Tom Smith, the lawyer for Mr. and Mrs. Wright, to advise him whether it would be best for the two Chavez children—Mario (aged ten years) and Fidel (seven years)—to remain with and be adopted by the Wrights or to be returned to their natural mother. Attorney Smith said that he hoped their report could establish that the Wrights were the psychological parents of the Chavez boys. But he added that what his clients wanted most to know was whether adoption by them would be in the best interests of the children. Unlike the lawyers in the class action suit, Smith did not press the experts to reach a particular result or to use their reputations to support claims that were beyond their professional expertise. And the experts, sensitive to the limits of their professional knowledge and conscious of the borders between their discipline and that of lawyers and judges, wrote the following report:

> This is our assessment of Mario and Fidel Chavez, who are presently residing with Mr. and Mrs. Wright.
>
> After interviews with Mr. and Mrs. Wright, the two boys and Mr. and Mrs. Diaz—the boys' natural mother and her new husband—and after psychological examination by Dr. Robin Rhodes, we have formed an opinion in response to your request that we advise you about whether it would be best for Mario and Fidel to remain permanently in the custody of the Wrights or to be returned to Mrs. Diaz:
>
> In May 1979 the boys, then living with their mother in El Salvador, were placed by her in the custody of Mr. and Mrs. Wright with the understanding that they would take them to America and adopt them. Together with the Wrights, Mario and Fidel arrived in the United States in June 1979 and were immediately placed in the home of Mrs. Wright's married sister in Connecticut. The Wrights (who had been living and working in El Salvador for many years) began their search for employment and a home in Massachusetts. They spent weekends with Mario and Fidel until March 1980 when they found employment and purchased a home in Springfield, Massachusetts. Then, with the assistance of a housekeeper, they assumed direct responsibility for the care of the boys, who are now living with them. For a period of 15 days in November 1980, the boys were separated from the Wrights. They had been flown to Florida by their mother and Mr. Diaz without the Wrights' prior knowledge or permission.*
>
> Because of the almost eighteen months separation from their mother and because of the instability and frequently changing custodial arrangements for their care since arriving in the United States, as well as the insecurity accompanying the litigation over their custody, Mario and Fidel do not at present have primary psychological ties to any adult.
>
> We find that the boys' attachment to the Wrights is not yet a primary psychological relationship. It might best be characterized by calling it a friendship growing out of less than two years of continuous and direct

---

*Mrs. Chavez had managed to enter the United States, and shortly thereafter, in January 1980, she married Alberto Diaz, a U.S. citizen.

custody. The children are comfortable in their present setting. Similarly, the boys do not at present have a primary psychological relationship to Mrs. Diaz. It may best be characterized as a substantial but residual tie damaged by the long separation and by the exigencies of growing up in a war-torn country. As a result of events outside of the control of any of the interested parties, the capacity of the children to make firm attachments has been impaired. They do not sense themselves as members of any family and look with anxiety upon any change. Thus, the assignment of custody cannot be based on an assumption that one adult has a more basic psychological and emotional relationship to these children than the other adult. In addition to a common language and cultural heritage, Mrs. Diaz, of course, has a longer period of experiential contacts, as well as the earliest continuous relationship that preceded and in turn is associated with deprivation and disruption.

The children's psychological tests and their good school performance reflect emotional and intellectual strengths from the past, as well as the nurturing environment in which they now live. An uninterrupted opportunity to establish primary psychological ties to someone they come to know as parent(s) offers the only real chance these children have to meet the difficulties of the developmental tasks that lie ahead.

The Wrights have a strong wish to provide and are providing affectionate care for these children. Mrs. Diaz has demonstrated her affection for the boys and evidenced great tenacity and ingenuity in safeguarding them until they left El Salvador and in seeking to reconstitute her family. Mr. Diaz seems to fully support his wife's efforts. We do not question the qualifications of either the Wrights to adopt or of Mrs. Diaz to resume her role as parent.

Our knowledge does not enable us to make long-term predictions about which placement might be best. For the long-term benefit of these children what remains critical is that doubt and uncertainty about their placement end as quickly as possible in making one of these choices permanent. Whatever the court decides, these children need to know that the court's decision is a permanent one. These children yearn for permanency.

It is clear that it would be corrosive and damaging to the children if the court were to postpone a final decision in the false hope that further investigation could produce what only hindsight may ultimately reveal.

When the psychological reasons for making a choice between two available alternatives are substantially in balance, the one remaining

critical factor for the long-term benefit of the children is that the choice
be made quickly and unconditionally and that the uncertainty and doubt
about whom they belong to be removed.

Dr. Abel testified as an expert witness at the court hearing. At the conclusion of his testimony, which was practically identical to the written report, the
trial judge turned to him and said, "Now doctor, just between us, tell me who
do you really think would make the better parents?" Dr. Abel replied, "I can't
answer that question, Your Honor," and thought to himself, The judge is
pressing me to step outside of my professional role. I do know which set of
parents I personally would prefer, but my preference rests not on my professional knowledge but on my middle-class notions of the 'good life.' I would
be abusing my professional responsibility were I to disclose my personal
opinion to the judge.

In both their report and testimony, these experts were careful not to draw
conclusions that went beyond their professional knowledge.

Working Together: A Judge Acting as a Judge, a Lawyer Acting as a Lawyer, and a Child Development Expert Acting as a Child Development Expert

Whoever represents a child and whoever determines her placement must decide whether to obtain and how to use knowledge of the developmental needs
of children. Joyce and James Robertson describe one way in which experts
might provide such knowledge—by serving not only as witnesses but also as
advisors to the child's legal representatives throughout a court hearing. Their
account of a foster care case illustrates how participants from different disciplines can interact effectively, and prevent each other from straying unnoticed beyond their professional borders:

A child had been with foster parents from [the age of] 6 months to [the
age of] 4 years, placed there by the local authority because of the
mother's unfitness to look after her. Mother and stepfather took a dis-
like to the foster parents and sought to have the child moved elsewhere.
The local authority, although they had no complaint against the foster
parents but were under [severe] pressure, decided to effect the change.
The foster parents challenged this decision. . . . The authority put the

child aged 4 years into the "neutral situation"* of a children's home pending the decision of the court, and the child had been there for 4 months.

There were therefore four parties to the hearing, each represented by counsel:

(1) The mother and the stepfather seeking to have the child removed from the long-term foster home to another.
(2) The local authority, proposing to make the move.
(3) The foster parents, resisting the move on grounds that it was against the interests of the child who was as if of their family.
(4) The 4-year-old child, legally represented by a *guardian ad litem* who had . . . [recommended that] the judge . . . accept the local authority's proposal to remove the child from her foster family.

[We] appeared as expert witnesses on behalf of the foster parents. We considered that the foster parents' plea was in the best interest of the child. But we would have preferred to have been standing behind the *guardian ad litem* [appointed by the state] instead of one of the contending parties.

After giving evidence, we did not leave the court but with the judge's permission, stayed throughout the hearing. . . . It was then that we realized the disadvantage to the young child of having only legal representation. Each of the other parties sat behind their counsel, and as evidence was led they could offer comment and correction which their counsel could use. But the child was not in court, and there was no one to tug at her counsel's sleeve;[†] and of course he was not equipped to perceive matters through the eyes of a child.

---

*The Robertsons commented further: "There is no neutral situation for a young child parted from those she loves. Feelings and needs do not go into suspension. That this child was removed from adequate substitute parents indicates failure to recognize that she was emotionally a child of the foster parents, with the certainty of acute distress and probably damage through being separated from them.

"The inescapable fact is that once a young child leaves the care of his family, however necessary that may be, he is emotionally at risk because of the rupture of his relationships. These will be broken again if, in due course, he has to give up a temporary caretaker to whom he has become attached, even to return to the mother. If leaving his family subjects him to a succession of caretakers the risks to his emotional health are compounded."[16]

†Even if the child were in court, her counsel might still have required someone with knowledge of child development to "tug at his sleeve" and to correct misreadings of her conduct.[17]

At various points where it seemed to us that the *guardian ad litem* was not reacting with knowledge of child development, we passed notes down to the foster parents' counsel and he used these effectively in interventions—technically in the foster parents' interests, but from our view ensuring that the status of the child was better understood.[18]

The judge utilized the Robertsons' presence to help him recognize when persons strayed into areas outside their competence. In this hearing, unlike that in Jason Rose's case, the "unprofessional" interpretation of facts did not go unchallenged:

Several witnesses were brought by the opposing sides to discredit the foster parents. For instance, a staff member from the children's home described the child as attention-seeking and having temper tantrums. These were proper observations, but when asked to do so she gave [her] opinion that the behavior indicated that the child had been badly reared by the foster parents.

We passed a note to our counsel saying that the behavior was typical of a young child separated from those she loved and placed in an institution. Counsel immediately used this information and the judge agreed that the witness was being led to make judgments which were outside his competence. . . . Again, a domestic gave evidence of emotional behavior in the [foster] mother said to indicate instability. . . . We passed a note saying that the foster mother was behaving appropriately for a woman under the great stress of having been deprived of a de facto daughter. This too was accepted by the court.

These two examples illustrate the very important point that because the *guardian ad litem* had only legal knowledge, those misinterpretations of the behavior of child and foster mother might have gone unchallenged and have weighed against the foster mother.[19]

The Robertsons conclude:

Although we had remained as observers only, we gradually found that we were being used by the court and brought into consultation by the judge. He was aware of the ongoing guidance we were giving to the foster parents' counsel, and in further sessions in the witness box he [sought clarification of the concept of] "psychological parent" and [its] implications for this child's best interests. After some days the counsel for the local authority and the *guardian ad litem* withdrew their submissions in explicit acceptance of the Robertson evidence. The judge then ordered that the child be returned to the foster parents, and in his summing up acknowledged his indebtedness to the guidance on emotional development given by the Robertsons.

The point of all this is that the court needed access to specialized knowledge of child development throughout the hearing, and that as the child had been given only legal representation this psychological knowledge would not have been available had we not remained in court.[20]

The problem is not, as the Robertsons suggest, that the *guardian ad litem* gave the child *only* legal representation, but that he did not give the child *full* legal representation. He failed to recognize that he did not know enough about child development and parent-child relationships to know whether to accept or to challenge the witnesses' interpretations of the behavior of the child and her primary caregivers.

Lawyers and judges abdicate their professional roles when they allow a court hearing to be limited to rubber-stamping (or, for that matter, to rejecting automatically) proposals made by child welfare agencies or local authorities. One of the arguments for providing a child with independent counsel in such cases is that the state cannot be presumed to represent the interests of the particular child. Judge Breitel has observed:

In custody matters parties and courts may be very dependent on the auxiliary services of psychiatrists, psychologists, and trained social workers. This is good. But it may be an evil when the dependence is too obsequious or routine or the experts too casual. Particularly important is this caution where one or both parties may not have the means to retain their own experts and where publicly compensated experts or experts compensated by only one side have uncurbed leave to express opinions which may be subjective or not narrowly controlled by the underlying facts.[21]

At the court hearing in which the Robertsons testified, counsel for the foster parents never lost sight of the purpose of the hearing. He challenged the position of witnesses for the local authority, even though he might have predicted that his client would lose. He recognized what may too often go unrecognized: The judge had a choice to make, and even if lawyers can reasonably predict on the basis of past decisions that the court will rule against what they consider the child's interest, they must prepare for and insist upon a full hearing.

It is true that lawyers are equipped by training and experience to predict the outcome of a case. They serve their clients well, for example, in a contract or even in a criminal case if they consider with them the costs of continued litigation against the benefits of prevailing. Even when they believe that right (as embodied by case law or statute) is on their side, they may advise their clients to settle, to drop the claim, or to bargain a plea. But when the well-being of a child is at stake, they do a disservice to her if they *use* their predictions to deny the trial judge or the appellate court a choice by withdrawing the claim on behalf of the child, or by not presenting every shred of evidence that they can gather to enable the judge to decide differently than predicted. Such predictions cannot justify the failure to uncover and present information that might cast doubt on the wisdom of the expected outcome.

Counsel for the foster parents recognized the limitations of his and the judge's knowledge of child development. He did what lawyers do in almost any other kind of case: He utilized experts to interpret facts or to question the interpretation of facts by others—including the judge—who were ill-equipped to do so without expert guidance. Aided by the child development experts during the hearing, counsel was able to demonstrate that crucial testimony by local authority witnesses was beyond their competence. By challenging the position of the local authority and by organizing and presenting relevant information to the judge, counsel for the foster parents gave full legal representation to his clients (which, in this case, served the child, since their interests coincided).

The *guardian ad litem,* on the other hand, failed to introduce independent expert testimony either to support or to challenge the local authority's position. He accepted, without question, eyewitness testimony about the behavior and the meaning of the behavior of foster mother and child. The *guardian ad litem* would, no doubt, have perceived the need for expert testimony in a case concerning a building rather than a child. Were the collapse of a walkway in a hotel a matter of legal concern, he would have recognized his own and the judge's need to be educated by experts in structural design. Such education would be needed to qualify them to determine whether the internal structural failures were caused by external stresses and could have been prevented. No lawyer or judge would accept unquestioningly the testimony of nonexpert eyewitnesses on the cause of the collapse.

Where human behavior is at issue, the need for experts to inform the judge as to its meaning and implications is less easily recognized than when the "behavior" of nonhuman structures is involved. This blind spot, which may result in less than full legal representation of the child's interests in placement cases, seems to stem from two different and conflicting attitudes. One attitude, shared by professional participants (particularly by lawyers and judges), is that human relationships are so complex that a court hearing cannot educate a judge sufficiently to make a decision; therefore judges and lawyers should simply defer to child care agencies. The other attitude is that human relationships are so much a part of ordinary knowledge that there is no need for experts to assess the conduct of a particular child or her caregivers.

The Robertsons' case demonstrates what seems to be easily forgotten, especially when one of the parties is a state agency or local authority "acting on behalf of the child." It is that the function of court hearings is to equip judges to make informed decisions about matters that they would otherwise be unqualified to decide. A child is put at unnecessary risk when her legal representatives assume that they "know" the child's needs, or that they "know" the decision the judge will make. A child is put at unnecessary risk when her legal representatives do not think about whether they need to engage child development experts to enable them—and, in turn, the judge—to make informed assessments of the facts when considered through the eyes of a child. A child is put at unnecessary risk when judges assume that they have no choice but to accept the proposal of a child care authority and do not use the hearing to educate themselves sufficiently to determine whether their decisions are indeed in the child's best interest.

CHAPTER 19

Crossing Professional Borders

I n the preceding chapter we emphasized how important it is that professional persons acknowledge and act within the ambit of their disciplines. In this chapter, while continuing to stress the separateness of the different disciplines, we recognize that they cannot and need not be rigidly compartmentalized. Indeed, the effectiveness of participation in the child placement process by persons of different disciplines depends on their learning from one another. A workable child placement process will provide for a conscious, restrained, open, and reviewable use by professional participants of knowledge acquired from a discipline not their own. The art of collaboration grows out of a recognition that borders do exist (even if they cannot always be sharply defined), and that under certain circumstances they may be crossed.

By working together and reading each other's writings, professional participants in child placement may acquire some special knowledge from or familiarity with practices of another discipline. For example, from their work with child development experts, family court judges and child advocates may learn that the custody of a child who has thrived in long-term care with the same foster family cannot be changed without harming her. From collaboration with agency lawyers and through attending court hearings, social workers may learn that certain judges usually deny petitions to free a battered child for adoption, though they will grant petitions for temporary custody. From testifying in custody cases and from reading court opinions, experts in child development may learn that their reports are not likely to be given credence if they fail to interview and psychologically test each child and adult involved—even when they know they have enough information to respond to the judge's questions without such tests.

Learning by experience from other disciplines does not necessarily justify professional persons acting on what they have learned. Their knowledge of another discipline may be no longer valid, or their acquired knowledge may be valid but not necessarily applicable to a particular case. And even valid, generally applicable knowledge from another discipline should be acted on only if doing so will not contravene the dictates of the participant's own professional training.

The cases that follow illustrate the kinds of questions professional persons should address in deciding whether and when to act on their acquired knowledge—to cross borders.

Law-Trained Professionals Using Their Knowledge of Child Development

Lawyer and Judge

In *Rivera v. Marcus,* a U.S. District Court held that a foster mother's constitutional rights had been violated when, seven years earlier, two children were removed from her care without due process.[1] The usual remedy in such cases is an order to return the children.[2] At the request of counsel for the children, however, the court did not automatically issue the order. Counsel advised the court that taking the children from their present foster family might be detrimental to them. On the basis of knowledge acquired by working with child psychiatrists and by studying the literature of child development, he was alert to the risk involved for these children. He advised the court that "the stability of [their] current situation and their bonds to their present foster parents should be carefully considered before uprooting them."[3] By agreeing to hold a hearing, the District Court judge demonstrated that he knew enough about a child's need for continuity of care not to move these children until he had heard expert testimony on the potential effect of such a move.

The children's lawyer and the District Court judge properly crossed professional borders. Their reliance on knowledge from child development was visible and open to challenge and did not conflict with or undermine their own professional roles. The lawyer did not cease to act as advocate for his clients, and the judge did not abdicate his judicial function.

Courts

In *Ross v. Hoffman,* the chancellor of a Maryland equity court decided to leave Melinda Ross, age nine, in the custody of Mr. and Mrs. Hoffman, her long-term foster parents. Mrs. Ross, Melinda's mother, argued that the Hoffmans had failed to overcome the presumption in law "that a child's welfare will be best served in the custody of the natural parents." She asserted that the chancellor erroneously relied upon the theory of "psychological parenthood" from *Beyond the Best Interests of the Child*.[4] The chancellor had said:

> [In] that book [the authors] point out that whether any adult becomes a psychological parent over the child is based upon a day-to-day interaction, companionship and shared experiences. And if you look at it from that view, Mrs. Hoffman . . . was the day-to-day person while Mrs. Ross . . . would go once or twice a week, . . . and there were . . . long periods of absences, and they say this role can be fulfilled by . . . any other caring adult, . . . whatever the relationship may be . . . .
>
> Further, there is something I use . . . from the Family Law Report on Child Custody Conciliation. . . . They talk about mothering the young child. They said the word "mothering" denot[es] *function* rather than a person. The function does not reside in the biological mother . . . .
>
> *   *   *
>
> It is the adults within the home of the child . . . with whom the child can interact meaningfully, . . . and I think that is what [the child psychiatrist] had in mind [when he said] why risk [moving Melinda,] because we know what this child can do in the home of the Hoffmans. She is well-developed and healthy, and if we change the custody we are not sure whether Mrs. Ross and her new husband and this child can interact meaningfully with her.[5]

On the basis of his acquired knowledge, buttressed by expert testimony applied to undisputed facts, the chancellor had recognized that the presumption in favor of Mrs. Ross as natural parent had been overcome.* For him to have accepted that presumption in this case would have defeated its function. As a New York court has observed, that function is to safeguard the "security, continuity and 'long term stability' . . . [that] are vital to the successful personality development of a child" and that biological parents usually provide.[6]

---

*In this case, the two sources of information on which the judge relied—"acquired knowledge" and "expert testimony"—happened to agree. But what if there is a conflict between, for example, what the judge has learned from reading and what he hears from an expert testifying at the trial? No more can be asked than that the judge articulate the basis of his finding, so that it can be reviewed and called into question during the hearing or on appeal by experts of the same or different schools of thought or even different disciplines.

An intermediate appellate court emphasized the importance of the chancellor having made visible the basis for his decision and thus leaving it open to challenge and review: "[He} reviewed at great length the facts and testimony upon which he relied [and] explained that his reasoning had, to some extent, been influenced by certain educational background factors to which he had been exposed extrajudicially. . . ."[7] The court acknowledged that the boundaries between disciplines may sometimes be crossed:

> To expect [a] judge . . . to erase from memory all that he has read or experienced, not specifically related to the facts of a case, before deciding a case is an absurdity so apparent as to deserve no rebuttal. Error would result when the reasoning was obviously distorted, but not when sound reasoning is influenced by prior experience or education. The soundness of the chancellor's reasoning here is apparent from the excerpt of his opinion. We do not find that he gave undue weight to that particular underpinning of his reasoning. Rather, we commend him both for recognizing and expressing that which helped him to decide.[8]

The Maryland Supreme Court affirmed the intermediate appellate court's decision. Its opinion reflects the way in which expert knowledge—here about a child's need for continuity—can gradually enter case law and in a limited way, as precedent, become a part of the professional equipment of judges and lawyers. The precedent established in *Ross v. Hoffman* incorporates generally accepted and generally applicable knowledge from the field of child development. In some cases, these precedents enable lawyers to argue against and qualify courts to overturn, without hearing expert testimony, the presumption in favor of natural parents. Lawyers and judges on their own can come to recognize many "parent"-child relationships that should not be disturbed.* Thus, through judicial precedent, the borders between the professions are opened and may legitimately be crossed under certain circumstances.

The highest Maryland court, the Maryland Court of Appeals, made several general observations reflecting its understanding of the knowledge it had acquired:

> The child may be so long in the custody of the nonparent that, even though there had been no [legal] abandonment or persistent neglect by

---

*The Supreme Court of Illinois failed to recognize this when it severed the relationship between baby Richard and his "adoptive" parents.[9]

the parent, the psychological trauma of removal is grave enough to be detrimental to the best interest of the child . . . . "Changes in conditions which affect the relative desirability of custodians . . . are not to be accorded significance unless the advantages of changing custody outweigh the essential principle of continued and stable custody of children."[10]

The court then listed specific criteria for determining whether someone other than the natural parent is the child's primary caregiver and should have custody of the child:

The factors which emerge from our prior decisions which may be of probative value . . . include the length of time the child has been away from the biological parent, the age of the child when care was assumed by the third party, the possible emotional effect on the child of a change of custody, the period of time which elapsed before the parent sought to reclaim the child, the nature and strength of the ties between the child and the third party custodian, the intensity and genuineness of the parent's desire to have the child, the stability and certainty as to the child's future in the custody of the parent.

*   *   *

[Here, practically all criteria were present.] His conclusion, that custody in the Hoffmans was in the child's best interests, was founded upon sound legal principles. . . .[11]

The intermediate appellate court itself had recognized the limits of its acquired knowledge. It cautioned that the knowledge of judges was insufficient to "fix a period for which a parent may [cast] off the robe of parental responsibility both inwardly and outwardly, before forfeiting the judicially espoused presumptive shield provided a natural parent.[12]

Legislature

Special knowledge from child development can also enter law by legislation. For example, in abolishing the maternal preference—the presumption that children, particularly of tender years, should remain in the custody of their mother—the Oregon legislature incorporated knowledge from child development in listing these factors to be considered in determining custody:

(a)   The emotional ties between the child and other family members;

(b)   the interest of the parties in and attitude toward the child; and

(c)   the desirability of continuing an existing relationship.[13]

Knowledge from child development is similarly reflected in those factors that the legislature listed as only secondarily relevant:

> In determining custody of a minor child . . . the court shall consider the conduct, marital status, income, social environment or lifestyle of either party *only* if it is shown that any of these factors are causing or may cause emotional or physical damage to the child.[14]

In applying these statutory guidelines, the Oregon Supreme Court in *Derby v. Derby* recognized the significance of identifying the primary caregiving parent regardless of gender:

> The undisputed evidence in this case was that the wife was not merely the mother, but was also the primary parent. During the marriage she was not working and performed the traditional and honorable role of homemaker. She cleaned the house, cared for the children, fed the family, nursed them when sick and spent those countless hours disciplining, counseling and chatting with the children that every homemaker should. For some families the husband may perform this role and be the primary parent. . . . In this family [he] played the traditional role of breadwinner, working eight to ten hours a day. In his off-hours he dedicated much time and attention to the children, but the lion's share of the child raising was performed by the wife. It is undisputed that the children were happy and well-adjusted and that the relationship between the wife and the children was close, loving and successful. Although the same relationship unquestionably existed to a degree with the husband, the close and successful emotional relationship between the primary parent and the children coupled with the age of the children dictate the continuance of that relationship.[15]

In Oregon, lawyers and judges thus no longer need expert testimony in every divorce-custody case before determining who is the child's primary caregiver. As with judicial precedent, in a limited way and for a limited purpose, special knowledge from child development has become part of the working knowledge of the law-trained participants. Similarly, were the guidelines to disposition proposed in Book One and the grounds for intervention proposed in Book Two incorporated in legislation or judicial precedent, some knowledge from child development would become part of the professional equipment of law-trained persons. Individual clinical examinations might no longer be necessary in order for a court to make a finding:

- that enforced separation of a four-year-old from the only parent she has known will have serious repercussions for her development;
- that a child's absent biological parent cannot, by virtue of blood ties alone, replace a long-term caregiver as psychological parent;
- that a murderous parental attack on a child will destroy the possibility of her feeling safe again in the care of that parent; or
- that a child's capacity to develop meaningful relationships will be undermined if she is forced to maintain contact with separated parents who are not in general agreement about visits.

These guidelines and grounds thus identify situations in which judges and lawyers representing children may cross professional borders. This acquired knowledge is, of course, highly visible and remains open to review and challenge in specific cases, as well as generally by legislative revision.

Court and Legislature

The Supreme Court of West Virginia has interpreted its legislature's decision to abolish "all gender based presumptions" for awarding custody to mean that a child's "primary caretaker parent" should be preferred. West Virginia's statute provided only that custody awards accord with "the best interest of the child."[16] Unlike the Oregon statute, it contained no guidelines for identifying the parent who would best serve the child. This lack of guidelines forced the court to analyze its reasons for having previously adopted the now-prohibited maternal preference. In *Garska v. McCoy,* it found that the preference had been designed to assure that the parent who through caregiving was "closest to the child" would be given custody. The West Virginia court turned to the child development–based legislative and judicial decisions of Oregon for guidance in establishing factors for deciding custody:

> [The] trial court shall determine which parent has taken primary responsibility for, *inter alia,* the performance of the following caring and nurturing duties of a parent:

(1) preparing and planning of meals;
(2) bathing, grooming, and dressing;
(3) purchasing, cleaning, and care of clothes;
(4) medical care, including nursing and trips to physicians;
(5) arranging for social interaction among peers after school; i.e., transporting to friends' houses or, for example, to girl or boy scout meetings;
(6) arranging alternative care, i.e., babysitting, daycare, etc.;
(7) putting child to bed at night, attending to child in the middle of the night, waking child in the morning;
(8) disciplining, i.e., teaching general manners and toilet training;
(9) educating, i.e., religious, cultural, social, etc.; and,
(10) teaching elementary skills, i.e., reading, writing, and arithmetic.[17]

These indicia of the primary caregiver, like those listed in *Derby v. Derby,* may or may not be acceptable to experts in child development or generally applicable in this or other cultural settings. What matters is that they—and, indeed, the primary-caregiving preference itself—are open to review, to challenge, and to change.

The court went on to explain the relationship between these factors and the need of children for continuity of care. Taking into account child development considerations practically identical to those reflected in the Oregon statute, the court said:

> While, as the trial court found, the educational and economic position of the father is superior to that of the mother, nonetheless, those factors alone pale in comparison to love, affection, concern, tolerance, and the willingness to sacrifice—factors about which conclusions can be made for the future most intelligently upon a course of conduct in the past. At least with regard to the primary caretaker parent there is a track record to which a court can look and where that parent is fit he or she should be awarded continued custody.[18]

Whether established by statute (as in Oregon) or by judicial precedent (as in West Virginia), the primary-caregiver guidelines explicitly identify the factors to be considered in terms of their function: assuring continuity of care for the child. They enable judges and lawyers to achieve a degree of literacy in child development—to gain some understanding of the reasons for the preference. Unlike the earlier preferences for the mother or for biological parents, the preference for the primary caregiving parent provides more than "mere assertions of end results."[19] The new preference is no longer divorced from the ideas, concepts, and theories that need to be understood in order to recognize its purpose.

Courts have from time to time recognized that the earlier presumptive preferences could be overturned if applying them would not serve the child's need for continuity of care. For example, in an 1889 case—long before the notion of continuity was formulated by experts in child development—the Court of Error and Appeals in New Jersey recognized that the judge's task was to "fix the future status of the child [Clara] with some stability and permanence" and that her welfare required that she be allowed to remain with her long-term foster parents rather than be forced, as the lower court had decreed, to live with her natural parents.[20] Although biological parents were presumptively favored, the court declared:

> Nature's provision of mutual affection commonly exists as the incentive to parental and filial duty and the bond of family union. It is the instinct of childhood to attach itself and cling to those who perform towards it the parental office, and they become endeared to it by the ministering to its dependence. . . . In a controversy over its possession, its welfare will be the paramount consideration in controlling the discretion of the court.[21]

And in overturning the presumption, the court explicitly identified those functions of natural parents which the foster parents had assumed in this case:

> They agreed to take it and rear it as their own child. They nursed and cared for it through helpless infancy. They watched over and provided for it as it grew in years. Whatever it has known of parental love and care is from them. It would be passing strange if it had not become bound to them, and the home they gave it, with a child's affection. They . . . are still willing and abundantly able to provide for it, and advance it in life.[22]

Because the mechanical application of the presumption would not serve its purpose, the court was willing to overturn it. Similarly, the Supreme Court of Kansas, in an earlier case, overturned the presumption in favor of fathers, after recognizing that evidence of the past performance of the parents and foster parents was the best guide to determine the custody of the child:

The right of the father must be considered; the right of the one who has filled the parental place for years should be considered. Perhaps it may not be technically correct to speak of that as a right; and yet, they who have for years filled the place of the parent, have discharged all the obligations of care and support, and especially when they have discharged these duties during those years of infancy when the burden is especially heavy, when the labor and care are of a kind whose value cannot be expressed in money—when all these labors have been performed and the child has bloomed into bright and happy girlhood, it is but fair and proper that their previous faithfulness, and the interest and affection which these labors have created in them, should be respected. Above all things, the paramount consideration is, what will promote the welfare of the child?

*   *   *

What the future of the child will be, is a question of probability. No one is wise enough to forecast, or determine absolutely, what or what would not be best for it; yet we have to act upon these probabilities from the testimony before us, guided by the ordinary laws of human experience.[23]

In 1958, a Missouri appellate court also examined the basis for a presumption. The court rejected a mother's claim over a father's for the custody of their two children, ages eight and five:

Although our courts have said many times that, "*all other things being equal*," custody of a child of tender years should be awarded to the mother . . . , the paramount and controlling consideration in every child custody case, to which all other principles and presumptions must yield is the welfare of the child. . . . There is no paucity of cases demonstrating that, where the best interests of a child will be served thereby, custody will be awarded to the father; and, clearly this should be and is true even where both parents are fit and proper persons to rear the child.[24]

The gender-related, the blood-tie, and the primary-caregiving-parent preferences are all meant to enable courts to identify who has been or is most likely to be responsible for the child's care. Only the primary-caregiver preference explicitly identifies the evidence essential for assuring that the underlying continuity function will be served. There is no need to overcome a presumption in order to harmonize a placement decision with its purpose.

The guidelines and the relatively objective factors to be considered are visible and open to challenge in courts and legislatures.

Family Courts

Family court judges, whether applying a gender-based preference or a preference for the primary parent, will continue to consider and in some cases require the testimony of experts in child development.* But as the appellate judge in *Ross v. Hoffman* emphasized, it is always necessary to question the basis of expert testimony. He warned that reliance on the work of psychiatrists, psychologists, and trained social workers "should not be too obsequious or too routine. . . ."[25][†]

A similar warning against overreliance on experts may be implicit in one family court judge's observation: "Whenever I ask the Child Guidance Clinic to make an evaluation, I know in nine cases out of ten what the report of the Clinic's psychiatrist-social worker team will recommend. That is why," he added, "I seldom send cases to the Clinic for assessment."

This statement could have several different meanings. The judge may mean that he does not want to hear what he "knows" the Clinic will report because it almost always conflicts with his personal preference for the outcome of a child placement case. Or he may mean that he does not believe in child development theory at all and that he automatically ignores what experts in the field have to say. Or he may mean that he believes that the Clinic's staff base their reports on personal as opposed to professional judgments, or that they are otherwise incompetent. Conversely, this family court judge may be pleased with the quality of staff work at the Clinic and mean that since the staff treats similar cases alike, he himself has become able over time to identify like cases in child development terms and is now equipped to decide many of them without hearing expert testimony. The meaning of the judge's reluctance to consult the Clinic must be disclosed and left open to review. Otherwise his own personal, nonprofessional, or outdated views may determine, without challenge, how he uses the "knowledge" he has acquired.

---

*Even experts in child development, recognizing the limits of their knowledge, may not be able to determine which of two psychological parents is primary. In such cases a judicially supervised drawing of lots between two equally acceptable psychological parents might be the most rational and least offensive and least disruptive process for resolving the hard choice.

†The caveat highlights that the social policy that the law is designed to serve is determined not by the experts but by society through law. For example, the legislature might declare a policy that makes the interests of parents or the family, not the child, paramount in the placement process. Or a legislature might enact a statute that gives a priority to a placement that makes the legal status of adoption superior to safeguarding a longterm relationship that cannot become adoptive.

In a limited way, then, the law may come to reflect explicitly in case law or in statute the "current" state of knowledge from child development. When guided by such judicial or legislative determinations, lawyers and judges perform tasks for which they are trained: construing statutes and interpreting precedents in applying them to individual cases. The law, however, does not adjust automatically to new discoveries in the source discipline. Moreover, law, to the extent that it reveals conclusions rather than information about the special knowledge that underlies it, is prone to misapplication. Therefore the basis for decisions in law (both statute and precedent) must remain highly visible and open to challenge in legislature and in court. Lawyers, judges, and legislators—indeed, all professional persons in the child placement process— must be careful to ask themselves the following questions:

- "Does the law reflect the current state of knowledge?"
- "Would the application of the precedent or statutory provision in this case serve the purpose for which it was fashioned?"

Child Development Professionals Using Their Knowledge of Law

Child Psychiatrist—Jane

Dr. Hague, a child psychiatrist, was engaged by the court-appointed lawyer for ten-year-old Jane to determine the visitation arrangements with her father that would best serve her interests. Her mother, who had custody, opposed all visits. Dr. Hague interviewed the child and her parents and found that she was suffering from a "destructive loyalty conflict." He concluded that Jane would be hurt more from shuttling between "two enemy camps" than from not seeing her father at all for the time being. Nevertheless, in his report to the court he recommended that she visit her father one afternoon each week.

Dr. Hague made this recommendation because he "knew" that the court never denied fathers the right to visit unless there was evidence of physical abuse, which was not the case here. He explained, "Had I come out against visits altogether, the judge would not only have ordered them anyway, but he also would probably have included overnight visits, which would have been even more difficult for Jane to tolerate than daytime visits."

By acting counter to his professional opinion, this child psychiatrist negated the basis for his participation in the proceedings. He denied the court information it ought to have had. In accord with his professional findings, Dr. Hague should have told the court that the least harmful alternative for Jane would be no visits, and said why this was so. He might have added that if the court did decide to order visits, they should not be overnight. In that way he could have used his acquired knowledge without increasing the risk of harm to the child, without depriving the court of his expertise, and without foreclosing the possibility of appellate or legislative review of the conflict between court and expert.[26]

Clinical Psychologist—Peggy

A divorce court judge asked Dr. Burns, a clinical psychologist, to conduct a family study to help him decide who should have custody of six-year-old Peggy. Her father had been a prisoner of war in Vietnam for the past five years, during which time she lived and thrived in the care of her mother. From these facts alone, Dr. Burns was able to conclude that it would be best for Peggy to remain with her mother. But she also knew from prior experience with this court that the judge always demanded that there be clinical assessments based on interviews and psychological tests of both parent and child. And she knew from a number of prior decisions that custody orders based on such assessments had a better chance of withstanding appellate scrutiny than those that did not. Although she thought that the court was infringing on her professional judgment as well as disserving Peggy's interests by requiring unnecessary tests, she conducted them.

Dr. Burns had no doubt that the possible harm to Peggy from these gratuitous intrusions was less than the harm that would result if the court were to reject her recommendation.* She decided not to risk Peggy's well-being by using the occasion to educate the court about the undesirability of superfluous examinations.† Unlike the decision of Dr. Hague in Jane's case, her action assured—rather than precluded—that the court would consider the information that she was specially qualified to give.

Social Worker—Maria Colwell

The *Report of the Committee of Inquiry* following Maria Colwell's murder by her stepfather uncovers some of the hazards facing child development professionals when they act on their knowledge of the law.[28] The report discloses

---

*Had Dr. Burns believed that there was a risk of substantial harm to Peggy from additional tests, conducting them merely to please the trial judge and to assure that the decision not be overturned on appeal would have been an unjustified use of her knowledge acquired from law.

†Dr. Burns's dilemma was like that confronting child care agencies whose policies, though designed to serve the well-being of children, may hurt a particular child if applied inflexibly.[27]

that at the time her mother and stepfather sought to recover custody of Maria, the child care agency had evidence that her trial visits to her parents had been disastrous, and it believed that no change in custody should be made.[29] Yet the professional staff of the agency decided not to oppose the parents' attempt to get custody. "Their reasoning appeared to be that if [the biological mother] did not succeed on this first occasion she would probably do so sooner or later and therefore it was better to accept the position and seek to control it. . . ."[30]

The "better to accept" position of the social workers was based not upon their social work expertise but upon their perception of the legal process. Their view was not idiosyncratic. "[I]t was generally believed," the Committee of Inquiry noted, "that natural parents had the 'right' to have their child back from care once they had established that they were fit to receive it and that this thinking influenced magistrates court."[31] The social workers' acquired knowledge of law, though well founded, should not have been acted upon. By using this knowledge, they denied the judge an opportunity to consider their professionally informed finding that moving Maria would be detrimental to her. They arrogated to themselves a decision that belonged to the judge—whether to accept or reject their opinions. Furthermore, they sanctioned an outcome that professionally they knew to be wrong.

If the social workers had been urged by the attorney for the local authority not to waste their or the court's time by opposing the mother's petition, they might have recognized that following this advice would be unprofessional. Yet without such outside pressure, they compromised their professional selves and thus subverted the hearing before the court.

Except in the event of disastrous consequences, like those in the Maria Colwell case, such use of knowledge about law often goes unnoticed. Therefore these experts must be especially alert to recognize when they are about to act on their knowledge from law—and not to do so if it would mean depriving the process of the expertise that alone justified their participation. That is true even when their "legal knowledge" is correct and can be applied to the case before them. Before using their acquired knowledge they should ask themselves in each case:

- "Will I be depriving the placement process of the expertise that is the basis for my participation?"
- "Will I be increasing the risk of harm to the child if I use or act upon my knowledge from another discipline?"
- "Have I made the basis of my position sufficiently visible so that others may question it?"

Law and Child Development Professionals Together Assessing Their Use of Acquired Knowledge—*Danny Byse*

Lessons learned from *Maria Colwell's* murder prompted both law- and non-law-trained participants to reexamine a child care agency's decision to withdraw its petition to terminate the parental rights of Danny Byse's mother.

Danny Byse was born in the infirmary of the state prison where his mother, Angela Byse, was serving a two-year sentence. Shortly after birth, Danny was placed in foster care with Donald and Mary Dumont. His father had no interest in him and was willing to surrender his parental rights. On her release from prison, Mrs. Byse took Danny out of foster care, but she was unable to care for him properly. Within weeks, seriously ill from neglect of his health needs, Danny was again placed with the Dumonts. He thrived in their care. Once every two months they took him to visit his mother, who had been reimprisoned on another offense. Two years later she was paroled to a halfway house and sought to reestablish her relationship with Danny.

The Child Care Agency responded with a petition to terminate her parental rights in order to give permanency to Danny's relationship with the Dumonts, who wished to adopt him. This decision rested on an assessment by his social worker that Mrs. Byse was unlikely to be able to give Danny the care that his fragile health demanded. The Agency's position was reinforced by court-ordered psychiatric evaluations of mother, child, and foster parents. The psychiatrist strongly recommended that Danny and his mother not be reunited. His letter to the court left no doubt that Danny's primary ties were with the Dumonts and that his return to Mrs. Byse would needlessly place him at risk of "undue emotional stress." More importantly, he warned that Danny's life would be jeopardized because Mrs. Byse had shown herself unable to meet his complicated medical needs.

At a pretrial proceeding, the judge who was assigned to hear the case said that he would deny the agency's petition because the mother "deserved a chance" to show what she could do with the child. On the advice of the state's attorney who acted as its lawyer, and with the concurrence of the lawyer for the child, the Agency withdrew the petition.

Following the Agency's action, the lawyer for Danny, the social worker assigned to his case, the lawyer for the Agency, and the psychiatrist met to discuss the decision to withdraw the termination petition. The psychiatrist explained why he believed that this decision ran counter to Danny's interests. The social worker said that while her professional knowledge led her to concur with the psychiatrist's assessment, she had agreed to the withdrawal because she was persuaded that "there was no chance of winning." She added,

"In any event, even if I had wanted to persist, there was no way of getting the Agency lawyer to pursue the matter." And, indeed, the Agency lawyer said, "I would have been unwilling to go forward with the petition under these circumstances even if the professional staff had pressed me to proceed."

Finally, Danny's lawyer said:

> Though I was persuaded by the social worker's report and by the psychiatric evaluation that Danny would be harmed if he were ever returned to his mother, I, too, wanted to withdraw the petition, because it was the wrong time strategically. I knew we would lose. On the basis of the expert opinions I knew that there was no parent-child relationship between Danny and his mother and that it would be harmful to try to forge a bond between them. But though these are statutory grounds for termination, the decision is a discretionary matter. I knew the trial judge meant it when he told us at the pretrial hearing that he would throw out the petition.[32] I also knew that I had no chance of winning an appeal under these circumstances.

When a child's well-being is at stake, a lawyer's prediction that the case will be lost, no matter how well informed, is not sufficient to justify abandoning the case.* Here the child care agency ought to have instructed the state's attorney to proceed. And the state's attorney should have pursued his client's wishes, even though he "knew" he would not win.† The social workers for the Agency should not have altered their professional behavior in anticipation of the court's decision. They should not have accepted their attorney's view of what would be best for the child. And the lawyer for Danny, informed by experts in child development about his client's needs, ought to have represented him by insisting on going forward.‡

---

*We recognize that limited financial and personnel resources of child care agencies and legal service agencies may make the likelihood of prevailing a factor in efficiently allocating resources. But such resource restraints should not be allowed to obscure the extent to which the interests of the child may be disserved.

A Connecticut judge emphasized the importance of social workers' pursuing the interests of the child: "When I instruct new . . . social workers, I urge them to seek the relief they feel is indicated, and if it is rejected let the buck stop at the judge's bench where the action taken (or denied) is on the record, appealable, and *visible*. . . . [It] is disheartening when time after time, [their requests] are denied by judges acting out of ignorance and seat-of-the-pants 'expertise,' but if the agency does not try for the action that may save the child from further harm, there is *no* chance that such action will be taken.[33]

†If the statute had prohibited termination in such cases the arena for challenge by the social workers would have been the legislature.

‡Professionals ought not to withhold information or avoid participation in court proceedings out of fear of being embarrassed either by cross-examination or by association with a "lost cause."

Fortunately, the Agency decided to reinstate its petition to terminate and to make visible its reasons for doing so. As a result of this decision, Danny Byse had an opportunity to have his best interests made secure—an opportunity that would otherwise have been foreclosed. And the judge, despite, and even because of, his pretrial position would be confronted with the evidence of the experts. This evidence, even if ignored by the trial judge, would help assure fair review on appeal and ultimately review by the legislature of how well its child placement law was working.

Professional persons who participate in the child placement process must strike a balance between too general and too specific a definition of disciplines. They must acknowledge the existence of borders and, despite the absence of firm guidelines, must differentiate between situations when they can and when they cannot go beyond those borders.

CHAPTER 20

Dual Role—Ambiguity and Ambivalence

I n the previous two chapters we examined situations in which professional persons might not have recognized that they were assigned or were assuming roles in the child placement process that they were not specially qualified to perform. In this chapter, our focus shifts to situations in which professionals are assigned or assume two potentially incompatible roles in relation to the same child or family.* For example, can a social worker use home visits for supportive work with a family and at the same time use those visits to investigate allegations of fraud or child abuse for a state welfare agency?[2] Can a mental health therapist who is treating an abusive parent evaluate, from the child's point of view, the desirability of returning the child to this parent? Can a lawyer effectively advocate (not just communicate) a child's preference for who her custodial parents should be and at the same time advocate what she herself believes, informed by expert advice and guided by case and statutory law, to be in the child's best interests? The answer to these questions is the same: The potentially conflicting loyalties inherent in such dual roles tend to prevent both assignments from being faithfully discharged.[3] The operative presumption for legislature, agency, and court ought to be against the assignment of dual professional roles. And the presumption for professional participants ought to be against accepting or assuming such roles. The cases that follow illustrate the hazards of dual assignments in the child placement process.

---

*Many of the cases discussed in Chapters 18 and 19 were not simply illustrations of professionals acting outside of their qualifications. It is possible, for example, that the judge in the *Jason Rose* case was trained not only in law but in child development as well. In that event he would have been qualified to be both judge and expert witness—but not in the same case. The social workers in the *Maria Colwell* case might have been trained in law or informed about law through their experience with the family courts, but they could not serve as professional advisers to the court about the child's need and at the same time decide what portion of their advice or evidence was relevant to the outcome of the case from the legal (as distinguished from the child development) point of view.[1]

Child Therapist Refusing to Serve as Consultant to the Court in a Custody Case Involving His Patient—*Johnny Sloan*

Johnny, a four-and-a-half-year-old child whose divorcing parents were involved in an intense court battle for his custody, had been in psychotherapy with Dr. Bernard Steele for several months. Dr. Steele was trying to understand Johnny's fear of falling asleep and to help him overcome it. In the course of the custody hearing, Judge Rachel Thomas learned that Johnny was in psychotherapy with Dr. Steele. She asked him to provide answers to the following questions about the child's relationship to his parents:

- "To which parent is Johnny most closely attached?"
- "If he is closely attached to both parents, which parent in the short run and which parent in the long run would best be able to serve his interests?"

Dr. Steele refused to carry out Judge Thomas's request. He said that to do so would jeopardize the therapeutic alliance essential to psychotherapy. The effectiveness of therapy, he explained, "rests on Johnny's belief that what he says and does when we are together is just between us and will be used only to help him to try to get over his fear of sleep. Also, if I have to concentrate on the court's questions, I cannot devote my full attention to my therapeutic function."

For Judge Thomas, the purist stance of Dr. Steele seemed unreasonable, especially since she suspected that he already had the information she wanted. Dr. Steele insisted that he could not function as Johnny's therapist if he took on an investigative/reportorial role for the court concerning the custody of his patient. No matter whether he made a fresh investigation or used what he had already learned in therapy, his working relationship with Johnny would be impaired. Indeed, it would become difficult for Johnny to benefit from treatment, even with a different therapist, after such a "betrayal." Further, Dr. Steele explained that his special relationship with Johnny might unintentionally cause him to be less than objective if he undertook to answer the court's questions. Thus, he would not serve either the court or Johnny well if he attempted to serve both.[4]

Though not entirely convinced by Dr. Steele's objections, Judge Thomas appointed Dr. Cynthia Fare, a child psychiatrist with no prior relationship to Johnny or his family, to do a custody evaluation.* Her report demonstrated

---

*Alternatively, Judge Thomas might have believed that the fact situation was clear enough without Dr. Fare's clinical evaluation, or might have asked Dr. Fare to use the fact situation itself as the basis for an expert opinion without burdening Johnny with another clinical examination.

yet another reason why it was good professional practice for Dr. Steele to have refused the court's assignment. The tests and interviews Dr. Fare had conducted revealed a number of details that might become useful in therapy by being clarified and interpreted over an extended time, but which were not otherwise usable. Dr. Fare could easily put these details aside. But Dr. Steele, having already begun to consider these fine points in therapeutic terms, would have found it difficult to disregard them when answering the court's questions. His information overload would have needlessly complicated his custody evaluation. At worst, such refinements could divert and confuse; at best, they were unnecessary. Deciding the question of custody required findings on which parent was primary and which parent "wanted" the child—not interpretations of Johnny's unconscious that might become useful in treatment but were too unreliable and tentative to be used as placement data.

Psychiatrist and Social Worker Assuming Dual Roles—*Karen Spencer*

After Karen Spencer had been murdered by her mother, Professor J. D. Mc-Clean issued a report to the Derbyshire County Council and Derbyshire Health Authority:[5]

> Karen Spencer was born on 4 December 1975. She had to remain in hospital for some 5 weeks but went home to her parents, Marilyn and David Spencer, on 9 January 1976. On 19 February 1976 she was admitted to hospital with injuries, including a fractured skull, inflicted by her mother. Karen remained in hospital until the end of March and during that time a care order was made, placing her in the care of the local authority, the Derbyshire County Council. On discharge from hospital Karen was placed with foster parents. She remained with them for twelve months, but was at home with her natural parents for visits most weekends and for longer periods at holiday times. The length of the visits gradually increased until at the end of March 1977 Karen was home on trial on a full-time basis. On 16 April 1977 she was again assaulted by her mother and sustained severe head injuries from which she died three days later.[6]

The Report disclosed that the social worker who was charged with Karen's welfare had also counseled her parents. The social worker and the Consultant Psychiatrist were anxious to give the Spencers "the feeling of progress, something to reward their initiative . . . something to avert the feeling that

'authority' was not committed to helping them, some incentive for greater efforts in future."[7] The Consultant Psychiatrist, it appears, had a dual role:

> In August and September the Consultant Psychiatrist received requests
> for a psychiatric assessment from the General Practitioner, the Social
> Worker, and from the Spencer's Solicitor. The formal position appears
> to have been that the Psychiatric Report was prepared at the request of
> the social services department, and it is addressed to the Social Worker.
> The two Solicitors were clear that the Consultant Psychiatrist was the
> department's witness. But not everyone shared that view. The Area Of-
> ficer annotated one copy of the report: "[The Consultant Psychiatrist]
> present in court and prepared to give evidence on behalf of mother," and
> the Consultant Psychiatrist himself was quite clear in his evidence to
> me that he was acting for Mrs. Spencer. When pressed he said that he
> was in a sense working with the Social Worker and taking a global view,
> but that he had been approached by her Solicitor and regarded himself
> as representing her; but all the professionals involved were friends, "all
> were trying to do what was best."

Professor McClean continued:

> I have presented in some little detail this interesting difference of em-
> phasis as to the Consultant Psychiatrist's role. I make it quite clear that
> I am not suggesting any impropriety, or even any real confusion. There
> is, I believe, always an element of tension, or ambiguity, when a pro-
> fessional (and it can be a lawyer as easily as a medical man or a social
> worker) owes duties to his client, with whom he will have a continuing
> relationship, and to the court and other agencies.[8]

We do not agree that there was no "real confusion." Indeed, the hazard of
assuming that the Consultant could at the same time adequately represent
Karen's needs and those of the parents who had abused her is apparent in his
psychiatric report:

> Having regard to Mrs. Spencer's personality and the tendency she has
> had to act impulsively when under stress, it would seem at first that
> there has been little time since February for her and her husband to de-
> velop a stable relationship which would reassure the Social Services
> that the child would no longer be at risk. On the other hand my feelings

after the interview were that they had responded fairly well to [the Social Worker's] counseling and I am more optimistic about their ability to cope in the future. I would agree that to have the baby home on a permanent basis immediately would be unwise but I think that they need more incentive than they are getting at the moment. In my view I do not think Karen would be at risk if the time she spent with her parents was increased. Mrs. Spencer seems willing and anxious to receive help and guidance and if this were available, I would think her confidence and her general ability in dealing with the day to day problems when looking after a child would develop. I also believe that it is important for the marriage that such an incentive be made available, the resentment which Mr. Spencer still feels would then dissipate more quickly.[9]

Neither the social worker nor the Consultant Psychiatrist should have been responsible for both *helping Mrs. Spencer regain custody* of Karen and *determining whether it was safe for Karen to be returned to her care.* The Consultant Psychiatrist should have recognized that he could not act on behalf of everyone who had approached him. The judge should have considered whether the psychiatric assessment of Karen's needs was contaminated by his joining the social worker in a "therapeutic plot" to help Karen's parents.[10] With this confusion about roles unresolved, neither the Spencers nor the social services department had reason to trust the Consultant Psychiatrist to do a good job. For the McClean Report to observe that the psychiatrist's "whole report [is] a touch optimistic"[11] understates the problem. In the "plot" and the "optimism" there was compromise in the worst sense. The consultant's obligations were split between making an investigation of Karen's need to be protected from the Spencers and providing the Spencers with help to save their marriage and to regain custody and care of Karen. That duality could not help but influence his interpretation of what he observed and what he reported to the court. As a result of the psychiatrist's dual and divided allegiances both Karen and her parents were ill served.

Two Canadian Judges Examine the Dual Role of a Lawyer for Children

In *In the Matter of Roy M. C., Jennifer C., Shannon C., and Jason C.,* the judge sought to clarify the role of counsel in child placement cases.[12] Lawyers for the Catholic Children's Aid Society, for the mother of four children, and for the Official Guardian each advocated a different position with regard to the care and custody of the children. With respect to the Official Guardian for the children, Judge Karswick asked:

> [D]oes counsel have an obligation to advocate the child's stated position or does he have the obligation to *also* state his own views of what is in the best interests of the child, discuss the evidence in support of that position and adduce all evidence which bears on the issue of the best interest of the child, even though it may be unfavorable to the child's views, preferences or instructions. . . .
>
> *   *   *
>
> When one considers the fundamental importance of this issue of custody for both the family and the community I do not think that the Court can, nor should it, direct the child's counsel to take a strict adversarial role and act as "mouthpiece," blindly advocating a view, preference or instructions which confound or shock his professional opinion of what is in the best interest of the child. It makes eminently good sense to have counsel take an active, real and positive role in the social context of the Family Court, and as Officers of this Court, assume the obligation to adduce all relevant and material evidence on the issue of what is in the best interest of the child, and, when called upon, to express a professional and responsible view of what that disposition should be.[13]

Judge Karswick apparently did not consider that though a lawyer may be able to *communicate* to a judge both the preference of his child client and his own professionally informed view of the child's "best interests," a lawyer cannot effectively *advocate* both unless they happen to coincide.

In *Re W.*, Judge Abella of the Ontario Provincial Court was specifically asked to clarify the task of the child's legal representative.[14] The child's lawyer had declared that she would support the application of the Children's Aid Society for Crown wardship of a seven-year-old girl. "She also stated that she would be representing the child by presenting not only the child's wishes, but her own perception of the child's best interests as well. It was to this duality of role that mother's counsel [who opposed the wardship application] addressed himself in requesting a clearer delineation of function in order to prepare his own case."[15] Judge Abella, unlike Judge Karswick, concluded that though a child's ambivalence or inability to instruct counsel required "a degree of flexibility in a child's lawyer's role as articulator of his or her client's wishes,"[16] that flexibility did not extend to the lawyer's advocating his own views when they conflicted with those of his child client. The judge observed:

> So long as the forum is the courtroom, the child's lawyer should represent his or her young client in a way which reflects equal participation with the other parties in this forum.
>
> Representing a client in these cases usually involves executing a client's instructions and, without being misleading, attempting to show through the evidence that these instructions or wishes best match the child's needs. In other words, a mother who wishes custody of her child expects her lawyer to present her case in such a way that her wishes are shown to be in the best interests of the child. it is, in most cases, an articulation of the client's rather than the lawyer's subjective assessment. It should be no different when the client is a child. Where, therefore, the child has expressed definite views, these views, rather than those of the child's lawyer, should determine what is conveyed to the court. The child's advocate is the legal architect who constructs a case based on the client's views.
>
> In its purest form, that means that the child's lawyer should present and implement a client's instructions to the best of his or her ability. And this, in turn, involves indicating to the court the child's concerns, wishes and opinions. It involves, further, presenting to the court accurate and complete evidence which is consistent with the child's position.[17]

Judge Abella said that the lawyer's role of *counselor* to her client is not inconsistent with her role as advocate of the client's wishes. At the same time, she warned that in the case of the child client, lawyers must be especially sensitive to the danger of abusing their counseling role:

> In the case of a child who is capable of coherent expression the lawyer's role in representing the child's wishes does not preclude the lawyer from exploring with the child the merits or realities of the case, evaluating the practicalities of the child's position and even offering, where appropriate, suggestions about the possible reasonable resolutions to the case. Offering advice is part of the lawyer's obligation to protect the client's interests. Obviously, however, given the vulnerability of most children to authority in general and given the shattered sensibilities in family disputes in particular, great sensitivity should be exercised during these exploratory sessions.[18]

Though we do not share Judge Abella's view of the lawyer's role as advocate of the child's wishes, we do share her, rather than Judge Karswick's, position that a lawyer cannot at one and the same time effectively advocate the child's preference and his own professionally informed assessment of "best interests." But in spite of this position she assigns a dual role to counsel for the child when she concludes:

> This case involves a seven-year-old girl who expresses ambivalence about where she wants to live. She has offered no clear instructions to her lawyer. Counsel's role in protecting her client's interests would include, therefore, articulating, exploring and attempting to explain this conflict to the court by evidentiary means [advocacy of the client's wishes]. Then, having heard the evidence of all parties, [counsel] could further assist the court by offering in final submissions her assessment of what the evidence reveals to be in her client's "best interests" [advocacy of lawyer's own perception of best interests].[19]

If the child's lawyer indicates that the child has no preference and if the court believes that it needs an "assessment of what the evidence reveals would be in the [child's] 'best interests,' "[20] that task should be assigned to a different lawyer.* Such an arrangement would diminish the risk of the child's lawyer finding "no clear preference" when his client's expressed preference conflicted with his own view of "best interest."

Professional participants must be alert to ask and answer this question:

- "Am I [Are you] assuming, assigning, or being assigned more than one role in relation to the same family or child?"

This need to confront and avoid dual assignments reflects one of the differences between the role of the professional person and that of "ordinary devoted" parents. In every intact family, for example, parents inevitably take some actions that appear to be for the primary benefit of mother, father, or a particular child, even though another child's interest, viewed in isolation, might call for different conduct. That is compromise in the best sense. By acting in the interest of the family as a whole, parents serve the overriding interest that each of the children has in the integrity of that family. But in the child

---

*Had Judge Abella adopted the view that counsel for the child was to advocate the child's best interests, rather than to be her "mouthpiece," no duality problem would have arisen.

placement process, dual role assignments result in compromise in the worst sense, serving no one's best interests. Whenever doubt exists about the incompatibility of two roles, they should be performed by different persons.[21] In the interests of the child, professional participants ought not to be handicapped by being placed—or by placing themselves—in professionally ambiguous positions.

CHAPTER 21

No License to Act as Parents

Professional participants in the child placement process do not, either individually or collectively, make or make up for a parent. They are specialists, not generalists. They are neither qualified nor authorized to act with a parent's discretion and prerogatives—yet they sometimes do. This may be because good professional work requires humanity as well as expertise and because their assignments often entail performing parent-like tasks that place them in ambiguous relationships with both children and parents.* Under such circumstances judges, lawyers, social workers, and child development specialists may unwittingly use their authority to act "the good parent," especially if they find a child (or, indeed, a parent) particularly appealing, annoying, or pathetic. The professionals' challenge, as nonparents, is how to be caring without taking unwarranted control of the life of the child for whom they do not and cannot take full responsibility. The ability to locate the line between the usurper of parental autonomy and the caring expert characterizes the good professional.[1]

Professional persons may unwittingly assume parental prerogatives *directly,* in their contacts with the child, or *indirectly,* by imposing their will on her parents. They may, for example, use their direct contact with a child to discipline her, not as psychologists might because they seek to further therapeutic goals, or as judges might because they must maintain order in the courtroom, but because they consider her "spoiled," "unruly," or "ungrateful." And professionals sometimes use their indirect relationships with children to make parental decisions about family lifestyle (for example, when trial judges order a joint custody arrangement that neither parent has sought).[2]

When professional persons, in direct contact with a child, must, as part of

---

*If parents choose to delegate to a day care center a role in raising their child, the day care professionals who assumed the parental role do not thereby exceed their authority. The freedom to delegate child care to others is a parental prerogative.

their assignment, perform parent-like tasks during home or office visits, the child can quickly become confused. Two child development experts were reminded of this problem when they interviewed Jim, age six. Having been asked to tell the court which of Jim's parents was his primary caregiver, they saw Jim in his own room at home. As part of their evaluation, they sat on the floor and, with evident pleasure, joined him in play. As Jim pushed a large toy automobile around the room, one of them asked:

"Where are you going?"

"On a picnic."

"Whom do you want most to go with you?"

"The two of you."

The semblance of the parental role is even more difficult to avoid when the professionals' direct contacts with the child are more intense and of longer duration than in a court-ordered evaluation. Therapists in particular face a special problem in their efforts to establish trust with a child patient.[3] A therapist in training said to a five-year-old boy, during a treatment hour, "I love you—I'll always love you even when you're naughty." During daily meetings this therapist let the child hug her and climb on her body. The therapist knew that this was for treatment purposes, but the child may not have understood that. He might have felt that she would always be available, like a parent. When this therapist stopped seeing him, not because his treatment was complete* but because she had completed her training, he had good reason to feel betrayed. The result of such betrayal is that a child's ability to trust may become impaired.[4]

Albeit to a lesser degree, lawyers representing children over an extended period of time may engender similar confusion in their child clients. This is illustrated by the comments of an Australian judge addressing a conference of child placement professionals. In praising counsel appointed by her to represent a child whose parents were separated, she said: "[It] came through to me in the process of hearing the case that one of the little girls who is the subject of a custody dispute wants an order whereby she can live somewhere near the instructing solicitor . . . [laughter]."[5] Such misperceptions by a child of the professional's role must be recognized and minimized.

---

*Completing treatment would include helping the child understand the limits and limitations of their relationship.

Parental authority is inevitably supervened to some extent whenever professionals implement, for example, laws that mandate the removal of neglected or abused children. But no matter how extensive such authorized supervention may be, the problem of gratuitous invasions of parental prerogatives remains. Judge Dembitz of the New York Family Court recognized the danger of unnecessarily assuming a parental role, albeit an indirect one, in the case of *Melissa M.*[6] She ordered the four-and-a-half-year-old child to be removed from her foster family and to be placed with her natural father and his new wife.* Melissa's foster parents then sought a court order allowing them to visit, but Melissa's new parents said that visits would disrupt their family life and confuse the child. Though Judge Dembitz believed that such visits would be beneficial for Melissa, she refrained from substituting her judgment for that of the custodial parents. Unwilling to intrude, even indirectly, on Melissa's relationship with her new parents, Judge Dembitz said that "the parental decision-making prerogative with 'freedom of personal choice in matters of . . . family life' should be maintained . . . unless there is strong reason for interference with it."[7] She recognized that professionals risk injury to parent-child ties if they ignore the meaning of family integrity for a child.[8]

The cases that follow illustrate how some professionals may disregard the fact that though their assigned tasks may be highly significant, their relationships to the children they serve are not permanent commitments. Unlike Judge Dembitz, they sometimes forget that the child is not their own.

Taking the Parental Prerogative in Direct Contact with the Child

Judges—Emily

In a post-divorce visitation dispute Emily, age ten, was interviewed by Family Court Judge Dixon in compliance with the statutory mandate that the preference of older children be taken into account. After the interview, Judge Dixon told her parents and their lawyers:

Emily is a very nice, bright little girl. She has told me what she feels about the visits and I have explained my decision to her—that visits with her father must continue. *I have also told her that if she has any problems with the visits*—if either her mother or her father make things

---

*The court had earlier rejected the psychiatrist's recommendation that Melissa remain with her foster parents.

difficult—*she may come to me at any time and talk to me.* I want both parents to know that I will not allow them to let this little girl suffer from their continued warfare.

Some months later Emily's father went back to court because his daughter refused to visit with him and her mother would not force her. The mother's lawyer asked Judge Dixon to hear the case because he had already interviewed Emily and was familiar with the circumstances. He refused. He said that he was about to go on an extended vacation and had no time. The lawyer explained that Emily was anxious to talk to him about the visits and reminded him of his promise that she might speak to him at any time. He replied, "Let her talk to Judge Clement, who will be hearing cases while I am away. He is as good a judge as I am."

Judge Dixon misled Emily into believing that he would be available, as a parent might be, when she needed him. He may have thought he was being understanding and sensitive when he made the promise. He may have felt that implicit in his invitation was the qualification, " . . . if I am not away and if I do not have too many other cases to work on." But Emily had no reason to perceive his "promise" that way. In effect, Judge Dixon invited Emily to trust him during a difficult time and then betrayed her.[9] While judges may consider themselves functionally interchangeable with one another, children do not necessarily see them that way. And even if the judge had honored his promise, a problem of gratuitous intrusion on Emily's relationship with her parents would remain. By interposing himself between Emily and her parents, Judge Dixon might have been undermining their opportunity to work out their own difficulties with the visits he ordered.[10]

The case was then heard by Judge Clement.* He was advised that Emily had been excused from school to talk with him, and that she was waiting in the corridor outside the courtroom, anxious to be heard. He decided, however, to hear her parents first. From them he learned that Emily was adamant in refusing to visit her father, though they disagreed about the reason for this. After several hours of testimony, Judge Clement announced that he would adjourn the hearing until the next day, because he now had to hear another case. The lawyer for Emily's mother reminded him that Emily had been waiting for a very long time and asked him to interview her before moving to the other case. Judge Clement replied, "Let her mother bring her back tomorrow. From

---

*When a child is passed from one judge to another, the new judge should be informed about any representations or promises made by other judges to the child.

what I have learned here today I think it may do Emily some good to make her wait."

He had apparently decided that she was a spoiled child and thought that keeping her waiting outside of his courtroom all day would teach her a lesson. He took a parent's liberties without authority and without a parent's knowledge of Emily. He might have believed that she needed disciplining, but he was not entitled to act on that belief. When Judge Clement interviewed Emily the following day, he told her: "You are too young to know what is good for you. You had better visit your father next Sunday; otherwise I will have your mother punished."

Though the judge had authority to order Emily to visit her father, he went beyond his authority and entered her parents' domain when he sought to "educate" her by saying that she was too young to know what was good for her. Further, he intruded on a parent's prerogative by telling Emily the probable consequences of her refusal to obey his order. Though parental autonomy is limited by law, it is the province of parents, not of judges, to translate for their children the demands of the law and how these should be met.

Both judges took parental license with Emily: Judge Dixon when he sought to comfort her, and Judge Clement when he attempted to discipline her and to give her insight about herself. Though the intrusiveness of such behavior is clear upon reflection, in practice it may easily go unnoticed by the offending, yet well-meaning, professional person and unchallenged by the intimidated or bewildered parent or child.

Foster Parents—Rosalie

A child's relationship with foster parents during the placement process is likely to be more intense and more protracted than that with a judge or a lawyer. Foster parents are intended to provide temporary care in a family setting. Their professional task may be to keep alive the foster child's ties to absent parents. Or it may be to prepare her for permanent placement with an adopting family. In both situations, their assignment requires them to provide full-time (day and night) care for the child in their home. They may not be able to maintain their professional identity for long; rather they may become "real" parents in their own as well as the child's eyes. Over time, their direct contact with the child may unavoidably obliterate the professional relationship and justify their assertion of parental prerogatives.[11]

Rosalie, a one-year-old child, had been abandoned at birth. Pending adoption, she had been placed by the state's Child and Youth Agency with Mr. and Mrs. Trager, who had successfully cared for several children while they were waiting to be adopted. The Tragers knew that they were supposed to help Rosalie develop to the best of her ability. They had every intention of cooperating in the adoption plan, as they had many times before. But this time they "failed." Rosalie needed a great deal of medical attention in the first few months and at one point almost died. In caring for her special needs, the Tragers became devoted to her, as did their own children. An intense and reciprocal feeling of closeness spread through the entire family. Indeed, one of the Trager children wrote the director of the Agency urging that they be allowed to adopt her. Mrs. Trager initially thought that they should "stick with" their agreement to provide only foster care and that her family was already large enough with three children. But Rosalie "won her over" and she "fell in love with her," as had Mr. Trager and the children.

The Tragers had, necessarily and unavoidably, ceased to be professional parents and had become Rosalie's real parents. Rosalie was thriving in their care and by this time could in no way have experienced it as temporary. Fortunately for her, the Agency decided not to oppose their petition for adoption.

Foster care is intended to be limited to placements that are temporary by a child's sense of time. As professionals, foster parents must be trained and prepared to give up the child even though they may have grown to love her during that "brief period." When the period of care is no longer temporary from the child's point of view, foster parents become "real" parents for the child and should be so recognized.[12]

Taking the Parental Prerogative in Indirect Contact with the Child
Judges—*Aki and Edgar*

In a post-divorce custody dispute between a Japanese mother and an American father, the father sought to regain care of their two children, Aki and Edgar. His action was triggered by his ex-wife's plan to move to another part of the United States. A report to the court by its family relations officer spoke unfavorably of the mother, in large part because she had the children sleep on the floor. Because of this sleeping arrangement, the judge requested a psychiatric evaluation and postponed the hearing. The psychiatric report said that the mother was the primary psychological parent and explained that Aki and Edgar slept on the floor on tatami mats in keeping with Japanese custom.

When the time came for the hearing, another judge presided. He announced that he did not believe in "psychiatric stuff" and refused to look at the report. He told the mother to raise Aki and Edgar as "good Americans" and instructed the father to help her do so by buying proper beds for them.

This judge infringed on the parental role by giving unsolicited instructions on how they should raise their children. Even if he believed that it was healthier to sleep in beds than on tatami mats, it was none of his business. His instructions were unrelated to any legitimate goal of the child placement process.[13]

Taking the Parental Prerogative in Direct and Indirect Contact with the Child

Child Psychiatrists and Judges—Randall Cooper

A professional person's contact with a child in the placement process may be both direct and indirect. Randall, age seven, whose parents were in bitter dispute over his custody, had a long history of poor behavior. Since his parents' separation a year earlier, he had been in treatment with Dr. Biddle, a child psychiatrist. The court asked another child psychiatrist, Dr. James, to prepare an evaluation to assist in determining which of his parents should have custody.* Dr. James was sensitive to the risks of intrusion—direct and indirect—on Randall's already troubled relationships with his mother and father, as well as on his relationship to Dr. Biddle. In his report to the court, Dr. James said that Randall had been "quickly able to form a relationship" to him during two diagnostic play interviews. He decided against additional interviews "because of Randall's growing attachment and his obvious confusion about my role." From these two play sessions he had learned enough, he said, to know that Randall was clearly attached to both parents, was torn between them, was near panic about the dispute, and needed to remain in treatment.

During the course of his interviews with each parent, Dr. James had recommended to them that Randall remain in therapy. He reported that Mrs. Cooper, who had originally engaged Dr. Biddle, shared his view that treatment continue; and that Mr. Cooper, though he had no objection to treatment, believed that it was unnecessary and did not intend to pay for it. Dr. James said that both Mr. and Mrs. Cooper were loving parents. However, he explained to the court that Randall's interests would be best served by his mother because she understood his need for therapy and because therapy was more likely to be effective with parental support.

Dr. James closed his report to the court by stating: "It is imperative that Randall remain in treatment." This sentence underlies his recommendation

---

*Dr. Biddle had declined to conduct the evaluation. He indicated that his therapeutic work with Randall would be jeopardized if it were not kept separate from the custody dispute.

that Mrs. Cooper continue as primary caregiver. He did not suggest that treatment be a condition for custody, but he used her attitude toward treatment as one criterion for selecting the custodial parent. His assertion that Randall needed treatment might, however, have been mistakenly read as a recommendation—something often found in psychiatric evaluations—that the court *order* the custodial parent to provide for therapy.[14] Such restraints invade a parental prerogative, usurping a decision that ultimately must be left to parents except, of course, in cases of proven neglect or other statutory grounds for intervention. Custody was determined, after all, in order to provide Randall with a parent responsible for deciding what he needed on a day-to-day basis.

Professional persons, whether in direct or indirect contact with children in the placement process, must avoid gratuitous assertions of parental prerogatives. The framework of the placement system makes this difficult. When the child placement process in invoked, parental autonomy is challenged, and the parental role is easily disrupted. Professional participants are made responsible by statute and by judicial precedent for ordering and enforcing conditions of custody with regard to matters that parents usually determine. Though professional persons may have "to live with their decisions in the sense that they know what they have done, they don't often know what it means to the people in the sense that they don't have to live with the people. . . ."[15] They don't have the opportunity to respond to changing needs in the give-and-take of a day-to-day family relationship and to correct, if they could, their mistakes of judgment. Restraint in the exercise of such parent-like authority is the hallmark of good professional work.

Therefore, professional participants in the child placement process must, in each case, ask themselves and each other:

- "Are we acting to further our professional assignments, or are we usurping a parental prerogative?"
- "How can we do our jobs without confusing the child about the extent and meaning of our relationships with her—without harming her relationship to her parents, to her family?"
- "Do we mean what we say to the child? Do we intend to keep the promise we made? Even if we do, should we make it?

By addressing these questions, professional persons can help assure that the degree of intrusion on family integrity will be no greater than that which is necessary to fulfill the function of the state's intervention. Minimizing this intrusion is in the child's best interest.

CHAPTER 22

Softhearted and Hardheaded

I n the last chapter we noted, without elaborating, that good professional work requires humanity as well as expertise. Put another way, the good professional person in the child placement process must be both softhearted and hardheaded. These attributes complement rather than contradict each other. The professional person whose facile sympathy interferes with making unpalatable, though necessary, choices is neither hardheaded nor softhearted. The expert who makes hard choices and implements them with kindness and sympathy to the adult or child whom they may hurt is both. The softhearted factor rests on the capacity of professionals to draw on their emotions in ways that are not exploitative either of themselves or of those they serve—promising or implying no more than they are able and willing to provide. Thus a judge who comforts a child about to be placed by assuring her that "you can come to see me any time and talk to me" must be prepared, as the judge who made that promise in Emily's case was not, to carry out his promise.

Softheartedness cannot be ritualized. It requires understanding, genuine humanness, and honest sympathy. Humanness is not evidenced when lawyers, doctors, social workers, nurses, and other professional persons think that they can establish rapport with new adult clients or patients by automatically calling them by their first names. It is not that the use of the first name is always inappropriate. Rather, such practices "generally applied (applied, that is, without consideration of differences) are experienced as indifference."[1] If softheartedness is to complement hardheadedness, professionals must be responsive to the *individual* needs, circumstances, and characteristics of the persons with whom they deal.[2] This capacity is illustrated by the three cases that follow.

Softheartedness in the Way a Judge Announces His Decision—*Maggie*

Judge Tim Murphy had to decide whether nine-year-old Maggie should remain with her foster parents, with whom she had lived since her eighth day of life, or be returned to her biological mother. Having found, following a four-day hearing, that it would not be in Maggie's interest to be returned to her mother, Judge Murphy asked the parties to come to his chambers. He immediately informed them of his decision. He departed from his usual practice of keeping the parties waiting until he had time to write and file his opinion. He modified this procedure in order to end as quickly as possible the painful uncertainty under which Maggie and her parents, both foster and biological, had been living. Thus he spared them long days and nights of anxiously wondering what their fates would be. This softhearted procedure in no way infringed on the hardheaded substantive choice he made.[3]

An Institution Promotes Softheartedness in Its Care of Children

The pediatric unit of the Royal Hobart Hospital in Tasmania, Australia, provides an example of how the softhearted factor can become an integral component of a hardheaded institutional setting. The hospital recognized that "child care requires that: (a) children receive rapid, efficient and effective investigation and management of the condition which necessitated their admission [the hardheaded factor]; [and] (b) provision is made for the other needs of children and their families. These needs must cover the intellectual, emotional, and social requirements of [these] children [the softhearted factor]."[4] The hospital recognized that "[m]odern therapy may be highly effective, but it often involves the usage of drugs and equipment which in themselves may produce stress to young patients and their relatives."[5]

To assure that the *individual needs of different children* are met, parents are asked to complete a personal information sheet containing such details as the child's food likes and dislikes, sleeping times and position, favorite toys and games, words for wanting to go to the toilet, perception of her illness, and preferred ways of being comforted when in distress.[6] Further, sensitive to the fears of *all children*:

> [In order to] make the atmosphere less threatening . . . doctors and medical students do not wear white coats and nurses wear attractive aprons over their uniforms. Children are no longer tied into bed, and foldup beds have been purchased so that parents can sleep beside their children. The window in single cubicles have been curtained and . . . have been turned into parent-child units. . . . We encourage one of the parents to stay with the child and, if space allows it, we take in both if that is what they want. We allow visiting at any time but we recommend suitable rest periods for the patients depending on their ages. Visitors can be

siblings, school friends, or any relative, and staff is encouraged to make them feel welcome.[7]

A Physician's Softheartedness Toward a Child in Surgery—*Larry*

Young Dr. Amos Eztin intuitively brought a softheartedness to his relationship with four-and-a-half-year-old Larry. Larry was hospitalized for anemia and weight loss. After examination and evaluation he was taken to surgery for removal of a malignant growth in his abdomen. There had been no explicit preparations for the hospitalization, anesthesia, or surgery. It was assumed he was too young to understand.

Larry cried as he was placed on the gurney, and he asked Dr. Eztin to stay with him. The young physician had become quite fond of this reflective, charming child and his parents. He accompanied Larry to the operating room, where Larry asked at each point what was going to happen next. Dr. Eztin answered as best he could. As the preparations were made to anesthetize Larry, the child was panic stricken. Looking at the masked men and women around him, glancing at those sitting on the benches of the old-fashioned amphitheater, he cried out, "What are you going to do to me?" Dr. Eztin became anxious and self-conscious, but his concern for Larry enabled him to take the child's hand and haltingly explain that the doctors and nurses wanted to help him with the growth in his tummy that made him feel weak and sick. Larry interrupted, crying, "No! Why does the man want me to blow away the funny stuff?" Dr. Eztin explained, "He wants to give you a smell medicine so you can sleep. Then it won't hurt while the doctor takes out the growth in your tummy." Larry cried, "I want Mommy to sing me to sleep!" Dr. Eztin explained, "Mommy can't be here." Larry sobbed, "You sing to me." The young doctor gulped and began to hum Brahms' "Lullaby." Larry quieted down, clutched his doctor's hand, and gradually accepted the anesthesia.

At a time of overwhelming fear, Larry was holding on to his yearning for and memory of a soothing, safe closeness to his mother. He made a desperate effort to use the past as he faced a frightening, dangerous present. Dr. Eztin responded to the child's need for the parent who could not be present.* Realizing that he had not been prepared for this challenge by his academic and clinical education, Dr. Eztin dipped into his own past for memories and experiences that would answer Larry's need. Dr. Eztin later reflected, "Isn't it

---

*Hardheaded policies, like softhearted ones, should be open to question. A review of this hospital policy might consider whether parents should be permitted to accompany their child into the operating room.

ironic that, after all my medical training, it was my mother who prepared me for that situation?"

A Child Care Worker's Softheartedness Toward a Child in a Residential Nursery—*Tony*

Tony's mother had died when he was three years old, following a long illness that had left her unable to care for him. Before coming to a residential nursery, Tony had passed through many foster homes. He had received one shock of separation after another and had finally withdrawn completely into himself. However, he gradually emerged from his shell and became fiercely attached to Mary, one of the nurses who looked after him. His soldier father visited him only rarely. On one such visit, when Tony was almost four, his father introduced a young woman to Tony as "your new mummy." When the visit was over, Tony, who was "greatly impressed by his father calling him 'son'," asked: "Mary, will you call me 'son' like my daddy does?" When she said that she would rather not, because he was really not her son, he agreed that she might continue to call him by her pet name for him, so long as she called no one else by the same name.[8]

Mary was able to respond to Tony's need for a special relationship with her, without encouraging him to think of her as his mother.

Professional participants, including the administrators and staff of institutions, must ask:

- "Is this routine procedure or policy essential to our task, or does it unnecessarily infringe on a child's relationship with her family?"
- "Am I about to say something that will unnecessarily undermine a child's relationship to her parents or other adult caregivers?"
- "Are my affectionate and positive feelings for the child interfering with my carrying out my professional work?"
- "Am I using the child as an outlet for my own emotional needs?"

If professional persons ignore the limits of their assignments; if they are guided by personal preferences rather than by professional training and experience; if, out of sentimental feeling for the child, they act as if they were the parent that they are not and cannot be, they are not being softhearted. Unaccompanied by hardheaded willingness to face facts, their actions can only bring disappointment to the child.

If professional persons are alert to the danger of exceeding their competence and authority—if they understand the need for drawing lines, and for making their actions both visible to themselves and open to challenge by others—they demonstrate hardheadedness that translates into softheartedness. They will help to ensure for the child whose interests they serve what she needs most: strong bonds with an autonomous parent.

PART NINE

The Compleat Professional

CHAPTER 23

In the Best Interests of the Child

G ood professional practice necessitates weighing, balancing, and resolving conflicting demands, expectations, and pressures. We have described, in their multiple guises, some of the quandaries that confront professionals in the child placement process:

- They ought not to be swayed from professional standards by personal preference or sympathy for a particular adult or child.
- They should not stray beyond the boundaries of their own professional training into the territory of another discipline.
- They should not act on experience-based knowledge from another discipline if to do so would contravene the dictates of their own professionally informed judgment or negate the basis for their participation in the process.
- They should recognize that they may not be able to perform two different roles in relation to the same family, though each role comports with their professional training.
- They should not confuse the child they serve by acting like the parent they are not.
- At the same time, good professionals are expected not to lose their humanness and to bring to their work the wisdom they have acquired through experience working with families and with other professionals.

It is in the best interests of the child for all of the professional participants to recognize that neither separately nor together do they make or make up for an ordinary, unperfect parent. Their special knowledge is general to all children, and their function in the placement process is to enhance each child's opportunity to have a parent whose knowledge is general but to whom the child is special.

REFLECTIONS

I n writing and rewriting this volume, we have been constantly aware of a pressure within us to use the legal system to meet every situation in which a child needs help. We had to remind ourselves that neither law, nor medicine, nor science has magical powers and that there is no societal consensus about what is "best" or even "good" for all children. More than that, we had to address the tension between the fear of encouraging the state to violate a family's integrity before intervention is justified and the fear of inhibiting the state until it may be too late to protect the child whose well-being is threatened.

We respect the parental rights that are based on the fact of reproduction. We see the biological connection as a powerful motivating force for most parents to provide their children with continuous affectionate and responsible care. But we recognize that a child's attachments and healthy development do not rest on biology alone. They ultimately depend on the adult caregiver's affection—reciprocated by the child—and day-to-day attention to the child's needs. Moreover, society's faith in the blood tie exists side by side with a growing apprehension about the general deterioration and dissolution of family life and about the plight of many children whose parents fail to discharge their responsibilities. Thus, moves *against* and *for* state-sponsored intrusion upon parental autonomy vie with each other in a world where parental authority is frequently abusive, harmful, and detrimental to the child; where the child's essential tie to her parents ceases to be beneficial in families torn internally by parental violence or indifference; where state interference, under the cloak of the child's best interests, is sometimes no more than the wielding of power by authoritarian figures who try to impose their own standards on differently minded parents; and where well-intentioned rescue attempts may serve merely to destroy remaining family attachments while failing to provide children with the necessary substitutes.

Under existing policies and practices, the courts and social service agencies can be charged with doing too little, and often too late, to safeguard children's growth toward healthy adulthood. Battered infants may be returned to the same parents who have harmed them, and who may do so again. Attempts on a child's life may not be considered sufficient to bar the same parents from later access to their victim, regardless of that child's lack of trust and fear of repetition.[1] A parent's abandonment of a helpless infant, leaving her to starve in a deserted apartment, does not automatically terminate that parent's right to delay or prevent her adoption or to visit her in her new "place of safety" and interfere with her caregiving.

Under existing policies and practices, state authorities may be charged with doing too much, or doing it without sufficient justification. Conditions deemed chaotic and unsanitary in a parental home may prompt authorities to disperse a family before inquiring into the members' ties to each other and without recognizing the distress caused by the disruption of these ties. In matters of health, judges may deem it their duty to impose their own medical preference without regard to that of the parents. Failure to recognize and respect cultural differences in the way parents interact with their children may result in removal of children from their parents based on a state agency's culture-bound perception of abuse.* The duty to report cases of suspected child battering, instead of being the benefit intended, may expose innocent parents to harassment and distress and may discourage them from seeking medical help for their child.

Under existing policies and practices, the combination of too much and too little official action is evident in the area of foster placement. By not doing enough to keep families together; by failing to restrict foster care to children who have a real chance of being returned to their absent parents in a "short time"; by moving children from placement to placement in the interests of absent parents; and by removing children in long-term foster or adoptive homes in order to return them to long-absent biological parents, the state interferes with the attachments that are essential for a child's well-being.

Under existing policies and practices, the child's placement may be explicitly used, not to serve the child's present interest, but to remedy a past wrong done to an adult by another adult or by agents of the state.

---

*See Appendix A, "We Want Our Children Back."

Under existing policies and practices, professional participants may overstep the boundaries of their expertise; they may fail to recognize that they cannot perform two different roles in relation to the same child or family; and they may fail to respect the difference between being caring experts and usurpers of parental autonomy, thus confusing the child by acting like the parents they are not.

This is the muddled situation that we have sought to address.

In doing so, we have tried to hold in check our rescue fantasies and to urge that the state be authorized to intervene if and only if it can provide the child in jeopardy with a *less detrimental alternative.* We had to acknowledge that safeguarding the well-being of every child will be frustrated by the limits of our knowledge, by the limitations of all those who seek to help, and consequently by society's need to restrict coercive intervention to "objectively" definable grounds. This has meant, as does the drawing of any line, leaving out some children whom we would wish to protect. To do otherwise would have required—if only because of the inherent ambiguity of words—the inclusion of many children and families whom it would be arbitrary, if not harmful, to cover. Overinclusion would have meant leaving agents of the state with too much discretion.

Because harm is inherent in every intrusion on family integrity, we decided to err on the side on nonintrusiveness. In a continuing reexamination of the implications of our preferences for minimum state intervention on *de facto* family relationships and for making the child's interests paramount, we sought always to place ourselves in the position of children of different ages, of different developmental phases, and of different backgrounds. We established the correlative principles of least intrusive invocation, least intrusive adjudication, and least intrusive disposition. These principles are to be applied always in relation to ongoing, not necessarily *de jure,* family units. From the child's vantage point as a member of a family, we sought always to restrict coercive intervention to actual and threatened harm about which there is a consensus, and only when there is a reasonable expectation that intrusion will be more beneficial than injurious to the child. In this way we sought to confront our fear of state and professional participants doing too little or too much, or acting too early or too late, being too hardhearted or too softheaded.

The law's commitment to respect parental rights does not mean that children are to be regarded as property. However, sometimes they are treated as such. This misperception is reinforced by language that emphasizes the rights rather than duties of adults. The filing of a birth certificate is thought of as an assignment of a child to adults rather than the other way around. Likewise, divorce decrees award custody of the child to one of the competing adults rather than awarding a custodial parent to the child.

The vocabulary of placement ought to be reconceptualized to force focus where it belongs—on parental responsibility to satisfy a child's fundamental right to caring parents.

In our search for a reasonably just law for children and their families we have been mindful of Grant Gilmore's observation:

> Law reflects but in no sense determines the moral worth of a society. A reasonably just society will reflect its values in a reasonably just law. The better the society, the less law there will be. In Heaven there will be no law and the lion will lie down with the lamb. An unjust society will reflect its values in an unjust law. The worse the society the more law there will be. In Hell there will be nothing but law and due process will be meticulously observed.[2]

Were we living in a better society, there would be no need for this volume. But there is a need to try to contribute, even in a small way, to making our world a little less unperfect for our children. Thus, by establishing guidelines for disposition in Book One; by defining, in relatively precise terms, justifications for state intrusion into family relationships in Book Two; and by emphasizing in Book Three that it is in the best interests of the child for all professional participants to recognize that neither separately nor together do they make or make up for a parent, we hope to have provided a basis for a more balanced view of the problem and for a more just regulation of decisions and procedures that will safeguard, for as many children as possible, their permanent membership in a caring family.

The child's best interests will be served by providing the least detrimental alternative.

Appendix A

"WE WANT OUR CHILDREN BACK"
ABC News *20/20* (August 18, 1995)

HUGH DOWNS: You are about to witness the destruction of a family. They came to this country determined to make a better life, foreigners imbued with the American spirit. They worked hard and long and finally achieved gratifying financial success. But then, a most outrageous turn of events shattered their happiness forever. The country that gave them so much took away their most precious possession—their two children. How could such a thing happen in America? Well, you'll see, as I did, that it was a clash of two very different cultures—ours and theirs.

[voice-over] Every Friday for most of his life, Sadri Krasniqi answers the ancient Islamic call to prayers, not in some distant land, but in Dallas, Texas. Prostrate before his God, he gives thanks to Allah and to America.

SADRI KRASNIQI: All people from all the world come here because thinking a free country, they can keep own religion.

HUGH DOWNS: [voice-over] A poor Albanian immigrant, he arrived here in 1971. Twenty years later, he had made it big, not in oil, but pizza.

SADRI KRASNIQI: We worked very long, seven days a week every day; 14, 13 hours a day.

HUGH DOWNS: [voice-over] It paid off. With his Albanian wife, Sabhete, at his side, the couple's English improved a little and their bank account a lot.

SABHETE KRASNIQI: Thanks a lot. You have a nice day.

CUSTOMER: You bet. You do the same.

HUGH DOWNS: [voice-over] With four thriving restaurants, Sadri and Sabhete became American citizens, Sam and Cathy. They had it all—a suburban home with a swimming pool for their two kids and friends. But for the past six years, the Krasniqis have fought

Show: *20/20* (ABC, 9:00 P.M. ET); transcript #1533-1. Used with permission.

229

Texas legal authorities over the future of their own children. Their oldest, Urtim, is nick-named Tim. At 10, he had a passion for Korean martial arts. Little Lema had a smile that lit up their lives. In Albanian, she called Sam 'bobbi'—daddy.

SADRI KRASNIQI: I remember one day, Saturday, when she come in my restaurant and I'd be so hot she'd jump at me and kiss me around. I says, 'Lema, don't do that because I am sweat and I stink.' She says, 'Oh, daddy, you smell so nice to me.'

HUGH DOWNS: [voice-over] Sam passed on his Muslim faith to his children. They were taught not to eat pork, to show traditional Albanian respect for the family home. His kids were his pride and joy.

SADRI KRASNIQI: I work only for those children, to make them happy, to get every-thing—to get a good life.

HUGH DOWNS: [voice-over] The good life crumbled in 1989 at this school gym. Tim was in a tournament. A parent had to attend. As Sam videotaped his son and played with Lema on his lap, a woman sitting behind him called the suburban Plano police. In a state-ment, the woman swore Sam had fondled Lema's most private parts. Two undercover cops confirmed the behavior. Sam Krasniqi was arrested on the spot, charged with a hideous crime—sexually molesting a child, his own four year old daughter.

SADRI KRASNIQI: How can I think about my children about sex, a girl four and a half years old, I just can't imagine. I just can't believe it.

SABHETE KRASNIQI: Everybody back home hugging and kissing and playing with their own children till they start in the school.

HUGH DOWNS: [voice-over] The day of his arrest, Sam said he had patted Lema in the genital area, but innocently and affectionately, in the custom of his homeland. The police case hinged on one question—was it only a cultural misunderstanding or brazen child abuse?

DR. PAUL PRESCOTT: My reaction was at first one of stunned disbelief. Sexual abuse is not something that occurs in public, as a rule.

HUGH DOWNS: [voice-over] Dr. Paul Prescott is the state's leading authority on abused children. He was the first medical doctor to examine Lema and Tim Krasniqi at the re-quest of the Texas Child Protective Agency. He found no evidence of mistreatment.

DR. PAUL PRESCOTT: Nothing that would substantiate a claim of sexual abuse.

HUGH DOWNS: [voice-over] Family court prosecutor David Cole didn't accept that finding. Dr. Prescott never testified in the case. Cole has no doubts that it was child abuse.

DAVID COLE: It's almost just impossible to believe that this sort of activity could be going on in a public gymnasium. But all of those witnesses who were there all came to the same conclusion and that was [that] the activity was taking place.

GARY NOBLE: They didn't try to understand Cathy and Sam Krasniqi.

HUGH DOWNS: [voice-over] Gary Noble is the Krasniqis' current attorney.

GARY NOBLE: They never tried to understand their folk ways and their mores. They simply imposed our folk ways and mores upon them and then they required them to figure it out and by the time they figured out what was going on, their children were gone.

HUGH DOWNS: [voice-over] Forbidden by a judge from seeing his children, Sam Krasniqi was in a daze. He was pressured to admit wrongdoing, but his faith in American justice and his sense of Albanian honor didn't allow it.

SADRI KRASNIQI: I have to go in front of the judge and to lie in court and I never lie in my life. Also, I have to lie to my children and my children would grow up who says, 'Daddy, why you said something like that and you never did it?'

HUGH DOWNS: [voice-over] For six months, Sam was kept away from Tim and Lema. Cathy finally gave in to her children's pleas and took them to see their dad at the restaurant. It was a direct violation of the court order.

DAVID COLE: There's a protection issue. The children were endangered by the mother's activity, and that's the standard for a termination in Texas.

HUGH DOWNS: [voice-over] Termination of parental rights. For Sam and Cathy, it was the legal equivalent of the death penalty.

[interviewing] If you had believed that the charges against Sam were true, what would you have done?

SABHETE KRASNIQI: I would kill him. He knows that.

HUGH DOWNS: [voice-over] In family court, the Krasniqis were tried as unfit parents. Judge Harold Gaither believes Sam's case was hurt when he denied touching Lema at all.

JUDGE HAROLD GAITHER: I think that destroyed his credibility.

HUGH DOWNS: Three doctors examined Lema and only one found possible evidence of child abuse. That same doctor testified against Sam Krasniqi here in family court. A therapist testified against him, too, the same therapist who insisted that Sam admit his wrongdoing, and finally, the jury did not see or hear from the Krasniqi children, but it didn't take them long to decide the family's fate. The Krasniqis' parental rights were terminated, their children lost to them forever.

JUDGE HAROLD GAITHER: This jury in this case decided that this man committed conduct which endangered the physical or emotional well being of his daughter and further, that terminating his parent-child relationship with her was in the child's best interest, the same question for the son.

THERAPIST: Has your therapist talked to you about your dad?

HUGH DOWNS: [voice-over] With their case on appeal, Cathy was allowed supervised monthly visitations with the two Muslim children, by then in foster care.

SABHETE KRASNIQI: I love you very much.

TIM: I love you, too.

HUGH DOWNS: [voice-over] During one visit, she was dismayed to see Tim wearing a Jesus T-shirt and Lema, a Christian cross. The foster family, she learned, made them attend Christian services and there was more.

SABHETE KRASNIQI: Why are you crying, huh? Why you not tell mommy why you cry?

HUGH DOWNS: [voice-over] In tears, Lema admitted she'd also eaten pork at the foster home, against her religion.

SADRI KRASNIQI: We are Muslim. We are Muslim. We no eat the pork and I don't know why they're giving—force the little children to eat the pork.

HUGH DOWNS: [voice-over] The strain, the Krasniqis say, drove Tim to the edge.

SABHETE KRASNIQI: He went to the second floor in the house where he was staying, in foster home, and he opened the window and he want to jump down. His sister ask him, 'Why you—what you doing, Tim?' 'I want to kill myself because I miss my mom.' Somehow, she pull his leg and she said, 'What I will do without you?'

HUGH DOWNS: [voice-over] The family's ordeal wasn't over. Sam now faced a second trial in criminal court. If convicted here of sexually molesting his daughter, he'd go to prison.

[on camera] In desperation, Sam flew here to Amherst to beg the help of a professor at the University of Massachusetts, a woman who spoke his language and who had studied Albanian culture for nearly four decades.

BARBARA HALPERN: He told me, 'I don't understand how Americans work. You want me to lie? I didn't do anything wrong. Is it wrong to love your daughter?'

HUGH DOWNS: [voice-over] Anthropologist Barbara Halpern immediately understood it was a collision of two cultures.

BARBARA HALPERN: He did nothing improper, but he had no idea that Americans might perceive his appearance of impropriety.

HUGH DOWNS: [voice-over] An expert on Albanian customs, Dr. Halpern told me child protective officials contacted her for guidance about the Krasniqi case. It was her expertise, years of studying and living with Albanians, that Texas social workers disregarded from the start.

BARBARA HALPERN: There's lots of kissing full on the lips, lots of hugging, lots of caressing, even fondling, what people might call fondling, but the important thing to understand is that there is no sexual intent.

HUGH DOWNS: [voice-over] Dr. Halpern showed me slides taken in the Krasniqis' homeland.

[interviewing] They're holding hands.

BARBARA HALPERN: These are two adult men holding hands. They might have embraced and kissed. Nothing extraordinary about that, and we see ordinary, everyday people in southern Europe doing exactly the same thing.

HUGH DOWNS: [voice-over] In America, too, as we found out when we visited the large Albanian community in Staten Island, New York. Like their forebears, these Americans remain an extraordinarily physical people. We also found the special affection between little girls and their fathers—the central issue in the Krasniqi case. In criminal court last year, Dr. Barbara Halpern's expert testimony made all the difference. Sam was found not guilty of molesting Lema. But it came too late. The family court decision was final and irreversible. Their children were gone.

[interviewing] Sam, would you have agreed to go to jail if it meant the children could stay with Cathy?

SADRI KRASNIQI: Absolutely, yes. I go for all my life in jail. Just to release my children.

HUGH DOWNS: In October, Tim and Lema Krasniqi were legally adopted by their foster parents and converted to Christianity. The Krasniqis were devastated and the Muslim community here outraged.

ALI SHEIK: This is incomprehensible to be happening in the United States of America.

HUGH DOWNS: [voice-over] Ali Sheik is a prominent Muslim businessman who learned of the children's plight last fall in a Dallas newspaper.

ALI SHEIK: This is considered absolute blasphemy in terms of forcibly conversion of somebody to another faith as far as the Muslim religion is concerned.

HUGH DOWNS: [voice-over] The Texas Child Protective Service declined to talk with us on camera. In a videotaped statement, a spokesperson summed up the case.

LINDA EDWARDS (Texas Department of Protective and Regulatory Services, Public Information Officer): Four and a half years later, after all court appeals by the parents were exhausted, the children were adopted. This is how our legal system works and we must work within the system we have.

HUGH DOWNS: [voice-over] Judge Gaither believes the children are better off in a Christian home.

JUDGE HAROLD GAITHER: It might be more damaging to the children to take them out of that stability that they've had and place them back with a Muslim family simply because they're Muslim.

ALI SHEIK: I think that's absolutely baloney. Absolutely trash. I think given the circumstances, that if these kids know that there are not going to be any pressures on them, I think they'll come back to their parents.

HUGH DOWNS: [voice-over] The kids don't have that choice. They're permitted no contact with their natural parents. The Krasniqis are left with home videotapes of children they no longer know. It's a record of the death of a family.

SABHETE KRASNIQI: Every moment it was happy being with those kids.

HUGH DOWNS: [voice-over] To pay legal bills, the Krasniqis sold off their restaurants and pizza equipment. They recently closed down the last one. Now without steady work, Sam cleans the pool he put in for the kids. Cathy keeps their rooms immaculate, hoping they'll return. She still prepares the ethnic dishes the whole family once loved. But without children, neither parent has much of an appetite for food or anything else in life.

SABHETE KRASNIQI: Our life is over anyway without kids. If we get the kids, we will make the best of it. We will make everything again. Without kids, there's no life for us anymore.

HUGH DOWNS: From the start, it seems there was a lack of common sense in the Krasniqi case. Would anyone really molest his own child in front of hundreds of people? Why didn't jurors hear from the doctor who first examined the children and found no evidence of abuse or get to see or hear from the children themselves and learn something of their culture? On top of that, it took only eight months for the Texas child protective system and the family court to permanently take away the Krasniqis' children. But it took five years before a criminal court acquitted Sam Krasniqi of all sexual abuse charges. It's hard to understand why, but the two systems are separate and their decisions independent and in this case, one system of American justice seemed too swift and too blind.

Appendix B

PREFACE

to *Beyond the Best Interests of the Child*

It happens often enough that two authors join forces in producing a publication in which their individual contributions are inextricably intermingled. It is much less frequent for three people to embark on such a task and to achieve a result which does justice to each writer yet creates the final impression of a unified whole. To observe such a venture from its inception is an unusual privilege which I enjoyed.

The three authors of this volume are authorities in their particular fields, though each has on previous occasions applied his specialized knowledge in collaborations with colleagues in adjacent fields. They are also representative of three different institutions, the Yale Law School, the Hampstead Child-Therapy Clinic, London, and the Child Study Center, Yale University.

The impact of the Law School was obvious in the choice of the problem—the criticism of the existing laws governing the disposal of children and the attempt to formulate a revised code. Experience gained in the Hampstead Clinic was condensed in the chapters and paragraphs defining the relations between children and their adult environment, as well as in many items dealing with their changing needs during the period of growth and development. The Child Study Center contributed a wealth of clinical experience gained from actual cases of broken families, displaced children, and mishandled decisions about their fate.

Observing the three authors at their work, I was most fascinated by those moments when individual opinions clashed and lively battles ensued during which each contributor obstinately clung to and defended a conviction of his own. Objections of this kind sometimes concerned minor points of mere terminology, such as the new use of the expression *wanted child,* which might lead to misunderstanding; at other times they raged around such vital issues as the complete abrogation of the biological parents' rights whenever these run counter to the child's welfare. But even disagreements which at first appeared insoluble were resolved after much discussion and argumentation and, sometimes, after an intervening night's sleep. In any event, the high excitement revealed the enormous investment in their joint venture and mutual collaboration. At moments of tension the atmosphere was also relieved by humor, for example, when one of them to his surprise discovered that what he stressed had not been forgotten and completely neglected; when another remembered nostalgically how easy and comfortable it had been to write books

235

all on her own; or when at a point of rare agreement somebody remarked that their concerted action sounded to him like that of a symphony orchestra.

What I witnessed, finally, was the emergence of the benevolent figure of an enlightened judge who in his person embodied the knowledge and many personal characteristics of the three authors, i.e., sound knowledge of the law combined with the hard-won psychoanalytic knowledge of child development.

The idea for a book was first discussed in 1969, when plans were made for a series of individual essays to be contributed and signed by each of the authors. At the next meeting in 1970 at Yale, New Haven, this plan was scrapped in favor of the present sequence, which presents the basic concepts and definitions, guidelines, and their applications. The common work continued at Rathmore near Baltimore, Eire and Maresfield Gardens, Hampstead, London, where the final working over took place in 1973. The fictitious New Haven–Hampstead Court bears witness to two of these locations, while the name of Baltimore given to the Judge is a reminder of the third.

—Dorothy Burlingham

PREFACE

to *Before the Best Interests of the Child*

R eaders may welcome some explanation why our three authors reversed the sequence of events by tackling the problems of *beyond* the best interests of the child earlier than those that do come *before.* I can only surmise that in 1973 the difficulties and mistakes surrounding child placement loomed so large and clamored so insistently for solution that the questions when and for what reasons these children find themselves at the mercy of state disposition were pushed into the background. However, as a listener to their discussions, I can testify that even at the earlier date the points concerning protection for the parent-child relationship or the necessary state intrusion into it were never absent from the authors' minds. They were merely biding their time, waiting for the already anticipated writing of a second book.

Three authors with different backgrounds and on the basis of different experiences cannot be expected to tackle one and the same task in one and the same manner. Again a common language had to be devised to satisfy the needs of two professions and of the lay reader. In addition, however, agreement had to be reached on a number of questions about the advantages and disadvantages of state intervention, about the merits and demerits of present-day parents in general, and about the risk when parents are entrusted with the final say in the serious matters of child rearing, which used to be their sole prerogative in bygone days.

Discussion, no doubt, profited from previous experience. While mutual stimulation, pressure toward logical argumentation, and detailed exposition of points had remained the same, the participants knew more of each other's preferences, convictions, and idiosyncrasies. Accordingly controversies, even though perhaps heated at the beginning, were solved more quickly and opinions merged more readily.

That every statement in this book has been weighed and doubted until confirmed by the working of three critical minds has, I trust, not detracted from the ease with which the book can be read and, therefore, from the reader's satisfaction and approval of the final formulations.

—Dorothy Burlingham

PREFACE

to *In the Best Interests of the Child*

T his book, one in a series by these authors addressed to the best interests of children in custody and placement situations, should make those of us now involved in such work look closely at ourselves and the way in which we approach and carry out our professional roles. For those entering the field it is an introduction to the challenges, complexities, and dangers that lie along the paths traversed by clinical and legal decision-makers. The authors have taken a giant step toward the delineation of practices for improving the lives of children who come to our attention.

The very beginning of the book sets the tone, opening with the statement that "The professional participants in the child placement process do not, either separately or together, make or make up for a parent." The final chapter is an eloquent summation of the attitudes, behavior, and wisdom the authors counsel us to strive for in the best interests of our child clients and patients: to recognize the crucial importance of the "ordinary devoted parent"; to distinguish between professionally informed belief and personal value preferences; to refrain from exceeding one's competence and authority; to learn to work with others who have responsibilities in the child placement process; to avoid the dangers of assuming dual roles in a single case; to recognize the difference between the caring expert and the usurper of parental authority; to be unafraid to incorporate the view that good professional practice requires softheartedness as well as hardheadedness.

The authors have brought to this book their sophistication as theoreticians of law and psychoanalysis and as practitioners with years of hands-on experience dealing with child placement issues and problems. An integral part of the process through which they have arrived at the present writing has been the Child Placement Conflicts Seminar at the Yale Child Study Center. As a participant with Joseph and Sonja Goldstein and Albert Solnit in those meetings since 1977, I am vividly aware of the process through which our group of lawyers, child psychiatrists, pediatricians, psychologists, and social workers struggled as each of us tried to clarify our professional responsibilities and boundaries around the real-life cases with which we were concerned. The discussions were wide-ranging in scope, certainly heated, and sometimes combative as we presented and argued about the clinical material, the social situations, the possible options, and the tasks we had undertaken. The complexity and poignancy of many of the situations—some horrendous beyond imagining—the fact that in many situations there was no solution that seemed beneficial for all parties involved, our dissatisfaction at the imperfections of our knowledge and our systems of care and protection beset us and often outweighed any satisfaction we might feel at having contributed to a constructive or least detrimental plan for a child. The clarity and conviction with which the issues are defined in this book, I believe, owe much to the fact that they were fired in the crucible of these seminars.

In the early years of their existence the seminar sessions were intense and exhausting. The reasons for the intensity and exhaustion, beyond the usual concerns about whether one has performed competently as a professional under the scrutiny of one's colleagues, can be clearly understood when one reflects upon the issues dealt with in this book. But an interesting and relieving state gradually came into being in the seminars at least among the veteran members. Though the individual cases are now no less complex and difficult or just plain awful, we have arrived at a stage in our professional growth when we experience the situations and feelings they engender as signals that alert us to problems without overwhelming us and that suggest certain professional directions and procedures based on what we have learned about child placement.

Among many important points made in this book there are two that in my view are of special significance for even the most experienced and competent professionals: the warning against the danger of allowing personal values to distort professional decisions, and the hazards of trying to perform dual roles in reference to one case. It may well be that we have the greatest difficulty in learning to resist the temptation to allow personal preferences to modify or determine professional judgment. It is a task more difficult than achieving reasonable mastery of the knowledge base of our professional practice. The risk of deciding what one prefers, then looking for data that support the preference can be so insidious as to capture the unwary. It is not easy for any of us to keep such things straight, especially since professional knowledge and personal values at times coincide. Because the hope that parents and children will not be lost to each other is very strong in most of us, there are times when hopes and wishes weaken carefully considered scientifically based opinions. One way of guarding against the clinical errors of wishful thinking is to share responsibilities with colleagues having agreed on the task each will undertake and helping each other to keep the roles clearly defined.

This book is, in the best sense, a state-of-the-art discussion and shows how many of our practices can immediately be improved while looking toward a continuing refinement in our professional knowledge.

—Sally Provence

Appendix C

ACKNOWLEDGMENTS
to Earlier Volumes

Beyond the Best Interests of the Child

In the preparation of this book many individuals and several institutions have encouraged and facilitated our efforts. We wish to acknowledge our appreciation for this support.

For critical comment on various drafts of the manuscript: Laura C. Coddling, Steven Goldberg, Sonja Goldstein, Hillary Rodham.

For their assistance: Alexander M. Bickel, Robert Burt, Marshall Cohen, L. de Jong, John Hart Ely, Max Gitter, John Griffiths, Jay Katz. Seymour L. Lustman, Sally A. Provence, Amos Shapira, Martha Solnit.

For encouragement and a peaceful atmosphere in which to work: Kingman Brewster, Jr., President, Yale University; Abraham S. Goldstein, Dean, Law School, Yale University; John Perry Miller, Director, Institution for Social and Policy Studies, Yale University.

For library assistance: Robert E. Brooks, Gene Coakley, James M. Golden, Isaiah Shein, Charles S. Smith.

For permission to reproduce provisions of the Uniform Marriage and Divorce Act, the Uniform Child Custody Jurisdiction Act, and the Revised Uniform Adoption Act: the National Conference of Commissioners on Uniform State Laws.

For financial assistance (travel, study, and research grants): the Field Foundation, the Ford Foundation, the Foundation for Research in Psychoanalysis, the Freud Centenary Fund, the Anna Freud Foundation, the Grant Foundation, the Institution for Social and Policy Study, the Andrew Mellon Foundation, the National Institute for Mental Health, and the New-Land Foundation.

For secretarial assistance: Yvonne M. Bowkett, Billie Hutching, Geraldine Formica, Gina Lewis, Sophie Powell, Elizabeth H. Sharp, Jean Yurczyk.

For creative and firm editing: Lottie M. Newman.

Before the Best Interests of the Child

Many individuals and several institutions have encouraged and facilitated our writing of this book. We wish to acknowledge our appreciation for their support.

For creative and demanding editorial assistance at all stages of writing and for helping to translate many of our proposals into statutory language: Sonja Goldstein.

For critical comment and elbow-to-elbow editorial help on various drafts of the manuscript: Lon Babby, David De Wolf, Steven Goldberg, Laird Hart, Paula Herman, Andrea Hirsch, Martha Minow, Donn Pickett.

For their thoughts: Bruce Ackerman, Robert Burt, Robert M. Cover, Owen Fiss, Paul Gewirtz, Barbara Grant, Lionel Hersov, Carol Larson, Howard A. Levine, Benjamin Lopata, Burke Marshall, Neil Peck, Sally Provence, Spiros Simitis, Martha Solnit, George Stroh, Jeff Thaler, Michael Wald, Andrew Watson, Stephen Wizner.

For encouragement and a setting in which to think at work: Abraham S. Goldstein and Harry Wellington, Deans, Law School, and Robert Berliner, Dean, School of Medicine, Yale University.

For careful and thoughtful editing and indexing: Lottie M. Newman.

For library assistance: Robert E. Brooks, Arthur Charpentier, Gene Coakley, Isaiah Shein, Charles S. Smith.

For unstinting, cheerful, imaginative, and highly skilled preparation of the many drafts of manuscript: Liz Modena and Elizabeth H. Sharp.

For secretarial and photocopying assistance: Gina Bon, Albert Dingle, Gweneth Endfield, Russ Hentz, Walter Moriarty, Bea Nirenstein, Geraldine Perillo, Sophie Z. Powell, Ivy Weaver.

For generous and gratifying sustenance at all of our London meetings: Paula Fichtl.

For financial assistance (travel, study, and research grants): Elizabeth Dollard, The Ford Foundation, The Free Press, The Edna McConnell Clark Foundation, and the Office of Maternal and Child Health, DHEW.

In the Best Interests of the Child

Many individuals and several institutions have encouraged and facilitated our writing of this book. We wish to acknowledge our appreciation for their support.

For critical comment and elbow-to-elbow editorial help on various drafts of the manuscript: Jane W. Ellis, Catherine Mary Newell, and Paul Michael Schwartz.

For their thoughts and suggestions: Judith Areen, Daniel Braverman, Fredericka Breneman, E. Donald Elliott, Henry A. Finlay, Owen M. Fiss, Joshua Goldstein, Kathryn Lowell, Sophie Lowenstein, Martha L. Minow, Donn Pickett, Sally Provence, James and Joyce Robertson, Nancy Schwartz, Spiros Simitis, Ben Solnit, Dean and Marie Tegeler, Philip Tegeler, and Stephen Wizner, and the participants in the Child Placement Conflicts Seminar, Yale Child Study Center, 1977–1984, and in the Family Law Seminar, Yale Law School, Fall 1982.

For encouragement and a setting in which to think and work: Harry Wellington, Dean, Yale Law School; Robert Berliner and Leon Rosenberg, Deans, Yale School of Medicine; Aubrey L. Diamond, Director, Institute of Advanced Legal Studies, London University; Anne Bohm, Secretary of the Graduate School, The London School of Economics; and Arthur S. Sachs, senior partner of the law firm Arthur Sachs, Schpero, Berman & Shure.

For careful and thoughtful editing: Lottie M. Newman.

For indexing: Bonny Hart.

For patient, good-humored, creative, and precise processing of manuscript to book: George A. Rowland.

For library assistance: Robert E. Brooks, Donald Carter, Martha Clark, Morris L. Cohen, Gene Coakley, Tony Henderson, Mike Hughes, James Kennealy, and Sandra Trent.

For unstinting, cheerful, imaginative, and highly skilled preparation of the many drafts of manuscript: Juliana Flower, Dolores T. Gee, Elizabeth H. Sharp, and Elizabeth Voionmaa.

For secretarial and photocopying assistance: Gina Bon, Russ Hentz, Joanne E. Kittredge, and Walter Moriarty.

For generous and gratifying sustenance at all of our London meetings: Paula Fichtl.

For travel, study, and research grants: Elizabeth Dollard, The Free Press, Edna McConnell Clark Foundation, Saul Z. and Amy S. Cohen Family Foundation, John Simon Guggenheim Memorial Foundation, Irving B. Harris Foundation, and Florence and John Schuman Foundation.

NOTES

Chapter 1. Child Placement in Perspective

1. See Phillipe Aries, *Centuries of Childhood* (New York: Alfred A. Knopf, 1962).
2. See Jeremy Bentham, *Theory of Legislation* (Boston: Weeks, Jordan, 1840), Vol. I, p. 248. See also the opinion written in 1889 by Justice Brewer in *Chapsky v. Wood,* 26 Kan. Report 650 (1881), excerpted in Book One, Chapter 7.

Chapter 2. The Child-Parent Relationships

1. See Lillian Hellman, *An Unfinished Woman* (London: Penguin Books, 1972, pp. 12–13):

> There was a heavy fig tree on the lawn where the house turned the corner into the side street, and to the front and sides of the fig tree were three live oaks that hid the fig from my aunts' boarding-house. I suppose I was eight or nine before I discovered the pleasures of the fig tree. . . . The fig tree was heavy, solid, comfortable, and I had, through time, convinced myself that it wanted me, missed me when I was absent, and approved all the rigging I had done for the happy days I spent in its arms. . . .

2. Such reactions include fantastic anxieties, denial or distortion of reality, and reversal or displacement of feelings.
3. On the concept of the "gestational father," see Barbara Bennett Woodhouse, "Hatching the Egg: A Child-Centered Perspective on Parents' Rights," 14 *Cardozo L. Rev.* 1747 (1993).
4. "[T]he Constitution protects the sanctity of the family precisely because the institution of the family is deeply rooted in this nation's history and tradition." *Moore v. City of East Cleveland,* 431 U.S. 494, 503 (1977) (Justice Powell for a plurality of the Court). The parental role is "basic in the structure of our society." *Ginsberg v. New York,* 390 U.S. 629, 639 (1968).
5. The deficits in the psychological development of institutionalized infants, some of whom received excellent physical care, have been documented by many studies. See

Margaret A. Ribble, *The Rights of Infants* (New York: Columbia University Press, 1943); René A. Spitz, "Hospitalism: A Follow-up Report" (*Psychoanalytic Study of the Child,* 2:113–117, 1946); René A. Spitz and K. M. Wolf, "Anaclitic Depression" (*Psychoanalytic Study of the Child,* 2:313–342, 1946); John Bowlby, *Maternal Care and Mental Health* (Geneva: World Health Organization Monograph No. 2, 1951); H. L. Rheingold, *The Modification of Social Responsiveness in Institutionalized Babies,* Monographs of the Society for Research in Child Development, Vol. XXI, Serial No. 63, No. 2, 1956; M. D. Ainsworth et al., *Deprivation of Maternal Care: A Reassessment of Its Effects* (Geneva: World Health Organization, Public Health Papers 14,1962); Sally Provence and Rose C. Lipton, *Infants in Institutions* (New York: International Universities Press, 1962); Jill Berrick et al., "Specialized Foster Care and Group Home Care: Similarities and Differences in the Characteristics of Children in Care" (*Children and Youth Services Review,* Vol. 15 ([6]:453–473, 1993).

6. See, e.g., Uniform Adoption Act (1994) §1-104, Legal Relationship Between Adoptee and Adoptive Parent After Adoption:

> After a decree of adoption becomes final, each adoptive parent and the adoptee have the legal relationship of parent and child and have all the rights and duties of that relationship.

Adoption cancels out the legal rights of the biological parents (except where the adoptive parent is a stepparent, in which case the parental rights of only the outside parent are terminated). See Uniform Adoption Act (1994) §§1-105, 4-102. To safeguard their interests, even in cases where these run counter to the child's interests, either parental consent or termination of rights is generally an essential preliminary to adoption.

7. See, e.g., Ohio Rev. Code §3107.13 (1989), Probationary Period:

> A final decree of adoption shall not be issued and an interlocutory order of adoption does not become final, until the person to be adopted has lived in the adoptive home for at least six months after placement by an agency, or for at least six months after the department of human services or the court has been informed of the placement, and the department or the court has had an opportunity to observe or investigate the adoptive home, or in the case of adoption by a step-parent, until at least six months after the filing of the petition, or until the child has lived in the home for six months.

The Ohio law is drawn from The 1969 Revised Uniform Adoption Act. The 1994 Act does not include the six-month probationary period; however, it does leave the adoptive parents and child in limbo for six months pending the appellate period. See Uniform Adoption Act (1994) §§3-706, 3-707.

8. See, e.g., *New Haven Register,* Thursday, November 2, 1972, p. 70, col. 1:

Dear Ann Landers:
> The people who adopted me are the only parents I have ever known. They have been wonderful and everyone tells me how lucky I am.
> But there's this big break in my life. I need to find my real parents. I have to

know what the circumstances were that made them give me away. My imagination runs wild when I think about what might have happened that made them abandon me.

I think about these things more and more. It's getting so that I don't think about anything else. I have to learn the truth about myself so I can stop brooding. Don't tell me to forget it because I can't. I need some advice.

—Confused in Chicago

See also *New Haven Register,* Tuesday, February 20, 1973, p. 38, col. 3–4:

Dear Ann:
    May I speak to the young man who wants to find his real parents?

Dear Confused:
    If you were the baby I gave away, don't come knocking on my door. You have no real parents here. Your REAL parents are the loving couple who wanted a child. I didn't.
    Frankly, I think you are selfish to want two families. Count your blessings and don't look back. The parents who raised you love you and they are entitled to your total devotion. Forget about me.

—Straight Arrow

9. Cf. Thesi Bergmann in collaboration with Anna Freud, *Children in the Hospital* (New York: International Universities Press, 1965, pp. 22–23):

Psychoanalytic child psychology leaves no doubt that children are emotionally dependent on their parents and that this dependence is necessary for purposes of normal development; also, that relationships in a hospital are, at best, poor substitutes for family relationships. Once these facts are accepted, relaxation of visiting rules becomes an inevitable consequence.
    In Rainbow [Hospital], parents were given every opportunity to visit their children any time they liked, and to observe them during stressful as well as during easy times, in periods of physical therapy, pool activity, exercises, school, play, etc. Care was taken that parents and children could interact as they do at home, a child occasionally preferring to play with other children while the mother visited with other mothers or the nurse. Young children were especially eager to be put to bed and tucked in by their mothers, while older children preferred to be up with their visitors as long as possible. . . .
    Family ties were maintained further by the children making telephone calls to their homes and by all, except those in body casts, if they had progressed sufficiently in convalescence, going home occasionally for weekends.

Also see Kevin R. Grigsby, "Maintaining Attachment Relationships Among Children in Foster Care," *Families in Society,* Vol. 75 (5): 269–276, May 1994; John E. Poulin, "Kin Visiting and the Biological Attachment of Long-term Foster Children," *Journal of Social Service Research,* Vol. 15 (3–4): 65–79, 1992.

10. Foster parents used to be excluded from consideration as adoptive parents, but this is no longer invariably the case. New York, for instance, requires that foster care agreements contain the following language:

It is duly acknowledged by the parties hereto that pursuant to the law of the state of New York, a foster parent shall have preference in any proceedings to adopt the child subject to this agreement upon such child having been in the custody of such foster parent for a period in excess of twelve months (1 N.Y. Soc. Serv. Law §374 (1-a) (1992)).

11. In some cases in some states, a foster child who is not legally adopted may still participate in the estate of an intestate foster parent, taking under a label such as "equitable" or "virtual" adoption, or "adoption" by estoppel. See, e.g., *McGarvey v. State of Maryland,* 533 A.2d 690, 692–93 (Md. 1987) (recognizing doctrine of "equitable estoppel" and noting that 27 other jurisdictions do same); Jeffries, "Equitable Adoption: They Took Him Into Their Home and Called Him Fred," 58 Va. L. Rev. 727 (1972). But see *Proffitt v. Evans,* 433 S.W. 2nd 876 (Ky. 1968): "The common law did not provide for adoptions. Strict compliance with the adoption statutes has always been required. . . . To recognize a 'de facto' adoption would bring a condition of chaos to the law."

12. *Painter v. Bannister,* 140 N.W. 2d 152 (Iowa 1966) is an interesting celebrated case in point. There, in a *habeas corpus* action, a biological father sought to regain the custody of his seven-year-old son, whom he had left with the child's maternal grandparents (following his wife's death in an automobile accident two and one-half years earlier). The household of the grandparents was described as "stable, dependable, conventional, middleclass, midwest" and that of the biological parent as "unstable, unconventional, arty Bohemian, and probably intellectually stimulating." "It is not our prerogative," the appellate court asserted, "to determine custody upon our choice of one of two ways of life within normal and proper limits and we will not do so." It concurred with the trial judge's finding that both parties were proper and fit to serve as parents. While acknowledging a preference in law for the biological parent, the court weighed more heavily the child's welfare and concluded that the existing psychological parent-child relationship should not be disturbed.

> Mark has established a father-son relationship with [the grandfather] which he apparently had never had with his natural father. He is happy, well-adjusted and progressing nicely in his development. We do not believe it is for Mark's best interest to take him out of this stable atmosphere in the face of warnings of dire consequences from an eminent child psychologist and send him to an uncertain future in his father's home. Regardless of our appreciation of the father's love for his child and his desire to have him with him, we do not believe we have the moral right to gamble with this child's future . . . [*id.* at 158].

13. These guidelines also have substantial implications for child placement in juvenile delinquency proceedings; however, we do not explore those implications in this volume.

Chapter 3. Placement Decisions Should Safeguard the Child's Need
for Continuity of Relationships

1. See Anna Freud, *The Harvard Lectures,* ed. Joseph Sandler (London: Karnac Books, 1992, p. 133) (from lectures originally delivered in 1952):

> [C]onflicts in the human being and in the child are inevitable; they are expressions of the structure of the personality. Do not aim at having a child without conflict, do not aim to spare the child conflict. Equally, frustrations are inevitable. Wish fulfillment on demand does not lead to a development from the pleasure principle to the reality principle, something which distinguishes human beings from animals. What a study of the defense mechanisms would show you is that it is not the absence and presence of conflict, but, rather, the ways and means used to solve the conflict between the ego parts of the personality and the id parts—the drives; and that it is the choice of solutions which decides the normality or the abnormality of the future adult.

2. A large number of the children billeted without their families in wartime England developed enuresis. Many specific examples of regression following separation are recorded by Anna Freud and Dorothy Burlingham in *Infants Without Families: Reports on the Hampstead Nurseries (The Writings of Anna Freud,* Vol. III; New York: International Universities Press, 1973).

3. A not uncommon case history is found in *Carter v. United States,* 252 F.2d 608 (D.C. Cir. 1957). See also Anthony Heath et al., "Failure to Escape: A Longitudinal Study of Foster Children's Educational Attainment," *British Journal of Social Work,* Vol. 24 (3):241–260, June 1994; Emily McFadden, "The Inner World of Children and Youth in Care," *Community Alternatives: International Journal of Family Care,* Vol. 4 (1):1–17, Spring 1992.

4. Sakinah Salahu-Din and Stephan R. Bollman, "Identity Development and Self-Esteem of Young Adolescents in Foster Care," *Child and Adolescent Social Work Journal,* Vol. 11 (2):123–135, April 1994.

5. In "Young Children in Brief Separation: A Fresh Look," (*Psychoanalytic Study of the Child,* 26:264–315; New York: Quadrangle Books, 1971), James and Joyce Robertson compare two forms of substitute care for young children whose mothers were confined to the hospital. One group of children received foster care in the home of the Robertsons; another child was placed in a residential nursery. See also the films made by James and Joyce Robertson, *Young Children in Brief Separation* (films Nos. 1, 2, and 4; London: Tavistock Child Development Research Unit; New York: New York University Film Library, 1967–1971) and *John: 17 Months* (film No. 3, *ibid.,* 1969).

6. See *Smith v. Organization of Foster Families,* 431 U.S. 816 (1977), for an illustration of a system where periodic review, though mandated, is routinized and ineffective. And see Michael S. Wald, "Termination of Parental Rights" in *When Drug Addicts Have Children,* 195 (D. Besharov ed., 1994).

7. We thus reject the approach taken in the Revised Uniform Adoption Act (1969), which requires a period of at least six months after an agency placement before an adoption decree can become final—a longer period is required for other adoptions (Section 12) and an appeal procedure based on that used in ordinary civil actions (Section 15(a)).

The more recent Uniform Adoption Act (1994) continues to delay the finality of an adoption decree for six months (§§3-706, 3-707(d)). However, the 1994 Act does provide that appeals "must be heard expeditiously" (§3-707(a)).

8. The Uniform Adoption Act of 1953 provided in Optional §17 that adoptive parents could petition to annul "[i]f within two years after the adoption a child develops any serious and permanent physical or mental malady or incapacity as a result of conditions existing prior to the adoption and of which the adopting parents had no knowledge or notice. . . ."

Neither the Revised Uniform Adoption Act (1969) nor the Uniform Adoption Act (1994) has such a provision.

But see Kentucky Rev. Stat. §199.540(1) (1965), which provides that an adoption can be set aside by a decree of annulment if within five years the adopted child "reveals definite traits of ethnological ancestry different from those of the adoptive parents, and of which the adoptive parents had no knowledge or information prior to the adoption. . . ."

9. See *In Re Marriage of Carney*, 598 P.2d 36 (Ca. 1979), where the California Supreme Court reversed the lower court's ruling that had changed custody from father, with whom the children had been living for five years, to mother because the father had become a paraplegic:

> In this case of first impression we are called upon to resolve an apparent conflict between two strong public policies: the requirement that a custody award serve the best interests of the child, and the moral and legal obligation of society to respect the civil rights of its physically handicapped members, including their right not to be deprived of their children because of their disability. As will appear, we hold that upon a realistic appraisal of the present-day capabilities of the physically handicapped, these policies can both be accommodated. The trial court herein failed to make such an appraisal, and instead premised its ruling on outdated stereotypes of both the parental role and the ability of the handicapped to fill that role. Such stereotypes have no place in our law. Accordingly, the order changing custody on this ground must be set aside as an abuse of discretion. *Id.* at 36–37.

And see *Newton v. Riley*, 899 S.W.2d 509 (Ky. App. 1995), where the court held that HIV status of child's stepfather was not a ground for modifying custody. But see *Roe v. Roe*, 324 S.E.2d 691 (Va. 1985) in which a homosexual father lost custody of his daughter who had lived with him for six years because of his "continuous exposure of the child to his immoral and illicit relationship." (at 691)

§409(a) of the Uniform Marriage and Divorce Act compromises the continuity concept while trying to respond to it by providing a fixed period during which decrees may not be modified:

> No motion to modify a custody decree may be made earlier than two years after its date, unless the court permits it to be made on the basis of affidavits . . . that there is reason to believe that the child's present environment may endanger seriously his physical, mental, moral, or emotional health.

This problem may be greatly exacerbated by conflicting laws between states and between countries.

10. We would thus oppose such provisions as the following from the Uniform Marriage and Divorce Act:
    §407 [visitation.]

    (a) A parent not granted custody of the child is entitled to reasonable visitation rights unless the court finds, after a hearing, that visitation would endanger seriously the child's physical, mental, moral, or emotional health.
    (b) The court may modify an order granting or denying visitation rights whenever modification would serve the best interests of the child; but the court shall not restrict a parent's visitation rights unless it finds that the visitation would endanger seriously the child's physical, mental, moral, or emotional health.

    §408. [Judicial Supervision.]

    (a) Except as otherwise agreed by the parties in writing at the time of the custody decree, the custodian may determine the child's upbringing, including his education, health care, and religious training, unless the court after hearing, finds, upon motion by the non-custodial parent, that in the absence of a specific limitation of the custodian's authority, the child's physical health would be endangered or his emotional development significantly impaired.

11. See *Brooks v. Parkerson,* 454 S.E.2d 769 (Ga. 1995), declaring the Georgia grandparent visitation statute unconstitutional in a case where the grandparents sought visitation over the objection of both parents:

    [A]s important as grandparents can be in the lives of their grandchildren, the relationship between parent and child is paramount. For this reason I can not believe in either the constitutionality or the political correctness of any law that allows a court using its own notions of what "special circumstances" are, to pierce the delicate, complex and sacred unity of parent and child against the wishes of fit parents and without a showing of absolute necessity . . .

    * * *

    . . . The rights that some grandparents may seek under the liberal rules of the statute invalidated today could separate fit parents from responsibility for and authority over their children, thereby undermining the privacy and primacy of the American family. (*Id.* at 778, 779–780 [Sears, J., concurring]).

    But see *Beckman v. Boggs,* 655 A.2d 901 (Md. 1995), in which paternal grandparents were allowed to petition for visitation under the Maryland grandparent visitation statute over the objections of the child's father (their son), who, following the death of the mother, had consented to adoption by the child's maternal grandparents.
    The importance of parental autonomy also militates against court-enforced visitation by other relatives, including siblings. See 750 Ill. Comp. Stat. Ann §5/607 (West 1993 & Supp. 1995); Conn. Gen. Stat. §46b-59 (1994) (providing that court may in its discretion and subject to the child's "best interests" grant visitation rights to "any person.")

12. See, e.g., N. Dembitz, "Beyond Any Discipline's Competence," 83 *Yale L. J.* 1304, 1310 (1974); Richard S. Benedek and Elissa P. Benedek, "Postdivorce Visitation: A Child's Right" (*Journal of the American Academy of Child Psychiatry,* 16:256–271, 1977); and Strauss and Strauss, "Book Review," 74 *Columbia Law Rev.* 996, 1004 (1974). On visitation or access as "a basic right of the child rather than a basic right of the [noncustodial] parent," see *M v. M* (1973) 2 All E.R. 81 (Family Div.).

13. See, e.g., *Grado v. Grado,* 44 A.D.2d 854, 356 N.Y.S. 2d 85 (1974) where the visitation order provided as follows:

> Every second and fourth weekend;
> Every first and third Saturday from 10:00 A.M. to 7:30 P.M.
> Every first and third Sunday from 10:00 A.M. to 11:00 P.M.
> Every Monday from 6:00 P.M. to 8:30 P.M.
> Every Wednesday from 6:00 P.M. to 9:30 P.M.
> Every holiday;
> Two weeks during the summer.

14. But see Eleanor E. Maccoby and Robert H. Mnookin, *Dividing the Child: Social and Legal Dilemmas of Custody* (Cambridge, MA: Harvard University Press, 1992). We agree with the authors' statement that their empirical studies of more than 1,000 divorcing families do "not resolve the most difficult policy questions concerning divorce; value judgments as well as data must always inform sound policy" (*Id.* at page 5). And we appreciate their making visible that their "conclusion is influenced by a value judgment that is quite independent of social science evidence. Because most divorced fathers have established a substantial relationship with their children before the breakup, we are sympathetic to the view that the father should ordinarily have the legal right to maintain some sort of ongoing relationship with the children after divorce, even though he was not the primary parent and no longer gets along with the mother. . . ." (*Id.* at pages 287–288).

However, we do not agree with their conclusion (nor does their data support it) that "the potential benefit of a general policy giving a custodial parent the legal right to terminate visitation would outweigh the potential cost," and that they would not "change existing legal standards which give a non-custodial parent the legal right to reasonable visitation" (*Id.* at page 288).

No matter how useful the findings of empirical studies of children in divorcing families may be for other such families and for those to whom these families come for counsel, they ought not to form the basis for state policy with regard to visits other than a "hands-off" one. Arranging (or not allowing) visits with a noncustodial parent, like other day-to-day decisions affecting an *individual* child's well-being, involves precisely the kind of value judgments that are the province of autonomous parents.

Maccoby and Mnookin also conclude that there should not be a state policy of court-ordered joint custody. They are "deeply concerned about the use of joint physical custody in cases where there is substantial parental conflict. . . . We do not think it good for children to feel caught in the middle of parental conflict. . . . To the extent that this custody arrangement is the result of encouragement by mediators, or judges for that matter, we think it unwise." (*Id.* at pp. 284–285). They have apparently failed to recognize that court-ordered joint custody is but one manifestation of court-ordered visitation.

15. See Frank Furstenberg and Andrew Cherlin, *Divided Families: What Happens to Children When Parents Part* (Cambridge, MA: Harvard University Press, 1991), pp. 75–76, recognizing the importance of parental cooperation in joint custody to the child's well-being:

> [T]he rationale for joint custody is so plausible and attractive that one is tempted to disregard the disappointing evidence and support it anyway. But based on what is known now, we think custody and visitation matter less for children than . . . two factors . . . : how much conflict there is between the parents and how effectively the parent (or parents) the child lives with functions. It is likely that a child who alternates between the homes of a distraught mother and an angry father will be more troubled than a child who lives with a mother who is coping well and who once a fortnight sees a father who has disengaged from his family. Even the frequency of the visits with a father seems to matter less than the climate in which they take place.
>
> [J]oint physical custody should be encouraged only in cases where both parents voluntarily agree to it. Among families in which both parents shared the childrearing while they were married, a voluntary agreement to maintain joint physical custody probably will work and benefit the children.

Since we see joint custody as little more than a synonym for visitation, we would apply their findings more broadly.

16. For a conflicting view, see J. B. Kelly and J. S. Wallerstein, "The Effects of Parental Divorce: Experiences of the Child in Early Latency" (*American Journal of Orthopsychiatry*, 46:20–32, 1976); J. S. Wallerstein and J. B. Kelly, "Divorce Counseling: A Community Service for Families in the Midst of Divorce," (*ibid.*, 47:4–22, 1977); and J. S. Wallerstein and J. B. Kelly, "The Effects of Parental Divorce: Experiences of the Preschool Child," (*Journal of the American Academy of Child Psychiatry*, 14:600–616, 1975).

17. *Braiman v. Braiman,* 378 N.E.2d 1019, 1020 (1978).

18. *Id.* at 1021, 1022.

19. On joint custody, see Annot., "'Split,' 'Divided,' or 'Alternate' Custody of Children," 92 A.L.R.2d 695 (1963).

20. Out of concern for equalizing the bargaining strength of separating parents, Mnookin and Kornhauser argue that visitation and joint custody agreements should be specifically enforceable in law. Their faith in the law's capacity to implement such contracts in situations where the law has already proved powerless to enforce marriage contracts seems unwarranted. The marriage contract is now generally construed to mean "till divorce do us part." It is a "binding" contract until either spouse wants out. Even if visitation is retained as a "bargaining chip," joint custody and visitation agreements will ultimately come to mean—at enormous cost to the children involved—specifically enforceable until either parent wants out. In any event, Mnookin and Kornhauser fail to make the child's interests paramount in their argument. R. H. Mnookin and L. Kornhauser, "Bargaining in the Shadow of the Law: The Case of Divorce," 88 *Yale L. J.* 950, 980–984 (1979).

21. As told to the authors.
22. The court that ordered the visits refused to help Mrs. Yerkovich regain custody of Joanna; state law, as interpreted by state officials, apparently did not treat such abductions as kidnapping and, therefore, their services were minimal. Beyond the state's boundaries, the FBI claimed not to have jurisdiction since a putative father could not "kidnap" his own child.

    Parents continue to be exempted from federal kidnapping law. See 18 U.S.C.A. §1201(a) (Supp. 1995). One court has interpreted this exemption to apply even to the biological parent whose parental rights have been terminated. See *United States v. Sheek,* 990 F.2d 150 (4th Cir. 1993). Where *state* law makes parental kidnapping a felony, however, it is a federal offense to abduct one's child and then flee across state boundaries to avoid prosecution. See 18 U.S.C.A. § 1073 (note) (Supp. 1995).

    See *Sorichetti v. City of New York,* 482 N.E.2d 70 (N.Y. 1985), involving suit by a custodial parent against the New York City police department for its failure to enforce a protection order against her estranged husband. When she delivered her daughter to him—pursuant to the protection order, which provided for limited visitation—he threatened the daughter's life. The mother then informed the police of his threats, showed them the protection order, and requested their assistance. It was denied. Later the father attempted to murder the child, who was found mutilated and disfigured.

    For another example of simplistic, albeit logical, thinking about visitation see *C.M. v. C.C.,* 377 A.2d 821, 824, 825 (Juv. & Dom. Rel. Ct., N.J.1977), granting visitation rights to the donor of semen for a child conceived by artificial insemination:

    > In this case there is a known man who is the donor. There is no husband. If the couple had been married and the husband's sperm was used artificially, he would be considered the father. If a woman conceives a child by intercourse, the "donor" who is not married to the mother is no less a father than the man who is married to the mother. Likewise, if an unmarried woman conceives a child through artificial insemination from semen from a known man, that man cannot be considered to be less a father because he is not married to the woman.
    >
    > * * *
    >
    > It is in a child's best interest to have two parents whenever possible. The court takes no position as to the propriety of the use of artificial insemination between unmarried persons, but must be concerned with the best interests of the child in granting custody or visitation, and for such consideration will not make any distinction between a child conceived naturally or artificially.

23. As reported in *New York Times,* August 28, 1984, section B, page 2, column 6.
24. As reported in Gannett News Service, March 15 and March 16, 1989.
25. *D'Onofrio v. D'Onofrio,* 305 A.2d 27, 29–30 (1976) (emphasis added).

Chapter 4: Placement Decisions Should Reflect the Child's Sense of Time

1. See, e.g., Anna Freud and Dorothy Burlingham, *Infants Without Families: Reports on the Hampstead Nurseries (The Writings of Anna Freud,* Vol. III; New York: Interna-

tional Universities Press, 1973, pp. 182–183) where they describe the violent reactions in a small child to the parting of his mother:

> The child feels suddenly deserted by all the known persons in his world to whom he has learned to attach importance. His new ability to love finds itself deprived of the accustomed objects, and his greed for affection remains unsatisfied. His longing for his mother becomes intolerable and throws him into states of despair which are very similar to the despair and distress shown by babies who are hungry and whose food does not appear at the accustomed time. For several hours or even for a day or two this psychological craving of the child, the "Hunger" for his mother, may override all bodily sensations. There are some children of this age who will refuse to eat or to sleep. Very many of them will refuse to be handled or comforted by strangers.
>
> The children cling to some object or to some form of expression which means to them at that moment memory of the material presence of the mother. Some will cling to a toy which the mother has put into their hands at the moment of parting; others to some item of bedding or clothing which they have brought from home. Some will monotonously repeat the word by which they are used to call their mothers. . . .
>
> Observers seldom appreciate the depth and seriousness of this grief of a small child. Their judgment of it is misled for one main reason. This childish grief is short-lived. Mourning of equal intensity in an adult person would have to run its course throughout a year; the same process in the child between 1 and 2 years will normally be over in 36 to 48 hours. It is a psychological error to conclude from this short duration that the reaction is only a superficial one and can be treated lightly.

See also Anna Freud, "The Concept of the Rejecting Mother" in *The Writings of Anna Freud,* Vol. IV (New York: International Universities Press, 1968), pp. 596–597:

> The first attempt at object love has been destroyed; the next one will not be of quite the same quality, will be more demanding, more intent on immediate wish fulfillments, i.e., further removed from the more mature forms of "love."

2. Ner Littner, "Discussion of a Program of Adoptive Placement for Infants Under Three Months" (*American Journal of Orthopsychiatry,* 26:577, 1956).
3. See *Sefkow v. Sefkow,* 427 N.W.2d 203, 212 (Minn, 1988), where the Minnesota Supreme Court acknowledged "unconscionable delay" in a four-year custody fight between divorcing parents, and further urged

> trial courts to bifurcate proceedings where custody is vigorously contested, deciding custody issues first and financial and other matters in a more relaxed manner. . . . We . . . believe that such bifurcation and expedient resolution will prevent a parent from manipulating the system to achieve personal goals which have little to do with the best interest of the child.

Such bifurcation comports with the concept of divisible divorce, which recognized that the official severance of personal relationships between the adult parties is divisible from (and need not be conditioned on or await a final determination of) property and support rights.

See, e.g., *Estin v. Estin,* 334 U.S. 541 (1948). Where an adult party to a divorce has sought to preclude a final decree of divorce until a final property settlement has been reached, courts have observed, e.g., that "[s]ociety will be little concerned if the parties engage in property litigation of a however long duration; it will be much concerned if two people are forced to remain legally bound to one another when this status can do nothing but engender additional bitterness and unhappiness." *Hall v. Superior Court of Los Angeles County,* 352 P.2d 161, 166 (Cal. 1960). Ending disputes about the child-adult relationships seems equally if not a more compelling reason for invoking the divisible divorce concept. *May v. Anderson,* 345 U.S. 528 (1953). That concept is implicit in the continuing jurisdiction courts retain over custody decisions, which, of course, we oppose.

4. See, e.g., Cal. Fam. Code §7822(a) (1995), Abandoned Child:

> A proceeding under this part may be brought where the child has been left . . . by both parents or the sole parent in the care and custody of another for a period of six months or by one parent in the care and custody of the other parent for a period of one year without any provision for the child's support, or without communication from the parent or parents, with the intent on the part of the parent or parents to abandon the child.

> See also Annot., "What Constitutes Abandonment of a Child by Its Parent or Parents Within the Purview of Adoption Laws," 35 A.L.R.2d 662, 668 (1954) and *Winans v. Luppie,* 47 N.J. Eq. 302, 305 (1890); *Hazuke's Case,* 345 Pa. 432 (1942); and *Lott v. Family and Children's Society,* Sup. Ct. of N.J. (1953), reprinted in J. Goldstein and J. Katz, *The Family and the Law* (*supra,* p. 1115).

5. See, e.g., N.Y. Soc. Serv. Law §384-b-7 (1994), which provides in pertinent part:

> "Permanent neglect" [is established when] the parent . . . has failed for a period of more than one year following the [placement] . . . substantially and continuously or repeatedly to maintain contact with and plan for the future of the child, although physically and financially able to do so, *not withstanding the [child-care] agency's diligent efforts to encourage and strengthen the parental relationship,* when such efforts will not be detrimental to the best interests of the child. [emphasis added]

6. See, e.g., *In the Matter of Sheila G.,* 462 N.E.2d 1139, 1140 (N.Y. 1984):

> When a child-care agency has custody of a child and brings a proceeding to terminate parental rights on the ground of permanent neglect, it must . . . prove by clear and convincing evidence that it has fulfilled its statutory duty to exercise diligent efforts to strengthen the parent-child relationship and reunite the family.

In that case, the New York court held that the agency had not met the threshold requirement of proving "diligent efforts" to reunite Sheila and her natural father, notwithstanding the lower court's finding that after six years with her foster parents,

Sheila suffered from "separation anxiety disorder" at the prospect of being reunited with her natural father.
7. See, e.g., *Davies Adoption Case,* 353 Pa. 579 (1946); *In re Graham,* 239 Mo. App. 1036 (1947). But see *In re Adoption of W.B.L.,* 681 S.W.2d 452 (Mo. 1984) (recognizing that parent may repent abandonment, but affirming trial court finding that mother's express intent to repent did not sufficiently negate her earlier and prolonged abandonment of child).

Chapter 5. Placement Decisions Should Take into Account the Law's Incapacity to Make Long-range Predictions and to Manage Family Relationships

1. See Jeremy Bentham, *Theory of Legislation* (*supra,* 1840), Vol. I, p. 254:

> [T]he natural arrangement, which leaves the choice, the mode, and the burden of education to the parents, may be compared to a series of experiments for perfecting the general system. Every thing is advanced and developed by the emulation of individuals, and by differences of ideas and of genius; in a word, by the variety of particular impulses. But let the whole be cast into a single mould; let instruction everywhere take the form of legal authority; errors will be perpetuated, and there will be no further progress. . . .

2. It has taken the law a long time, for example, to realize that its power to deny divorce cannot establish a healthy marriage, or preclude the parties from separating, or even prevent new "relationships" from maturing. See J. Goldstein and M. Gitter, "On the Abolition of Grounds for Divorce: A Model Statute and Commentary" (*Family Law Quart.,* 3:75–99, 1969).
3. See *Lott v. Family and Children's Society,* Sup. Ct. of N.J. (1953), reprinted in J. Goldstein and J. Katz, *The Family and the Law* (New York: Free Press, 1965, p. 1115).
4. The law, seeking to safeguard the privacy of family relationships and the private ordering of one's life, has adopted a policy of minimum state intervention consistent, of course, with the state's goal of safeguarding the well-being of children, protecting them from exploitation by adults. See J. Goldstein and M. Gitter, "On the Abolition of Grounds for Divorce: A Model Statute and Commentary" (*Family Law Quart.,* 3:75–99, 1969). See also Justice Douglas's dissent in *Wisconsin v. Yoder,* 406 U.S. 205 (1972).
5. See Anna Freud, "Child Observation and Prediction of Development: A Memorial Lecture in Honor of Ernest Kris" (*Psychoanalytic Study of the Child,* Vol. 13, pp. 97–98; New York: International Universities Press, 1958):

> I name three [factors which] make prediction difficult and hazardous. (1) There is no guarantee that the rate of maturational progress on the side of ego development and drive development will be an even one; and whenever one side of the structure outdistances the other in growth, a variety of unexpected and unpredictable deviations from the norm will follow. (2) There is still no way to approach the quantitative factor in drive development, nor to foresee it; but most of the conflict solutions within the personality will, in the last resort, be determined by quantitative rather than by qualitative factors. (3) The environmental happenings in a

child's life will always remain unpredictable since they are not governed by any known laws.

6. N. Dembitz, "Beyond Any Discipline's Competence," 83 *Yale L. J.* 1304 (1974).

Chapter 6. Placements Should Provide the Least Detrimental Available Alternative for Safeguarding the Child's Growth and Development

1. For a codification of the ambiguity and ambivalence that have come to surround this standard, see §402 of the Uniform Marriage and Divorce Act:

> The court shall determine custody in accordance with the best interests of the child. The court shall consider all relevant factors including:
>
> (1) the wishes of the child's parent or parents as to his custody;
> (2) the wishes of the child as to his custodian;
> (3) the interaction and interrelationship of the child with his parent or parents, his siblings, and any other person who may significantly affect the child's best interests;
> (4) the child's adjustment to his home, school, and community; and
> (5) mental and physical health of all individuals involved.

To this general codification of existing law the drafters of the Uniform Act have added:

> The court shall not consider conduct of a proposed custodian that does not affect his relationship to the child.

2. *In the Matter of the Petition of John Doe and Jane Doe, Husband and Wife, To Adopt A Baby Boy, A Minor,* 627 N.E.2d 648 (Ill. App. 1993), rev'd 638 N.E.2d 181 (Ill. 1994), cert. denied 115 S.Ct. 499 (1994), subsequent habeas corpus pet. den'd 115 S.Ct. 891 (1995). John and Jane Doe are, of course, fictitious names used to refer to the adopting parents. The court also uses the name Richard to refer to the child. We follow both conventions.
3. In other jurisdictions, the Does could be recognized as de facto parents. The California Supreme Court, for instance, has stated that

> [t]he fact of biological parenthood may incline an adult to feel a strong concern for the welfare of his child, but it is not an essential condition; a person who assumes the role of parent, raising the child in his own home, may in time acquire an interest in the "companionship, care, custody and management" of that child. The interest of the "de facto parent" is a substantial one. . . . (*In re B.G.,* 523 P.2d 244, 253 (1973))

The same court defined "de facto parent" as "that person who, on a day-to-day basis, assumes the role of parent, seeking to fulfill both the child's physical needs and his psychological needs" (*Id.* at 253 n.18).

4. 627 N.E.2d at 651–54.

Justice Rizzi also stated:

[O]ur holding as to the best interest of the child is consistent with what the Illinois Supreme Court has stated:

> In *Giacopelli v. The Florence Crittenton Home,* [158 N.E.2d 613], we stated . . . : "It is always recognized that a natural parent has a superior right to the custody of his child. That right, however, is not absolute and must yield to the best interest of the child. Such a superior right only obtains when it is in accord with the best interest of the child."
>
> "The best interest of the child is the standard and it is not necessary that the natural parent be found unfit or be found to have legally forfeited his rights to custody, if it is in the best interest of the child that he be placed in the custody of someone other than the natural parent. —— The parents' natural rights must give way to the welfare and best interest of the child." *People ex rel. Edwards v. Livingston* (1969), 247 N.E.2d 417, 421.[627 N.E.2d at 652 n. 2]

5. 627 N.E.2d at 656.
6. Justice Rizzi had already observed:

> If there is a conflict between Richard's best interests and the rights and interests of his parents *whomever they may be,* the rights and interests of the parents must yield and allow the best interest of Richard to pass through and prevail. *This tenet allows for no exception.* [*Id.* at 652]

But by addressing the question of Otakar's fitness to withhold consent to the adoption, Justice Rizzi allowed for the possibility of an exception. He shifted his focus from child to adult, from Richard's needs and interests to Otakar's rights and possible entitlement, as biological parent, to prevent the adoption. By implication Richard's interests were no longer paramount; they were to be outweighed by Otakar's interests if he was not an "unfit" parent as defined in the adoption statute.

7. *Id.* at 656.
8. Justice Rizzi concluded:

> We therefore affirm the judgment of adoption and the orders inherent to the validity of the judgment of adoption for the reasons that Otakar was an unfit person to have a child and his consent to the adoption was not required. [*Id.* at 656]

9. *In re Custody of Townsend,* 427 N.E.2d 1231, 1235–36 (Ill. App. 1981).
10. Justice Tully said:

> [I]n a most egregious departure from all evidence presented in the record, the majority declares: "Otakar was content 'to just let his child be born' without any interest, concern or responsibility——" and "Otakar was apparently content to go on with his life never truly knowing whether he had a child who was living or had a child who had died." [T]he majority in this case has employed judicial sophistry in

creating an untruthful scenario of the "big, bad and unfit" biological father in this case. [*Id.* at 657]

11. *Id.* at 664. Both judges evidence a concern about the hazards of delay. Justice Rizzi wrote:

> . . . Richard's story is the account of a helpless child caught in the quagmire of a judicial system that in attempting to resolve his problem became part of his problem. It has taken two years and five months for this case to sluggishly move through our judicial system. In a case of this nature, where plainly time is critical, it is a sad commentary on our judiciary.
>
> It shamefully took one year and almost two months from the time that the petition for adoption was filed to the time that the judgment of adoption was entered. It has shamefully taken one year and three months from the time that the notice of appeal was filed to decide this case in the appellate court. [*Id.* at 656]

12. 638 N.E.2d at 182–83.
13. See, e.g., *Sefkow v. Sefkow,* 427 N.W. 2d 203 (Minn. 1988), a divorce custody case pending before the courts for four years: "We think that under the circumstances of this lengthy litigation over Laura's custody, the events of the past [post-separation] four and one-half years are not only relevant, but indeed are crucial in determining the child's best interest." *Id.* at 212.

Chapter 7. The Rothman Decisions

1. Art Buchwald, the distinguished humorist, who himself was a foster child, recalled in a speech celebrating the 150th Anniversary of the Jewish Child Care Association in April, 1972 (unpublished):

> The status of a foster child, particularly for the foster child, is a strange one. He's part of a no-man's land.
>
> . . . The child knows instinctively that there is nothing permanent about the setup, and he is, so to speak, on loan to the family he is residing with. If it doesn't work out, he can be swooped up and put in another home.
>
> It's pretty hard to ask a child or foster parent to make a large emotional commitment under these conditions, and so I think I was about seven years old, when confused, lonely and terribly insecure I said to myself, "The hell with it. I think I'll become a humorist."
>
> From then on I turned everything into a joke.

Chapter 8. Why Should the Child's Interests Be Paramount?

1. See, e.g., *In re Baby Girl B.,* 618 A.2d 1 (Conn. 1992). And see *Stubbs v. Weathersby,* 869 P.2d 893 (Or. Ct. App. 1994), where the court held that a person is estopped in an adoption case when her conduct or silence precludes her from "asserting a right which she otherwise might have had when it is her duty to speak" and that conduct results in "detrimental reliance" by the adoptive parents. Here the biological mother

initiated the contact between the child and the adoptive parents, and she did not express her intent to revoke until after the adoption proceedings were commenced. The adoptive parents relied on her silence to their detriment. The court pointed out: "As a result of mother's conduct, the [adoptive parents] brought the child home, treated her as their own child, invested their energy and financial resources in her well being and initiated the adoption proceeding at their cost."

Adoptive parents cannot make a full commitment to a child unless they know that the biological parents' consents will become final at some point. In this case, the biological mother's consent became final before she tried to revoke it. According to the court, "Mother should not be permitted to renege on her initiated and carefully conceived plan to have her child adopted when the [adoptive parents] have relied on her proposal to their detriment."

2. See D. Dwork, *Children with a Star,* (New Haven, CT: Yale University Press, 1991).

Chapter 9: The Problem and Our Convictions

1. U. Bronfenbrenner, "Discovering What Families Do," in *Rebuilding The Nest,* ed. D. Blankenhorn, S. Bayme, and J. Elshtain (Milwaukee: Family Service America, 1990, p. 29).
2. While everyone may have different standards for what it means to shoulder the responsibilities of "being adult," and we have our own personal criteria for evaluating who lives up to them, the law in a secular society looks only to an objective criterion— chronological age—to determine who shall have the rights and responsibilities of being an "adult." These privileges may be forfeited by certain failures, notably criminal behavior, but to have reached the statutory age in law is to be adult. Concerning the distinction between being "adult" and being "an adult," see Joseph Goldstein, "On Being Adult and Being an Adult in Secular Law" (*Daedalus,* 105:69–87, 1976).
3. Jeremy Bentham, *Theory of Legislation* (Boston: Weeks, Jordan, 1840, Vol. I, p. 248).
4. Sigmund Freud, "Inhibitions, Symptoms and Anxiety" [1926], *Standard Edition,* 20:154–155 (London: Hogarth, 1959).
5. See Anna Freud, "Adolescence" [1958], in *The Writings of Anna Freud,* 5:136–166 (N.Y., 1969), Peter Blos, *On Adolescence* (New York: Free Press, 1962), *idem,* "The Second Individuation Process of Adolescence," in *Psychoanalytic Study of the Child,* 22:162–186 (New York: International Universities Press, 1967); *idem,* "The Genealogy of the Ego Ideal," in *Psychoanalytic Study of the Child,* 29:43–68 (New Haven, CT: Yale University Press, 1974); Erik H. Erikson, "The Concept of Ego Identity" and "The Problem of Ego Identity," in *The Psychology of Adolescence,* ed. Aaron H. Esman (New York: International Universities Press, 1975, pp. 178–192, 318–346).
6. See J. Bowlby, *Maternal Care and Mental Health* (Geneva: World Health Organization, Monograph Series No. 2, 1952); Alice Balint, *The Early Years of Life* (New York: Basic Books, 1954); S. Ritvo and A. J. Solnit, "Influences of Early Mother-Child Interaction on Identification Processes," in *Psychoanalytic Study of the Child,* 13:64–85 (New York: International Universities Press, 1958); Mary D. Ainsworth, R. G. Andry, Robert G. Harlow, S. Lebovici, Margaret Mead, Dane G. Plugh, and Barbara Wootton, *Deprivation of Maternal Care* (Geneva: World Health Organization, Public Health Papers 14, 1962); Anna Freud, "The Theory of the Parent-Infant Relationship" [1962], in

The Writings of Anna Freud 5:187–193 (New York: International Universities Press, 1969); *idem,* "The Emotional and Social Development of Young Children" [1962] (*ibid.,* pp. 336–351); *idem, Normality and Pathology in Childhood* (*ibid.,* Vol. 6, 1965); Milton J. E. Senn and A. J. Solnit, *Problems in Child Behavior and Development* (Philadelphia: Lea & Febiger, 1968).

But see Michael Rutter, "Psychosocial Resilience and Protective Mechanisms," in *Risk and Protective Factors in the Development of Psychopathology,* ed. Jon et al., (New York: Cambridge University Press, 1990). Michael Rutter, *Maternal Deprivation Reassessed* (Middlesex, England: Penguin Books, 1972); Richard B. Kearsley, Philip R. Zelazo, Jerome Kagan, and Rebecca Hartmann, "Separation Protest in Day Care and Home-Reared Infants," *Pediatrics,* 55:171–174, 1975; Ann M. Clarke and A. C. B. Clarke, *Early Experience: Myth and Evidence* (New York: Free Press, 1976); Barbara Tizard, *Adoption: A Second Chance* (London: Open Books, 1977); and Jerome Kagan, Richard B. Kearsley, and Philip R. Zelazo, *Infancy: Its Place in Human Development* (Cambridge, MA: Harvard University Press, 1978). Many of these and other behavioral psychologists emphasize the resilience of cognitive functions, claiming that intellectual performance is relatively resistant to differing social environmental stimuli and deprivation in early childhood. Building their theory of child development not on emotional but mainly on cognitive or group social assessments, they question the detrimental impact on a young child of being separated from or not having a primary psychological parent. However, their reliance on the resilience of cognitive function as evidence of the child's well-being is simplistic.

7. This is not unlike what Chafee had in mind when he said that "the First Amendment and other parts of the law erect a fence inside which men can talk. The lawmakers, legislators and officials stay on the outside of that fence." Zechariah Chafee, Jr., *The Blessings of Liberty* (Philadelphia: J. B. Lippincott, 1956, p. 108).

8. Justice Harlan dissenting in *Poe v. Ullman,* 367 U.S. 497, 551–52 (1961); later relied upon in his concurrence in *Griswold v. Connecticut,* 381 U.S. 479, 499–500 (1965).

9. See, e.g., *Stanley v. Illinois,* 405 U.S. 645 (1972); and see *Smith v. Organization of Foster Families,* 431 U.S. 816, 844–45 (1977), where the Court said:

> [T]he importance of the familial relationship, to the individuals involved and to the society, stems from the emotional attachments that derive from the intimacy of daily association, and from the role it plays in "promot[ing] a way of life" through the instruction of children, *Wisconsin v. Yoder,* 406 U.S. 205, 231–233 (1972), as well as from the fact of blood relationship. No one would seriously dispute that a deeply loving and interdependent relationship between an adult and a child in his or her care may exist even in the absence of a blood relationship. At least where a child has been placed in foster care as an infant, has never known his natural parents, and has remained continuously for several years in the care of the same foster parents, it is natural that the foster family should hold the same place in the emotional life of the foster child, and fulfill the same socializing functions, as a natural family. For this reason, we cannot dismiss the foster family as a mere collection of unrelated individuals.

Justice Powell, in striking down a zoning ordinance that made it unlawful for a mother, son, and two grandchildren to occupy the same dwelling as a family unit, in

Moore v. City of East Cleveland, Ohio, 431 U.S. 494, 503–504 (1977), observed for a plurality of the United States Supreme Court:

> [T]he Constitution protects the sanctity of the family precisely because the institution of the family is deeply rooted in this Nation's history and tradition. It is through the family that we inculcate and pass down many of our most cherished values, moral and cultural.

See also *Commonwealth ex rel. Children's Aid Society v. Gard,* 66 A.2d 300, 306 (Pa. 1949), an opinion recognizing that ties of blood may weaken over time:

> To take this nearly 65 month old girl . . . away from the only parents she has known since she was an infant of eighteen months would be exactly the same in its effect on her and on the man and woman who have stood in a parental relationship to her for nearly four years as would the separation of any well cared for child from its own parents. Nothing could be more cruel than the forceable separation of a child from either its real or foster parents by whom it has been lovingly cared for and to whom it is bound by strong ties of affection; to a child it is equally cruel whether the separation is brought about by "kidnapping" or by legal process.

10. For discussion of the limitations of law in child placement, see pp. 45–48.
11. Orphanages in the past, for example, and other institutions have proved thoroughly disappointing as a solution for the uprooted and physically challenged child. Although offering physical care and survival, they usually failed to grant their inmates relationships that are necessary for the development of self-esteem, of internal mechanisms for impulse control, and of the capacity for maintaining meaningful personal relationships. See S. Provence and R. C. Lipton, *Infants in Institutions* (New York: International Universities Press, 1962).
12. See *In the Matter of Jacob, an Infant,* 660 N.E.2d 397 (N.Y. 1995).

> Kaye, Chief Judge:
> Under the New York adoption statute, a single person can adopt a child (Domestic Relations Law Sec. 110). Equally clear is the right of a single homosexual to adopt. . . . These appeals call upon us to decide if the unmarried partner of a child's biological mother, whether heterosexual or homosexual, who is raising the child together with the biological parent, can become the child's second parent by means of adoption.
> Because the two adoptions sought—one by an unmarried heterosexual couple, the other by the lesbian partner of the child's mother—are fully consistent with the adoption statute, we answer this question in the affirmative. To rule otherwise would mean that the thousands of New York children actually being raised in homes headed by two unmarried persons could have only one legal parent, not the two who want them . . .
> The adoption statute must be strictly construed. What is to be construed strictly and applied rigorously in this sensitive area of the law, however, is the legislative purpose as well as legislative language. Thus, the adoption statute must be applied

in harmony with the humanitarian principle that adoption is a means of securing
the best possible home for a child. . . .

. . . This profound concern for the child's welfare is reflected in the statutory
language itself: when "satisfied that the best interests of the child will be promoted
thereby," a court "shall make an order approving the adoption" (Domestic Relations Law Sec. 114 . . .)

This policy would certainly be advanced in situations like those presented here
by allowing the two adults who actually function as a child's parents to become the
child's legal parents. The advantages which would result from such an adoption include Social Security and life insurance benefits in the event of a parent's death or
disability, the right to sue for the wrongful death of a parent, the right to inherit under the rules of intestacy . . . and eligibility for coverage under both parents' health
insurance policies . . .

Even more important, however, is the emotional security of knowing that in the
event of the biological parent's death or disability, the other parent will have presumptive custody, and the children's relationship with their parents, siblings, and
other relatives will continue should the coparents separate. Indeed, viewed from
the children's perspective, permitting the adoptions allows the children to achieve
a measure of permanency with both parent figures. . . .

The pattern of amendments since the end of World War II evidences a succes-
sive expansion of the categories of persons entitled to adopt regardless of their marital status or sexual orientation. . . .

And see *In re Tammy,* 619 N.E.2d 315 (Mass. 1993). But see *In Matter of Alison D.
v. Virginia M.* 572 N.E.2d 27 (N.Y. 1991).

Chapter 10. The Framework

1. This phrase comes from a talk by E. James Anthony, "A Mind That Lost Itself: A
   Prospective Study of Mental Decompensation from Birth to Breakdown," at the Yale
   Child Study Center in New Haven, Connecticut (April 9, 1977).
2. U.S. Constitution, Fourth Amendment.
3. Interventions to establish and to correct violations of these provisions are perceived
   and explained not exclusively in terms of *parens patriae* or the child's best interests,
   but rather in terms of "reasonable and proper exercises of police power"—of "compelling state interests" in protecting employment opportunities for adults and in assuring for the state a minimally literate and healthy citizenry.

   See generally *Wisconsin v. Yoder,* 406 U.S. 205 (1972), and R. H. Mnookin, *Child,
   Family and State* (Boston: Little, Brown, 1978).

   With regard to vaccination, see, e.g., *Jacobson v. Massachusetts,* 197 U.S. 11, 26
   (1905), upholding the constitutionality of a compulsory smallpox vaccination law:

   [T]he liberty secured by the Constitution of the United States to every person
   within its jurisdiction does not import an absolute right in each person to be, at all
   times and in all circumstances, wholly freed from restraint. There are manifold restraints to which every person is necessarily subject for the common good.

4. Alexander M. Bickel, *The Least Dangerous Branch* (Indianapolis: Bobbs-Merrill, 1962, p. 151); see also *Bowers v. State,* 389 A.2d 341, 349 (Md. Ct. App. 1978):

> [In amending the child abuse statute to impose liability on a parent or custodian who causes his child or ward, to sustain physical injury "as a result of cruel or inhumane treatment or as a result of other malicious acts" the Maryland legislature employed terminology] sufficiently explicit to survive even strict scrutiny under the Due Process Clause. First, it meets the requirement of notice, such that persons of common intelligence need not guess at its meaning or speculate as to its application. . . . Parents of ordinary intelligence are made aware that they do not subject themselves to the statute by merely engaging in corporal discipline for the purpose of punishment or correction. Only when the line is crossed and physical injury is intentionally and maliciously or cruelly inflicted does criminal responsibility attach. In short, the statute provides fair warning; it sets no trap for the unwary or innocent parent. [This is so even though they may not know, at the time they act, that their conduct is prohibited.] Police, court and jury are precluded from reacting to nothing more than their own subjective ideas of child discipline.

On the absence of fair warning and consequently of power restraint in child welfare legislation in England, see Lord Justice Sachs in *Hewer v. Bryant* [1970] 1 Q.B. 357, 371 (1969):

> In the end, so far as comprehensibility . . . is concerned, one finds that this voluminous and well-intentioned legislation has created a bureaucrat's paradise and a citizen's nightmare.

5. "Poor families, the only families that receive close supervision from child protective systems, are often disrupted, without adequate attention to the harms of family separation." P. C. Davis, "The Good Mother: A New Look at Psychological Parent Theory," *Rev. of Law and Social Change* (forthcoming, 1996).
6. B. D. Underwood, "The Thumb on the Scales of Justice: Burdens of Persuasion in Criminal Cases," 86 *Yale L. J.,* 1299, 1300–01 (1977):

> [A] factual issue is close for decision if the two sides are in equipoise; in that event, neither side can be said to have a preponderance of evidence and therefore the party with the burden loses.

7. See Milovan Djilas, *The Unperfect Society* (New York: Harcourt, Brace & World, 1969, pp. 4–5)

> [S]ociety cannot be perfect. Men must hold both ideas and ideals, but they should not regard these as being wholly realizable. We need to comprehend the nature of utopianism. Utopianism, once it achieves power, becomes dogmatic, and it can quite readily create human suffering in the name and in the cause of its own scientism and idealism.

8. For a discussion of the suspended judgment notion in another context, see J. Goldstein, "The *Brawner* Rule—Why? Or No More Nonsense on Non Sense in the Criminal Law, Please!" 1973 *Wash. U. L. Quart.*, 126, 131 (1973).

Chapter 11. Parental Requests to Determine Placement

1. The following from the Uniform Marriage and Divorce Act §403 (Second Tent. Draft 1970) was rejected by drafting committee of National Conference of Commissioners on Uniform State Laws:

> Unless the court finds that the child's physical health or emotional stability will be significantly jeopardized by the award the court shall find that the best interest of the child will be served by awarding custody: (a) to the person selected by the parents. . . .

And see R. H. Mnookin & D. Kelly Weisberg, *Child, Family and State* (Boston: Little, Brown, 3d. Ed., 1995, pp. 806–807).

2. See discussion of *Comerford v. Cherry,* 100 So. 2d 385 (Fla. 1958), Chap. 13, p. 109, text accompanying n. 4.

3. *Prince v. Massachusetts,* 321 U.S. 158, 166 (1944). And see *Moore v. City of East Cleveland,* 431 U.S. 494, 499 (1977) and cases cited therein. See also *Kilgrow v. Kilgrow,* 107 So.2d 885 (Ala. 1959), holding that courts have no jurisdiction to settle differences of opinion between parents as to what is best for their child when the parents and child are living together as a family group.

4. See *Velasquez v. Jankowski,* 5 F.L.R. 2088, 2089 (N.Y. Sup. Ct. 1978), in which even a natural parent, after the death of his ex-spouse, is denied custody because it would require separating two half sisters who went to live with their aunt and uncle following their mother's death. The court said:

> What does exist in the matter at bar . . . upon which the court makes its determination, is that "rare, extraordinary circumstance which could drastically affect the welfare of the child. . . ." I cannot and will not award the older child, Mary, to the petitioner. If I were to award Frances [petitioner's child], there would be perforce, a separation of these two sisters that would be disastrous to both of them. I was able to discern the fear on their faces and voices at the prospect of their separation. It would be cruel and heartless to both of these girls to separate them and a separation would be destructive to their future. Courts should be reluctant to permit separate custody of siblings and separations between siblings is frowned upon [cases omitted]. "Young brothers and sisters need each other's strengths and association in their everyday and often common experiences, and to separate them unnecessarily, is likely to be traumatic and harmful." (*Obey v. Degling,* 36 N.Y.2d 768)

5. See *In re Janet G.,* 94 Misc.2d 133, 143–44, 403 N.Y.S. 2d 646, 652–53 (Fam. Ct. 1978), holding that the natural mother had not voluntarily, informedly, or knowingly surrendered her child for adoption:

Waiver is suspect, and the courts are zealous in their concern with "the involuntariness or unintelligence of a waiver" even in those cases involving only property interests. . . . *A fortiori,* where the agreement surrenders parental rights to the State, where the agreement is between the State and a minor [parent], where the minor is not aware or made aware of the legal significance of the provisions, where the minor does not know that she need not sign the papers presented to her, where the instrument is a maze of fineprint, complex, technical provisions [the waiver is void].

6. Cf. Iowa Code §232.116 (1995) which provides for "termination of both the parental rights with respect to a child and the relationship between the parent and the child,"

a. [When t]he parents voluntarily and intelligently consent to the termination of parental rights and the parent-child relationship *and* for *good cause* desire the termination.

For the apparent use of the "best interest standard" as the guide to determining "for good cause," see, e.g., Del. Code Ann. titl. 13, §§1103–1108 (1993). Section 1104 explicitly provides that parents desiring to terminate their parental rights may themselves petition the court. After a filing of a social study and report on the petition by an authorized agency or the Health and Social Services Department, the Delaware courts may, after a hearing, terminate the rights of the parents to their child, *provided that such termination is found to be in the best interests of the child.* Once a termination order has been made, the code authorizes the transfer of parental rights "to some other person or persons or the Department [of Services for Children, Youth and Their Families] or a licensed agency. . . ." See §§1107–1108.

7. *In re Janet G.,* 94 Misc.2d 133, 143, 403 N.Y.S.2d 646, 652 (Fam. Ct. 1978).
8. Page, "The Mother's Decision" (*Child Adoption,* 75:45, 52, 1974).
9. Richard A. Posner, *Economic Analysis of Law* (Boston: Little, Brown, 2nd ed., pp. 112–113).
10. Herbert Wieder, "On Being Told of Adoption" (*Psychoanal. Quarterly,* 46: 1–22, 1977); David Brodzinsky and Marshall Schechter, eds., *The Psychology of Adoption,* (New York: Oxford University Press, 1990); Herbert Weider, *Handbook of Adoption: A Psychoanalytic View* (New York: Wiseacre Books, 1995).

Chapter 12. Safeguarding Familial Bonds Between Children and Long-term Caregivers Who Are Not Their Parents

1. John Locke [1690], *The Second Treatise of Government* (London: J. M. Dent & Sons, 1924, p. 147):

Nay, this [paternal] *power* so little belongs to the father by any peculiar right of nature, but only as he is guardian of his children, that when he quits his care of them, he loses his power over them, which goes along with their nourishment and education, to which it is inseparably annexed, and it belongs as much to the *foster father* of an exposed child, as to the natural father or another; so little power does the bare *act of begetting* give a man over his issue, if all his care ends there, and this be all the title he hath to the name and authority of a father.

See Chapter 2, pp. 14–15 and *Smith v. Organization of Foster Families,* 431 U.S. 816 (1977).

2. Object constancy is the psychoanalytic term for describing a child's capacity to retain the memory and emotional tie to her parents, and to feel their nurturing, guiding presence even when they are sources of frustration or disappointment or when they are absent. This is the second of two stages in child-parent bonding. The first stage is a need-satisfying attachment of infant to mother, an opportunity beyond the biological connection to begin reciprocal psychological relationships. Toward the end of her first year, as the child becomes capable of differentiating strangers from those who care for her on an hour-to-hour basis and later herself from them, she has entered into the stage of object constancy when she can retain the emotionally charged memory of the constant or primary love objects.

   Unpredicted and prolonged separation experiences in the first and second years of life could exceed the infant's capacity to hold on to the parent emotionally and cognitively. Object constancy may never be achieved, or, even if achieved, would be lost in children exposed to repeated or prolonged separations or periods of emotional deprivation such as those in large institutions or in multiple foster home placements.

   Object constancy is a crucial achievement, a condition for internalizing the care and attitudes of the psychological parents, enabling the child to identify with her parents in order to become increasingly active in shaping her own environment and in developing her own autonomous personality. See Selma Fraiberg, "Libidinal Object Constancy and Mental Representation," in *Psychoanalytic Study of the Child,* 24:9–47 (New York: International Universities Press, 1969). Also see note 8 (this chapter); A. Solnit, "Developmental Perspectives on Self and Object Constancy," *Psychoanalytic Study of the Child:* 37:102–110, Dec. 1982; A. Solnit & P. Neubauer, "Object Constancy and Early Triadic Relationships," *Journal of the American Academy of Child Psychiatry,* 25:23–29, Jan. 1986.

3. For a literary reflection of the "psychological child" notion, see George Eliot, *Silas Marner* (London: Shenval Press, 1953).

4. *Louisville Gas v. Coleman,* 277 U.S. 32, 41 (1928) (dissenting opinion).

5. This book's grounds for intervention and the guidelines in Book One incorporate principles of general application that have been distilled from psychoanalytic theory and from an extensive body of diagnostic and therapeutic work in child development. Both the grounds and the guidelines have been designed to enlarge the number of situations in which courts and other agencies of decision can determine a particular child's placement without a clinician's examination of her and of the adults seeking her custody.

   The court should no longer need such examinations to confirm the fact, for example, that enforced separation of a four-year-old from the only parent she has ever known will have serious repercussions for her development; or that the child's absent biological parent cannot, by virtue of blood ties alone, replace the long-term caregiver as psychological parent; or that murderous parental attacks on a child will destroy the possibility of her ever feeling safe again in the care of the assaulting parents; or that a child's capacity to develop meaningful relationships will be undermined if she is forced to maintain contact with separated parents who are not in agreement about her visits.

Clinicians will, however, continue to be called by courts and counsel to make assessments, particularly at the disposition stage. For example, courts will require an evaluation of a child's relationships to the competing adults who are entitled to claim custody under the special exception to this chapter's long-term-caregiver ground. And clinical examinations may be required of persons who wish to qualify as foster or adopting parents, as well as of the particular child for whom they are to be selected.

Experts are and will continue to be engaged because their training has equipped them with the interview skills to approach individual adults as well as children, because of their capacity to talk to people (particularly to children in their own language). Through such interviews and the understanding of verbal and nonverbal expressions, clinicians create an intimacy in which light can be thrown on the needs and wishes of children and their parents, as well as on their strengths and weaknesses, successes and failures, and on their deviant behavior (i.e., clinicians are called on as consultants and investigators to describe and evaluate such phenomena).

6. See, e.g., *Bennett v. Marrow,* 399 N.Y.S.2d 697, 699–700 (1977), where the appellate court affirmed the trial court's findings in just such a hearing. Although eight-year-old Gina Marie had been living in the home of her natural mother for the past fifteen months, the trial court determined that Gina Marie's primary psychological bond continued to be with the foster parents with whom she had lived for the preceding six years. After observing that the hearing in the trial court extended over a four-week period and contained the testimony of some twenty-six witnesses, the appellate court said:

Addressing itself then to the relationship between the respondent and Gina Marie, the court gave credence to the testimony of a witness called by the Law Guardian, Dr. Sally Provence, a child psychiatrist from Yale University. Finding her to be "certainly the most impressive expert witness who appeared in this proceeding," the hearing court accepted Dr. Provence's testimony that a psychological parent-child relationship had developed between respondent and the child and the court noted that such bond "appears as strong today as [before Gina Marie went to live with her mother]." It was Dr. Provence's further testimony, in substance, that to remove the child from such a relationship would endanger the development of the child in many ways and could affect her academic success and her motivation to learn.

7. In the Child Custody Act of 1970, codified as amended MCL §§722.21–722.28 (1993), the Michigan state legislature established that a factor in determining "the best interests of the child" in custody cases is the "length of time the child has lived in a stable, satisfactory environment and the desirability of maintaining continuity" MCL §722.23(d). The Act bars removing a child from an "established custodial environment" unless there is "clear and convincing evidence" that the change is in the best interest of the child. MCL §722.27(c), Without adopting statutory time periods, as we propose, the Michigan legislature recognized the importance of *time with* the same caretaker by providing:

The custodial environment of a child is established if over an appreciable time the child naturally looks to the custodian in that environment for guidance, discipline, the necessities of life, and parental comfort [MCL §722.27(c).]

For a construction of this provision, see *Bahr v. Bahr,* 230 N.W.2d 430 (Mich. App. 1975). But see *Drummond v. Fulton County Dept. of Family & Children's Services,* 228 S.E.2d 839 (Ga. 1976), *cert. denied,* 432 U.S. 905 (1977), in which foster parents were denied a petition to adopt their two-and-a-half-year-old child, who had lived with them since he was one month old. The court said that the foster parents

> misconstrue the Georgia law in assuming that the best interests of the child rule ap-plies to foster parents. Without this test and its focus on the child, there is no basis for recognizing any right in the "psychological parents." Since the focus in deter-mining whether a third party is entitled to custody is on the natural parents and whether or not they have forfeited their rights or are unfit . . . any relationship between the child and his foster parents is primarily irrelevant [228 S.E.2d at 842–43].

8. See, e.g., *In the Matter of Baby Girl Clausen* ("Baby Jessica"), 501 N.W.2d, 193 (Mich. App. 1993), and see *DeBoer aka Baby Girl Clausen, By her Next Friend, Peter Darrow v. DeBoer,* 114 S.Ct. 1 (1993). Justice Stevens, as Circuit Justice, said "Be-cause I am convinced that there is neither a reasonable probability that the Court will grant certiorari nor a fair prospect that, if it did so, it would conclude that the decision below is erroneous, I have decided to deny the application [to stay the enforcement of the order of the Supreme Court of Michigan, moving Baby Jessica from the DeBoers to the Schmidts]." And see *Certain Named and Unnamed Non-Citizen Children and Their Parents v. State of Texas,* et al. 448 U.S. 1327, 1332 (1980), vacating a stay pend-ing appeal because "it is not unreasonable to believe that [the Supreme Court] may agree with the decision of the District court" and because the applicants "also have presented convincing arguments that they will suffer irreparable harm if the stay is not vacated."

   See also *Matter of Bennett v. Jeffreys,* 40 N.Y.2d 543, 544 n. 1 (1976), where the court approved taking an eight-year-old child from the person with whom she was placed as a newborn baby, and leaving her with her natural mother pending determi-nation of the mother's petition to regain custody; *Bennett v. Marrow,* 399 N.Y.S.2d 697 (1977), discussed in note 6, *supra.*

9. Amici Curiae Brief for A Group of Concerned Persons for Children at 15, *Smith v. Or-ganization of Foster Families,* 431 U.S. 816 (1977).

   See *Stanley v. Illinois,* 405 U.S. 645, 647, (1971), where the Supreme Court held that an unwed father was entitled to a hearing before the state could take custody of his two children after the death of the mother.

> This Court has not, however, embraced the general proposition that a wrong may be done if it can be undone. . . . Surely, in the case before us, if there is a de-lay between the doing and the undoing [the father] suffers from the deprivation of his children, and the children suffer from uncertainty and dislocation.

> But see *Eason v. Commissioner of Welfare,* 370 A.2d 1082 (Conn. 1976), where a six-year-old child who had lived with foster parents since shortly after birth was re-moved directly from school by the Welfare Commissioner and returned to the natural mother without even preparation for this separation; and *Drummond v. Fulton County Dept. of Family & Children's Services,* 563 F.2d 1200 (5th Cir. 1977) cert.

denied, 437 U.S. 910 (1978), where the agency, without a hearing, removed a two-year-old child of mixed race from his "excellent" white foster parents (who wished to adopt him) in order to place the child with then-unidentified black parents.

On holding agents of the state accountable for such actions, see *Before the Best Interests of the Child* (1979), Appendix II, para. 10.14, defining "Violation of Family Integrity," para. 10.15, defining "Child Abuse by the State," and para. 40.0 on "Immunity from Liability."

10. See also *N.Y. Times,* February 17, 1996, p. 25, Jose Sexton, "A Failure to Teach and Protect: How a School for Child Welfare Workers Fell Apart."

11. See Book One, p. 21, for a description of the relationship between long-term care-givers and the child as a "common-law adoptive parent-child relationship."

12. For an account of an early warning system that did *not* work properly, see *Smith v. Organization of Foster Families,* 431 U.S. 816 (1977).

13. What foster care arrangements might be made for two to three weeks, possibly more, for a child between eighteen and thirty months of age is suggested by the work of James and Joyce Robertson. Foster "parents" would be required to discuss, whenever possible, with the infant's natural or adopted parents the child's eating, sleeping, and toilet habits and preferences, as well as the ways in which the child is comforted. The foster parents would have an opportunity to observe how the real parents talk, play, and generally handle their child. Plans might be made for the child to have with her in her foster home her own bedding, favorite toys, even a photograph of her parents and of her own room. Plans would be made, where possible, for either or both of the real parents to visit or be visited by the child. Efforts to do this would be facilitated by trying to arrange foster placements in the neighborhood of the child's real home. For the school-age child, continuity of neighborhood surroundings, for example, would facilitate maintaining ties with school and friends. The variations for trying to meet an individual child's as well as her parents' fundamental needs not to break the ties between them are countless. See James and Joyce Robertson, *Young Children in Brief Separation (supra).* See also Jean Adnopoz, "Complicating Theory: The Application of Psychoanalytic Concepts and Understanding to Family Preservation," *Psychoanalytic Study of the Child,* Vol. 51, 1996 (forthcoming).

Chapter 13. Failures of Parental Care

1. *Welfare Commissioner v. Anonymous,* 364 A.2d 250 (Conn. Super. 1976).

2. *Id.* at 251–252.

3. Indeed, the court recognized the undesirability of the Commissioner initiating an adjudication. He observed that "the court would not adopt [the Commissioner's construction] for a reason of 'policy.' That 'policy' reason is that, in construing a statute concerning the relationship of children to biological or nonbiological parents, courts should prefer that construction which minimizes state intervention" [*id.* at 252].

But see *Matter of D,* 547 P.2d 175, 182 (Ct. App. Or.1976) construing the following statutory exception in ORS 109.322 to the general rule that the consent of parents is a prerequisite to issuance of an adoption order:

> If either parent . . . is imprisoned in a state or federal prison under a sentence for a term of not less than three years, there shall be served upon such parent, if he has not consented in writing to the adoption, a citation in accordance with ORS 109.330 to show cause why the adoption of the child should not be decreed. . . . Upon hearing being had, if the court finds that the welfare of the child will be best promoted through the adoption of the child, the consent of the . . . imprisoned parent is not required, and the court shall have authority to proceed regardless of the objection of such parent. . . .

4. *Comerford v. Cherry,* 100 So.2d 385, 390 (Fla. 1958). The court also said:

> The courts have always seen to it that the property of a testator was received by those whom the testator indicated. The upbringing of minor children is a matter which concerns every thoughtful human being more vitally than the disposition of his worldly possessions when he has passed on.

   The same reasoning should hold for honoring the request by a parent for appointment of a "standby" guardian when the parent anticipates early death or disablement. See, e.g. *In Re Estate of Herrod,* 1993 WL 382464 (Ill. App. 1 Dist), involving such a request by an HIV-infected mother.

5. See, for example, *People v. Banks,* 641 N.E.2d 331, 334 (Ill. 1994), affirming the defendant's murder conviction for starving his infant stepdaughter over a three-month period. The defendant also severely malnourished his two older children, allowing them to eat only two or three times per week.

6. This statement is based on first-order inferences from clinical experiences. See, e.g., Byron Egeland, L. Alan Sroufe and Martha Erickson, "The Developmental Consequences of Different Patterns of Maltreatment." *Child Abuse and Neglect,* 7: 459–469, 1983; J. Lawrence Aber and Joseph P. Allen, "Effects of Maltreatment on Young Children's Socioemotional Development: An Attachment Theory Perspective." *Developmental Psychology,* 23 (3): 406–414, 1987; Charles Zeanah and Paula Zeanah, "Intergenerational Transmission of Maltreatment: Insights from Attachment Theory and Research." *Psychiatry,* 52:177–196, May 1989; Robin Malinosky-Rummell and David Hansen, "Long-Term Consequences of Childhood Physical Abuse." *Psychological Bulletin,* 11 (1): 68–79, 1993.

7. It is, however, a matter for legislation to prohibit teachers, at least in a compulsory education system, from using corporal punishment as a mode of discipline. Though the authority to use such punishment may not violate some constitutions, there is no justification for its continued legalization. In *Ingraham v. Wright,* 430 U.S. 651, 664, 97 S.Ct. 1401, 1405 (1977), the U.S. Supreme Court upheld the constitutionality of corporal punishment in the public schools. Cf. "Child Care in Sweden," *Fact Sheets on Sweden,* June 1994 ("Swedish law prohibits corporal punishment. . . .").

   Clitoridectomy—excision of the clitoris and perhaps part of the vaginal lips—is practiced in the United States by some immigrants from the forty or more countries in the Middle East and Africa where such mutilation is prevalent. The procedure is performed in order to have the girl be socially acceptable and marriageable. How should our society seek to end this practice—by legislation, or by the "enlightenment" that comes with being a part of this society? See New York Times INTERNATIONAL, Sunday, December 10, 1995, p. 18.

8. Institute of Judicial Administration/American Bar Association Joint Commission on Juvenile Justice Standards, *Standards Relating to Abuse and Neglect* (Cambridge, MA: Ballinger, 1981, §2.1C, at pp. 67–70:

> C. [Coercive intervention should be authorized when] a child is suffering serious emotional damage, evidenced by severe anxiety, depression, or withdrawal, or untoward aggressive behavior toward self or others, and the child's parents are not willing to provide treatment for him/her.
>
> *Commentary*
> . . . The definition should place sufficient constraints on expert testimony and judicial decisionmaking so that it will not be based solely on individual views regarding proper child development. It is possible that in practice this definition will prove either too broad or too narrow. These standards should not be considered frozen. Periodic review to see how they are working and to incorporate new knowledge is essential.
> The standard limits intervention to situations where the child is actually evidencing the symptoms. Intervention may not be premised on the prediction of harm. . . .
> The standard does not require that emotional damage be caused by parental conduct. If a child evidences serious damage and the parent is unwilling to provide help, intervention is justified regardless of the cause of the harm [*id.* at 57–58].

> See also Wald, "State Intervention on Behalf of 'Neglected' Children: A Search for Realistic Standards," 27 *Stan. L. Rev.,* 985, 1019 (1975).

9. R. K. Uviller, "Child Abuse And Snooping," *New York Times,* April 20, 1977, p. A25, Col. 2.
10. The statute continues to include nearly identical language. See Conn. Gen. Stat. §46b-120 (1994).
11. This is based on an actual case.
12. *Roe et al. v. Conn,* 417 F. Supp. 769, 775 (M.D. Ala. 1976).
13. Deposition of patrolman L. T. Conn, Sept. 1975 (pp. 250–56) in *Roe et al. v. Conn,* Civ. No. 75-232-N (M.D. Ala. 1976).
14. *Roe et al. v. Conn,* 417 F. Supp. 769, 774–75 (M.D. Ala. 1976). Judge Rives held that the Alabama Code provision "which authorizes summary seizure of a child 'if it appears that . . . the child is in such condition that its welfare requires,'" violates procedural due process under the Fourteenth Amendment of the United States Constitution." He said:

> The facts of this case dispel any notion that the State was faced with an emergency situation. As we earlier found, Officer Conn's investigation revealed that Richard Roe was clothed, clean and in "fairly good" physical condition with no signs of physical abuse. The Wambles' home was "relatively clean" and stocked with "adequate food." Without danger of immediate harm or threatened harm to the child, the State's interest in protecting the child is not sufficient to justify a removal

of the child prior to notice and a hearing. Additionally, even in the event summary seizure had been justified, a hearing would have had to follow the seizure "as soon as practicable" and not six weeks later as it did in the present case . . . [*id.* at 778].

See *Palmore v. Sidoti,* 466 U.S. 429, 432–433 (1983). Reviewing a state court judgment that had divested a divorced mother of the custody of her infant child because of her remarriage to a person of a different race, Chief Justice Burger for the Court wrote:

> The court correctly stated that the child's welfare was the controlling factor . . . [It] made no effort to place its holding on any ground other than race . . .
>
> A core purpose of the Fourteenth Amendment was to do away with all governmentally imposed discrimination based on race . . . Classifying persons according to their race is more likely to reflect racial prejudice than legitimate public concerns; the race, not the person, dictates the category . . . Such classifications are subject to the most exacting scrutiny; to pass constitutional muster, they must be justified by a compelling governmental interest and must be "necessary . . . to the accomplishment" of their legitimate purpose.

15. *Alsager v. District Court of Polk County, Iowa,* 406 F. Supp. 10 (S.D. Iowa 1975).
16. Daniel St. Albin Greene, "They Lost Their Kids for Six Years," *National Observer,* May 29, 1976, p. 1 and p. 14, col. 2.
17. *Alsager v. District Court of Polk County, Iowa,* 406 F. Supp. 10, 13 (S.D. Iowa 1975).
18. *Id.* at 22.
19. *Id.* at 23. The U.S. Court of Appeals affirmed the U.S. District Court's holding that the termination of parental rights proceedings were unconstitutional. However, it limited its finding of unconstitutionality to the procedures that were followed and did not address the question of whether the Iowa statute was unconstitutionally vague. The District Court had held that the statute was void for vagueness. *Alsager v. District Court of Polk County, Iowa,* 545 F.2d 1137 (8th Cir. 1976).

    Following the District Court's decision, the four youngest children were returned to their parents. The two oldest children had previously been returned. See William E. Farrell, "Family Gets 4 Sons Back After 6-year Court Fight," *New York Times,* December 31, 1975, p. 11.
20. This is based on an actual case.
21. This is based on an actual case.
22. This is based on an actual case.
23. See S. Freud, "Three Essays on the Theory of Sexuality" [1905], in *Standard Edition,* 7:173–179, 222–231 (London: Hogarth, 1953); Lauretta Bender and Abraham Blau, "The Reaction of Children to Sexual Relations with Adults," *American Journal of Orthopsychiatry,* 7:500–518, 1937); Ruth S. Kempe and C. Henry Kempe, *Child Abuse* (Cambridge, MA: Harvard University Press, Developing Child Series, 1978); A. Freud, "A Psychoanalyst's View of Sexual Abuse by Parents," in *Sexually Abused Children and Their Families,* ed. Patricia B. Mrazck and Henry Kempe (New York: Pergamon, 1981, pp. 33–35).
24. See S. Freud, "Katharina" [1893–95], in *Standard Edition,* 2:125–34 (London: Hogarth, 1955); Melvin Lewis and P. M. Sarrel, "Some Psychological Aspects of Seduction, Incest, and Rape in Childhood," *Journal of American Academy of Child*

Psychiatry, 8:606–619, 1969; A. Katan, "Children Who Were Raped," in *The Psychoanalytic Study of the Child,* 28:208–224 (New Haven, CT: Yale University Press, 1973); A. Rosenfeld, C. Nadelson, M. Krieger, and J. Backman, "Incest and Sexual Abuse of Children," *Journal of American Academy of Child Psychiatry,* 16:334–346, 1977.

25. Hans Loewald, "The Waning of the Oedipus Complex," in *Papers on Psychoanalysis,* (New Haven, CT: Yale University Press, 1980, pp. 384–405); M. Gitelson, "Re-Evaluation of the Role of the Oedipus Complex," *International Journal of Psycho-Analysis,* 33:351–354, 1952; J. Lampl–de Groot, "Re-Evaluation of the Role of the Oedipus Complex," *ibid.,* 33: 335–342, 1952; Lilli Peller, "Libidinal Phases, Ego Development and Play," in *Psychoanalytic Study of the Child,* 9:178–198 (New York: International Universities Press, 1954).

26. Ray E. Helfer and C. Henry Kempe, *Child Abuse and Neglect* (Cambridge, MA: Ballinger, 1976, p. 148):

It is evident that typical community intervention in incest cases, rather than being constructive, has the effect of a knockout blow to a family already weakened by serious internal stresses.

The case of the Krasniqi family illustrates the difficulty in distinguishing appropriate from inappropriate displays of affection. See Appendix A.

27. In 1981, the American Bar Association Commission on Juvenile Justice Standards proposed that coercive intervention should be authorized when "a child has been sexually abused by his/her parent, or a member of his/her household" (or alternatively, with the addition of "and is seriously harmed physically or emotionally thereby"). Such proposals do not satisfy the requisites of fair warning and power restraint, especially as "sexual abuse" goes undefined. Institute of Judicial Administration/American Bar Association Joint Commission on Juvenile Justice Standards, *Standards Relating to Abuse and Neglect* (*supra,* §2.1D, at p. 70).

If there were to be a sexual-abuse-specific ground, both its substance and procedure would need to be carefully circumscribed in order to prevent state interventions that are unwarranted or that cannot provide a less detrimental alternative for the child. With respect to substance, for example, such a statute might provide: "It is a ground for coercive intervention if a child's parent, or a member of his/her household has sexually abused, or attempted to sexually abuse the child. For purposes of this ground, sexual abuse is defined as (i) vaginal intercourse; (ii) anal intercourse; (iii) fellatio by penetration, however slight, by an object manipulated into the genital or anal opening of the child's body; or (iv) cunnilingus."

28. These are the facts as reported by District Judge Hurley in *Tenenbaum v. Williams,* 862 F Supp. 962, 965–67 (E.D.N.Y. 1994). The Tenenbaums sought money damages from the individuals and entities involved pursuant to 42 U.S.C. §1983. They claimed deprivations of their rights to (1) "family integrity" as a component of substantive due process, (2) procedural due process, in the summary removal of Sarah from their custody, and (3) freedom from unreasonable and warrantless searches, in Sarah's removal and examination. Judge Hurley dismissed most of the claims under the principles of qualified immunity for public officials. However, he held that the plaintiffs

could go forward with certain claims against the municipality, which is not entitled to immunity.

29. See J. Goldstein, A. Freud, and A. J. Solnit, *Before the Best Interests of the Child* (New York: Free Press, 1979, pp. 62–65), which proposed such a ground. For cogent reasons for not relying on the criminal system for safeguarding the child's best interests, see Michael Wald, "Thinking About Public Policy Toward Abuse and Neglect of Children: A Review of *Before the Best Interests of the Child*," 78 *Mich. L. Rev.* 645, 684–685; Michael Wald, "State Intervention on Behalf of 'Neglected' Children: A Search for Realistic Standards," 27 *Stan. L. Rev.* 985, 1026–1027.

30. *In re Vulon Children,* 288 N.Y.S.2d 203, 56 Misc.2d 19 (1968).

31. *Id.* at 206–209, 56 Misc.2d at 21–24. Judge Dembitz noted:

> No formal opinion was rendered at the time of dismissal, though the reasons therefor were indicated. In view of a notice of appeal by the Bureau of Child Welfare and the often expressed appellate view that a statement of the trial court's reasons is important for adequate review, this opinion setting forth more fully the grounds for dismissing the petition is now rendered [*id.* at 205, n. 1, 56 Misc.2d. at 205, n.].

32. Under §483-d of the New York Penal Law (McKinney's 1967), doctors and surgeons treating a child have a duty to report to an appropriate public welfare official any case where there is "reason to believe that such child has had serious injury or injuries inflicted upon him or her as a result of abuse or neglect. . . ." As to the social desirability of such reporting laws, see Paulsen, "Child Abuse Reporting Laws," 67 *Colum. L. Rev.,* 1 (1967).

Mandatory reporting has swelled the number of complaints for neglect and abuse that must be investigated by the state. In most states a third or more of these complaints are for alleged neglect that does not involve imminent risk of serious bodily injury. Investigations in such cases frequently constitute an unwarranted intrusion into family privacy, weakening the integrity of the families involved. Two-thirds of the mandated reports are for alleged physical or sexual abuse or for children at imminent risk of serious bodily injury. Coercive inquiries follow even when the state does not have adequate homemakers, social workers, psychiatric, emergency, foster, medical care, or other backup services. The overbroad and vague base for mandatory reporting and inquiry has led to overreporting, to unnecessary demands on services that are inadequate even for those children at greatest risk of serious bodily injury. Thus, those already at serious risk are put at greater risk, and damaging coercive intrusion is encouraged into families of children whose needs, if real, can best be served—and perhaps can only be served—by a range of voluntary services that would be available, accessible, and attractive to families who are or tend to be disorganized.

For other views about mandatory reporting, see Douglas J. Besharov, *Recognizing Child Abuse: A Guide for the Concerned* (New York: Free Press, 1990); Ruth S. Kempe & C. Henry Kempe, *Child Abuse* (Cambridge, MA: Harvard University Press, Developing Child Series, 1978); Ray E. Helfer & C. Henry Kempe, *Child Abuse and Neglect* (Cambridge, MA: Ballinger, 1976).

Chapter 14. Refusal by Parents to Authorize Lifesaving Medical Care

1. See J. Goldstein, "Psychoanalysis and Jurisprudence," 77 *Yale L. J.* 1053, 1059 (1968).
2. These standards are anchored in such common-law notions as that of plain duty. See Justice Field's jury charge regarding criminal liability for acts of omission in *United States v. Knowles,* 26 F. Cas. 800, 801 (N.D. Cal. 1864) (No. 15, 540):

> [T]he duty omitted must be a plain duty, by which I mean that it must be one that does not admit of any discussion as to its obligatory force; one upon which different minds must agree, or will generally agree. Where doubt exists as to what conduct should be pursued in a particular case, and intelligent men differ as to the proper action to be had, the law does not impute guilt to any one if, from omission to adopt one course instead of another, fatal consequences follow to others.

3. *In the Matter of Joseph Hofbauer,* Saratoga County Family Court, June 28, 1978, *aff'd,* New York Supreme Court, November 22, 1978 (slip opinion) presents an example in which the criteria for intervention under this ground were not met.

   Eight-year-old Joseph was diagnosed as having Hodgkin's disease. After refusing medical treatment consisting of radiation and possibly chemotherapy, Joseph's parents placed him in a course of nutritional or metabolic therapy that included the use of laetrile. The State of New York, through its Commissioner of Health and of Social Services, charged that by doing so, the Hofbauers had neglected Joseph, and sought to remove Joseph from his home. During the neglect hearing, doctors for the state testified that radiation with or without chemotherapy was the conventional treatment for Joseph's disease, that such treatment presented serious risks, and that no scientific foundation for metabolic therapy existed. Doctors testifying for the Hofbauers asserted that positive evidence for such therapy exists.

   Family Court Judge Loren N. Brown, in a thoughtful opinion, found that the Hofbauers are "loving parents who have devoted more time and energy and have given more thought and concern to the care of their child than would be expected of the ordinary parent," and that the requirement of providing adequate medical care only requires that parents place their child under the care of a licensed physician. Of several treatment alternatives, the Hofbauers had simply chosen that "least acceptable to the conventional medical establishment." Under these circumstances, therefore, where concerned parents chose for their child medically supported though unconventional treatment, the court refused to override that choice and find Joseph a neglected child.
4. *In re Pogue,* No. M-18-74 (D.C. Sup. Ct. Nov. 11, 1974), reported in the *Washington Post,* November 14, 1974, sec. C, p. 1, col. 1.
5. Kelsey, "Shall These Children Live? A Conversation with Dr. Raymond S. Duff," *Reflection,* 72:4, 7, 1975. For other expressions of Dr. Duff's views, see R. S. Duff and A. Y. M. Campbell, "Moral and Ethical Dilemmas in the Special-Care Nursery," *New England Journal of Medicine,* 289:885,1973; *idem,* "On Deciding the Care of Severely Handicapped or Dying Persons: With Particular Reference to Infants," *Pediatrics,* 57:487, 1976.
6. See Shelley Geballe, "Toward a Child-Responsive Legal System," in *Forgotten Children of the AIDS Epidemic* (New Haven, CT: Yale University Press, 1995); S. Provence and

R. C. Lipton, *Infants in Institutions* (New York: International Universities Press, 1962, pp. 159–166).

For a description of the conditions in one institution, New York's Willowbrook State School for the Mentally Retarded, see Judge Judd's opinion in *New York State Ass'n for Retarded Children, Inc. v. Rockefeller*, 357 F. Supp. 752, 755–57 (E.D.N.Y. 1973). Referring to the "inhumane" conditions at the school, Judge Judd mentioned the "loss of an eye, the breaking of teeth, the loss of part of an ear bitten off by another resident, and frequent bruises and scalp wounds" as typical complaints.

For an effort to reverse the course of the past, see *Consent Judgment in the Willowbrook Case*, No. 72 Civ. 356/357 (E.D.N.Y. Apr. 30, 1975). Similarly, see *Wyatt v. Stickney*, 344 F. Supp. 387 (M.D. Ala. 1972), which has been described as "dealing with a remote, rural state institution in Alabama housing some five thousand retarded children in conditions of unrelieved horror." Burt, "Developing Constitutional Rights of, in, and for Children," *Law and Contemporary Problems*, 39:118, 138, 1975. And see Statement of D. S. Days, III, Assistant Attorney General, Civil Rights Division, before the committee on Human Resources, Subcommittee on Child and Human Development, U.S. Senate, Concerning the Abuse of Children, Jan. 24, 1979.

7. From a conversation with James H. Lincoln, Judge of the Probate Court, Juvenile Division, Wayne County, Michigan.
8. J. E. Schowalter, J. B. Ferholt, and N. M. Mann, "The Adolescent Patient's Decision to Die," *Pediatrics*, 51:97–98, 1973.
9. For a discussion of emancipation of children for health care purposes, see J. Goldstein, "Medical Care for the Child at Risk: On State Supervention of Parental Autonomy," 86 *Yale L. J.* 645, 661–664 (1977). Also see, e.g., *In Re Roger* S., 19 C.3d 921, 929, 141 Cal. Rptr. 298. 302, 569 P.2d 1286,1290 (1977), in which the court acknowledged that since it is within a parent's power to place the child in a state-operated mental hospital and require him to remain there, just as he may place the child in a public hospital for treatment of a physical condition, it follows that he may waive these due process rights that the child might assert if the state sought hospitalization. But the court held that "as to minors 14 years of age or older, the parental power is not this comprehensive. The consequences of confining a person, minor or adult, involuntarily in a mental institution . . . impinge much more directly on the liberty interest of the patient than does confinement for treatment of physical illness."

For an interesting illustration of a parental decision to respect the wishes of their ten-year-old child not to continue treatment, see the *Denver Post*, Sunday, December 4, 1978, p. 38, col. 3:

> Shawn, who died of a rare form of cancer . . . had discussed his decision in a tape-recorded session with the Rev. Richard Olson of the First Baptist Church in Racine. "Mom and Dad came in, and the doctors came in . . . they said it probably wouldn't work, and if it did work, it would stop working sooner or later and I would die. Or I could just go off treatment, you know, and just, you know, stay at home and just die.
>
> * * *
>
> "When I found out I had cancer, I just thought, 'God'll take care of that,' . . . And he did. Not the way I wanted him to. . . . He always answers a prayer, but not always the way you want him to answer it."

Shawn died of Rhabdomyosarcoma, a fast spreading cancer that attacks the soft-muscle tissue. Radiation and chemotherapy treatments helped only temporarily, his mother said. By the time the disease was discovered, it already had invaded his lungs.

About a month ago, doctors suggested a more extreme, physically taxing drug treatment that would offer no hope for a cure but might prolong his life. "At the most it would give him some more time," [they said]. But the Bonenbergers asked that Shawn make his own decision, and he decided to live a day at a time.

"You just have as much fun as you can and make use of it," Shawn told Olson. "It's like each day is a gift. Like if you say, 'I'm going to clean my room tomorrow,' tomorrow you might not be here. You never know. You just live one day at a time.

* * *

I've never really accepted the fact that I have cancer. It's just hard. . . . A lot of people, when they find out they have cancer, they just give up. I definitely didn't do that."

10. *In re Sampson,* 65 Misc. 2d 658, 317 N.Y.S.2d 641 (Fam. Ct. 1970) *aff'd,* 437 App. Div. 2d 668 323 N.Y.S. 2d 253 (1971), *aff'd,* 29 N.Y.2d 900, 278 N.E.2d 918, 328 N.Y.S.2d 686 (1972).
11. *Id.* at 660, 317 N.Y.S.2d at 644.
12. *Id.,* 317 N.Y.S.2d at 644. According to Judge Elwyn, a psychologist had found Kevin to be extremely dependent. The staff psychiatrist reported that Kevin demonstrated " 'inferiority feeling and low self concept.' " *Id.,* 317 N.Y.S.2d at 644.
13. *Id.* at 672, 317 N.Y.S.2d at 655.
14. Id. at 673, 317 N.Y.S.2d at 656 (quoting *In re Seiferth,* 309 N.Y. 80, 87, 127 N.E.2d 820, 824 (1955) (J. Fuld, dissenting). For a contrary view of the importance of a child's preference regarding surgery, see *In re Green,* 448 Pa. 338, 292, A.2d 387 (1972). After a mother refused to correct her son's spinal curvature because the surgery would require blood transfusions, the Pennsylvania Court remanded for a determination of the child's wishes. The trial judge found that the child did not want the operation; his wishes were honored. *Green Appeal,* 452 Pa. 373, 307 A.2d 279 (1973).
15. 65 Misc. 2d at 674, 317 N.Y.S.2d at 657.
16. *In re Seiferth,* 309 N.Y. 80, 127 N.E.2d 820 (1955).
17. Letter from William G. Conable, attorney for Seiferth, to Joseph Goldstein (Apr. 20, 1964), quoted in J. Goldstein and Jay Katz, *The Family and the Law* (New York: Free Press, 1965, p. 993).
18. Letter from Mr. Elmer R. Weil, county attorney of Erie County, to Joseph Goldstein (Apr. 28, 1964), quoted in *id.* at 993–94.
19. *Hart v. Brown,* 29 Conn. Supp. 368, 289 A.2d 386 (1972).
20. The doctors were willing to rely on parental consent, without court review, to remove both of Kathleen's kidneys and thus leave her with "no potential kidney function" and with the "prospect of survival . . . because of her age, at best questionable." *Id.* at 372, 289 A.2d at 388. Compare *In re Nemser,* 51 Misc. 2d 616, 621–25, 273 N.Y.S.2d 624, 629–32 (1966), where the judge criticized the modern tendency for doctors to seek judicial approval for planned operations, even in emergency situations, rather than proceed without the written permission of the patient's guardian.

21. It may be that parental consent to surgery for the irreversible sterilization of a child ought not to be sufficient to authorize the operation without court review. In *A.L. v. G.R.H.,* 325 N.E.2d 501 (Ind. App. 1975), the court held that a parent does not have a common-law right to have a minor child sterilized. But see *Stump v. Sparkman,* 98 S. Ct. 1099 (1978), holding that the mother who requested the sterilization of her daughter without the daughter's knowledge and the judge who ordered it were immune from suit by the daughter for damages.

22. 29 Conn. Supp. at 378, 289 A.2d at 391 (emphasis supplied). For another view of the issues presented by this case, see M. Lewis, "Kidney Donation by a 7-Year-Old Identical Twin Child: Psychological, Legal, and Ethical Considerations," *Journal of American Academy of Child Psychiatry,* 13: 221–243, 1974). See generally Nolan, "Anatomical Transplants Between Family Members: The Problems Facing Court and Counsel" [1975], *Fam. L. Rep.* (BNA) 4035.

23. For a discussion of these concerns see Wald, "Thinking About Public Policy Toward Abuse and Neglect of Children: A Review of *Before the Best Interests of the Child,*" 646 *Mich. L. Rev.* 645 (1980).

Chapter 15. The Child's Need for Independent Legal Representation

1. In *Ingraham v. Wright,* 430 U.S. 651, 670, (1977), Justice Powell alludes to the insulating function parents may serve:

   The schoolchild has little need for the protection of the Eighth Amendment. . . . Even while at school, the child brings with him the support of family and friends and is rarely apart from teachers and other pupils who may witness and protest any instances of mistreatment.

2. See *Beyond the Best Interests of the Child* (1973, p. 100, para. 30.4). Also see Institute of Judicial Administration/American Bar Association Joint Commission on Juvenile Justice Standards, *Standards Relating to Abuse and Neglect (supra,* 5.1E at p. 96):

   E. Appointment of counsel for child. Upon filing, the court should be required to appoint counsel at public expense to represent the child identified in the petition, as a party to the proceedings. . . .
   Commentary
   This subsection mandates the appointment of counsel for the child named in the petition. There are good reasons to believe this guarantee is constitutionally mandated in light of the significant consequences to the child if court wardship were ultimately imposed. . . . The reasoning underlying The Supreme Court's mandate of counsel for minors in *In re Gault,* 387 U.S. 1 (1967) thus applies readily to minors involved in wardship proceedings (though *Gault* itself applied only to proceedings in which the child was charged with conduct that would be criminal if performed by an adult). . . .

3. Children who are adjudicated to be the responsibility of their long-term caregivers, under the ground described in Chapter 12, would not require counsel because disposition would generally be automatic. Except for the special category of older children

for whom the question of custody requires a hearing, not to appoint counsel would accord with the least-intrusive-disposition principle.

Lawyers for children may unnecessarily contribute to the litigiousness of placement proceedings. See Strauss and Strauss, Book Review, 74 *Colum. L. Rev.* 996 (1974), and Dembitz, Book Review, 83 *Yale L. J.,* 1304 (1974).

We share Professor Guggenheim's view:

> What are a child's substantive rights in custody proceedings? The obvious answer is they have a right to be placed with the caregiver who will best serve their interests. . . . However, children also have the right to be protected from their parents when their parents fall below the minimal standard of care established by law. Their right to state protection, in other words, is conditional. If, and only if, a parent is inadequate, should the state interfere with the parents' and child's right to familial integrity.

Guggenheim, "A Paradigm for Determining the Role of Counsel for Children," 64 *Fordham Law Review* 1399 at 1426, 1429 (1996).
4. See *Beyond the Best Interests of the Child* (p. 100, para. 30.4).
5. See Amici Brief for a Group of Concerned Persons for Children at 12–13, *Smith v. Organization of Foster Families,* 431 U.S. 816 (1977):

> Just as appointment of counsel for children in a divorce custody dispute or neglect proceeding does not foreclose the right of separating or allegedly neglecting parents to speak for their children, so the appointment of Helen L. Buttenwieser [by the court to represent foster children as a class] does not vitiate the standing of the longterm foster parents in this case to speak for the children entrusted to their care. A scrupulous concern for possible conflict of interest led to the appointment of *separate* but *not of exclusive* representation for the children.
>
> Separate counsel for the foster children [as a class, not as individuals] was appointed because the District Court believed that counsel for the foster parents could not "provide effective assistance to the court in defining, articulating and exploring those interests of the children which are potentially adverse to those of the foster parents." Her function was to serve as a fail-safe mechanism—to insure that all points of view were presented. But her voice was not intended to silence all others. None of her clients, not even the originally named foster children, could instruct her as to their desires, ignore her advice, express dissatisfaction with her representation or engage other counsel. She could not be and was never intended to be the final arbiter of the interests of even one child—much less a whole class of children.

Rule 23(c) of the Federal Rules of Civil Procedure, to assure fairness, requires that notice in some class actions be given to all members of the class, the exclusion of persons who so request from the class, and the allowance of appearance through counsel by any member of the class. See Rule 23 of the Federal Rules of Civil Procedure (class actions), and discussion in Wright, 7 *Federal Practice and Procedure* §1786 2d ed., 1986.

6. This is based on an actual case.

7. See, e.g., *In The Interest of: Gregory Kingsley, a minor,* in the Circuit Court of the Ninth Judicial Circuit in and for Orange County, Florida, Case No. Ju29–5245.

   The word "divorce" carries with it the implication that children are not only persons in their own right, but that they are emancipated persons who are as free as adults to decide what is in their own best interest. It seems to imply that children seeking such "divorce" are free to hire (or fire) legal counsel of their own choice—not that of their parents, their guardians or of the court. It seems to imply that children who "divorce" are free to be "single"—that is, unattached to a family and free of any parental control. It obscures the fact that the court—not the child—decides with what family—with which adults—the "divorce-seeking child" will be placed.

   See also the *London Times,* November 17, 1992, Features section.

   > [I]n a New York custody battle involving an 11-year-old boy, described as "extremely intelligent, articulate and sensitive," the child sought permission to select his own lawyer. The father supported the child's request to retain Martin Guggenheim, a well-known professor of family law at New York University Law School. Professor Guggenheim told the judge that the child "believes he has a constitutional right to be represented by counsel of his choice."

   What these cases have in common is a misunderstanding of what should constitute "children's rights."

8. Counsel must avoid becoming rubber stamps for court or agency. See, e.g., *Wisconsin ex rel. Memmel v. Mundy,* 75 Wis. 2d 276, 277, 249 N.W.2d 573, 574 (1977), where the parties stipulated that "all persons involuntarily committed to the [Milwaukee County mental health center] . . . had been denied their constitutional rights to effective assistance of counsel and due process of law." In *de Montigny v. de Montigny,* 70 Wis. 2d 131, 141, 233 N.W.2d 463, 468–69 (1975), the court held:

   > The guardian *ad litem* is more than an adjunct to the court. He is the attorney for the children and their interests. He must perform his duties in accordance with the standards of professional responsibility adopted by this court. Code of Professional Responsibility, 43 Wis. 2d, December 16, 1969. Nominal representation that fails to assure that children are treated as parties to the action is insufficient and constitutes a breach of the duties of professional responsibility.

   The Code of Professional Responsibility, Canon 7, EC 7–12, states:

   > If the disability of a client and the lack of a legal representative compel the lawyer to make decisions for his client, the lawyer should consider all circumstances then prevailing and act with care to safeguard and advance the interests of his client.

9. *G. v. G.,* Conn. Super. Ct. No. 11 28 46 (April 6, 1977) (unreported opinion).

10. See J. Goldstein, "On Being Adult and Being an Adult in Secular Law," *Daedalus,* 105:69, 71, 1976.

11. See Cal. Family Code §§7000 ff. (1994):
§7000. Short Title
§7002. Emancipated minor; description

A person under the age of 18 years is an emancipated minor if any of the following conditions is satisfied:

(a) The person has entered into a valid marriage, whether or not the marriage has been dissolved.
(b) The person is on active duty with the armed forces of the United States.
(c) The person has received a declaration of emancipation pursuant to Section 7122.

§7050. Purposes for which emancipated minors are considered an adult
An emancipated minor shall be considered as being an adult for the following purposes:

(a) The minor's right to support by the minor's parents.
(b) The right of the minor's parents to the minor's earnings and to control the minor.
* * *
(e) The minor's capacity to do any of the following:
  (1) Consent to medical, dental, or psychiatric care, without parental consent, knowledge, or liability.
  (2) Enter into a binding contract or give a delegation of power.
* * *
  (4) Sue or be sued in the minor's own name.
* * *
  (6) Make or revoke a will.
  (7) Make a gift, outright or in trust.
* * *
  (15) Establish the minor's own residence.
  (16) Apply for a work permit pursuant to Section 49110 of the Education Code without the request of the minor's parents.
  (17) Enroll in a school or college.

§7120. Petitions for declaration of emancipation; contents

(a) A minor may petition the superior court of the county in which the minor resides or is temporarily domiciled for a declaration of emancipation.
(b) The petition shall set forth with specificity all of the following facts:
  (1) The minor is at least 14 years of age.
  (2) The minor willingly lives separate and apart from the minor's parents or guardian with the consent or acquiescence of the minor's parents or guardian.
  (3) The minor is managing his or her own financial affairs. As evidence of this, the minor shall complete and attach a declaration of income and expenses as provided in Section 1285.50 of the California Rules of court.

(4) The source of the minor's income is not derived from any activity declared to be a crime by the laws of this state or the laws of the United States.

§7122. Findings of court; issuance of declaration of emancipation

(a) The court shall sustain the petition if it finds that the minor is a person described by Section 1720 and that emancipation would not be contrary to the minor's best interest.
(b) If the petition is sustained, the court shall forthwith issue a declaration of emancipation, which shall be filed by the county clerk.
(c) A declaration is conclusive evidence that the minor is emancipated.

12. Many state statutes require consideration of a child's wishes in custody proceedings. See generally R. H. Mnookin, *Child, Family and State* (Boston: Little, Brown, 1978, pp. 638–641).
    For an example of an opinion that directly clashes with ours, see the reported comments of a Michigan attorney in 4 F.L.R. 1203, 2842 (1978):
    The speaker pointed out several areas in which legal aid lawyers should lay plans for precedent changing litigation, and urged the directions in which it should go—one of these being establishment of the absolute right of the child to have a lawyer who is nothing but a partisan advocate and makes no attempts at objective judgments about the best interest or welfare of the child or question the child's judgment.

Chapter 16. The Problem and Our Questions

1. The phrase *ordinary devoted parents* is from D. W. Winnicott, *The Ordinary Devoted Mother and Her Baby* (London: Tavistock Publications, 1949).
2. James and Joyce Robertson, *Baby in the Family* (London: Penguin Books, 1982, p. 122) (paragraphing omitted).
    Tillie Olson has described these parental feelings in her story "I Stand Here Ironing," reprinted in *Motherlove,* ed. S. Spinner (Laurel, 1978, p. 216):

    She was a beautiful baby. She blew shining bubbles of sound. She loved motion, loved light, loved color and music and textures. She would lie on the floor in her blue overalls patting the surface so hard in ecstasy her hands and feet would blur. She was a miracle to me, but when she was eight months old I had to leave her daytimes with the woman downstairs to whom she was no miracle at all. . . .

    Another anecdote provides a picture of the parental task not unlike that perceived by the "woman downstairs." Early in the Second World War, a young refugee woman was employed as a mother's helper in an English household. After several weeks she plaintively described her job:

    At 7 o'clock in the morning I have to wake the older children. Then I have to help them to get dressed. As soon as I've done that, I have to run down the stairs to cook breakfast. Hardly have I finished with that, I have to run up the stairs to bathe and dress the baby. As soon as I've done that I have to run down the stairs to serve the breakfast. Then I'm expected to wash the dishes. No sooner have I finished with that, it's time to walk the older children to school. Hardly have I returned to the house than it's time to run up the stairs and feed the baby and make the beds. As soon as I've finished with that I have to run down the stairs and cook the lunch, serve the lunch, wash the dishes, walk the baby, prepare high tea, fetch the children from school, serve the tea, wash the dishes—and so it goes on all day; up the stairs, down the stairs, in the house, outside the house, cleaning, cooking, serving meals, feeding children, dressing children, playing with the baby, reading bed-time stories—until I go to bed exhausted. And the next day it starts all over.

Though parents have similar thoughts at times, their love for their children usually lightens the burden.

Chapter 17. Untangling Professional and Personal Beliefs

1. Justice Stewart, in his dissenting opinion in *Griswold v. Connecticut,* 381 U.S. 479, 527 (1965), recognized the need to separate personal commitment from professional knowledge:

> Since 1879 Connecticut has had on its books a law which forbids the use of contraceptives by anyone. I think this is an uncommonly silly law. As a practical matter, the law is obviously unenforceable, except in the oblique context of the present case. As a philosophical matter, I believe the use of contraceptives in the relationship of marriage should be left to personal and private choice, based upon each individual's moral, ethical, and religious beliefs. As a matter of social policy, I think professional counsel about methods of birth control should be available to all, so that each individual's choice can be meaningfully made. But we are not asked in this case to say whether we think this law is unwise, or even asinine. We are asked to hold that it violates the United States Constitution. And that I cannot do.

2. E. E. Maccoby and R. H. Mnookin, *Dividing the Child* (Cambridge, MA: Harvard University Press, 1992, pp. 287–288) (emphasis supplied).
3. Testimony of Leon E. Rosenberg, M.D., Professor and Chairman, Department of Human Genetics, Yale University Medical School, before the Committee on the Judiciary, Subcommittee on Separation of Powers, U.S. Senate, Concerning the Human Life Bill (April 24, 1981).
4. C. E. Lindblom and D. K. Cohen, *Usable Knowledge* (New Haven, CT: Yale University Press, 1979, pp. 12, 13) (paragraphing omitted). For a fascinating discussion on the differences between the "ordinary" observer/policymaker and the "scientific" observer/policymaker, see B. A. Ackerman, *Private Property and the Constitution,* chapter 2 (New Haven, CT: Yale University Press, 1977).
5. M. Shapiro, *Law and Politics in the Supreme Court* (Glencoe, IL: Free Press, 1964, p. 21).

6. See S. Ritvo, "Discussion," in J. Goldstein and J. Katz, *The Family and the Law* (New York: Free Press, 1965, p. 1032).

7. As do Lindblom and Cohen, (*supra* n.4) we use *disciplined* (systematic) and *professional* to separate occasional and superficially practiced activities such as classification, conceptualization, generalization, speculation, fact gathering, and policy analysis, in which all people engage, from the presumably more sustained, elaborate, and skilled practice of these activities by professional persons bearing such designations as social scientist, statistician, systems analyst, or researcher. But we remain open to the argument that the difference is often extremely small or even nonexistent.

See also the observation of Abraham Kaplan, *The Conduct of Inquiry* (San Francisco: Chandler, 1964, p. 126), reproduced in *Id.* (pp. 15–16):

> Scientific observation is deliberate search, carried out with care and forethought, as contrasted with the casual and largely passive perceptions of everyday life. It is this deliberateness and control of the process of observation that is distinctive of science, not merely the use of special instruments (important as they are)—save as this use is itself indicative of forethought and care. Tycho Brahe was one of the greatest of astronomical observers though he had no telescope; Darwin also relied heavily on the naked eye; De Toqueville was a superb observer without any of the data-gathering devices of contemporary social research.

8. J. Goldstein, "On Being Adult and Being an Adult in Secular Law," *Daedalus* 105: 69, 71 (1976). See also John Ely, *Democracy and Distrust* (Cambridge, MA: Harvard University Press, 1980, p. 134): "One reason we have broadly based representative assemblies is to await something approaching consensus before government intervenes." Even with consensus about "scientific findings," there is the danger that they may be used in law to perpetuate grave injustices on child and family. See Stephen J. Gould, "Carrie Buck's Daughter," *Natural History,* pp. 14–18, July 1984, reproduced in full in Appendix I, pp. 127–141 of *In the Best Interests of the Child* (Free Press, 1986). See also *Matter of Guardianship of Hayes* 608 P.2d 635 (Wash. 1980) (court addressed the question of whether it had authority to grant mother's petition for sterilization of her severely retarded sixteen-year-old daughter).

Chapter 18. Professional Boundaries

1. For an edited transcript of the hearing and the judge's opinion, see Judith Areen, *Family Law,* pp. 339–425, 459–461 (New York: Foundation Press, 2nd ed., 1985) (hereinafter cited as Areen, *Family Law*).

2. Areen, *Family Law* (pp. 460–461).

3. See, e.g., *Gallo v. Gallo,* 440 A.2d 782, 787 (Conn., 1981): "The trial court has the great advantage of hearing the witnesses and in observing their demeanor and attitudes to aid in judging the credibility of testimony." And see 3A Wigmore, *Evidence* §946 (Chadbourn rev., 1970): "The demeanor of the witness on the stand may always be considered by the jury in their estimation of his credibility."

4. Using a witness's demeanor in evaluating his testimony is not equivalent to judging his character. See, e.g., *Kovacs v. Szentes,* 33 A.2d 124, 126 (1943):

"[The] trier's right to take into account its observation of the demeanor of witnesses is limited to the observation of such genuine and spontaneous reactions by them in the courtroom as bear upon the credibility to be accorded to their testimony given under oath. . . ." Some of these findings [e.g., the wife found to be "under the domination of the defendant"] went beyond any question of credibility of witnesses . . . [and so constituted] error.

5. Areen, *Family Law* (pp. 459–461).
6. *Garska v. McCoy,* 278 S.E.2d 357, 361 (W.Va. 1981).
7. *Id.* at 361–363. The Connecticut Supreme Court has apparently seen less need for statutory presumptions than the West Virginia court did in *Garska v. McCoy.* In response to the allegation that the divorce custody statute was unconstitutionally vague because of its failure to provide guidelines for trial judges more specific than the "best interest" standard, the Connecticut Supreme Court said:

> We continue to adhere to the view that the legislature was acting wisely in leaving the delicate and difficult process of fact-finding in family matters to flexible, individualized adjudication of the particular facts of each case without the constraint of objective guidelines. [*Seymour v. Seymour,* 433 A.2d 1005, 1007 (1980)]

8. 9 Wigmore, *Evidence* §2569 (Chadbourn rev., 1981). Wigmore goes on to say:

> The dilemma sometimes . . . has given rise to much discussion over extreme cases—particularly the celebrated problem once put by a King of England, whether a judge could lawfully respite a convicted person whom he personally knew to be innocent. But it is now well enough understood that there is no impracticable dilemma. If the judge, as a man and an observer, has any personal knowledge, he may (and sometimes morally must) utilize it by taking the stand as a witness and telling in that capacity what he knows . . . ; this solves the dilemma without either injuring justice or violating principle.

9. *Kovacs v. Szentes,* 33A.2d 124, 126 (Conn. 1943). See also Guggenheim, "The Right to Be Represented But Not Heard: Reflections on Legal Representation for Children," 59 *New York University Law Review* 76, 102–103 (1984):

> [A] critical difference in the role played by lawyers [as champions advocating their *personal* views of best interest] and psychiatrists and other experts in cases involving children [is that] expert witnesses are subject to cross examination by the other party's counsel. Under a skillful cross examination, the expert's knowledge and competence will be tested, and his prejudices and biases, if he has any, will be revealed to the fact-finder. [*Id.* at 103]

10. *Rose v. Rose,* Areen, *Family Law,* p. 553. On the basis of uncontradicted expert testimony the judge found:

> Jason is emotionally unstable and depressed beyond that to be expected from a child his age. . . . [Diane] became inclined toward periods of wide emotional

swings. At times she would become enraged. Though this was probably not directed at Jason in a physical sense, he did have to experience it. She sometimes sank into depression, at other times acted more like the child's friend than mother, and then could swing into an aggressive mood. . . . [She] became unstable. I think Jason suffered from this inconsistency as much as from the frequent visitations. . . . [Steven] was more consistent in his parenting of Jason. . . . Above all, he has been a good father to Jason on a consistent basis.

The judge then observed that the history of Jason's relationship with his parents meant that less weight should be given in this case to the "continuity of care, stability, and psychological parenthood [that] go hand in hand with the in-custody parent." "There is," he said, "less continuity to be disturbed, little stability, and no single psychological parent." And he concluded that Diane was disqualified—unfit—to be the custodial parent and that "Jason's best interest lies with his father as primary custodian. He is more stable and offers Jason the best chance to make progress towards normalcy" (*id.* at 553).

11. *Id.* at 551, 553, 554.
12. 405 N.E.2d 1289 (Ill. App. 1980). The child's name is not given in the report of the case. We call her Rachel.
13. See *Schottenstein v. Schottenstein,* 384 So.2d 933, 936 (Fla. App. 1980), in which the appellate court vacated the trial court's order for psychiatric counseling in a custody case. It said: "We have searched the record to determine the basis for the trial court's decision. Interspersed with colloquy bearing on varied subjects, we find this:

Mr. Schottenstein: . . . I have a concern that they will have too much money. I want them to grow up to have a right sense of values. . . . If anything, they have too much money and they should learn to handle it better.

The Court: There are problems and there are problems. Maybe there is too much money. I have seen very wealthy children end up in dope and kill themselves.

I believe in psychologists and I believe in psychiatrists. If you want you make the children go.

* * *

They are smart children and let's get this resolved.

Do the children come back upset after they visit with him?

Ms. Schottenstein: Sometimes.

The Court: Doesn't that indicate to you the children ought to talk to a professional? How many fathers do they have? If the children are upset, *I think they should talk to a professional.*

The appellate court then observed: "While the trial judge may be a proselyte of psychological evaluations and consultation for every minor child of divorced parents, we cannot ignore the countervailing right of a person to be free from a compulsory mental examination" *(ibid.).*
14. Anna Freud, "On the Difficulties of Communicating with Children," in J. Goldstein and J. Katz, *The Family and the Law* (New York: Free Press, 1965, pp. 261–262).

15. Dept. of Health and Social Security, *Report of the Committee of Inquiry into the Care and Supervision Provided in Relation to Maria Colwell* (London: Her Majesty's Stationery Office, 1974, ISBN 0 11 320596 1), pp. 59, 60, 67; reprinted in J. Goldstein, A. Freud, and A. J. Solnit, *Before the Best Interest of the Child* (New York: Free Press, 1979, pp. 144–186).
16. James and Joyce Robertson, "The Psychological Parent," *Adoption & Fostering* 87:19, 21–22 (Issue No. 1, 1977).
17. See Anna Freud, "On the Difficulties of Communicating with Children," n. 14, *supra*.
18. The Robertsons' report appears in *The Emotional Needs of Infants and Young Children: Implication for Policy and Practice,* ed. Graham Martin (Adelaide, South Australia: Association for the Welfare of Children in Hospital, 1979, p. 251). Words in brackets were added by the Robertsons (London, July 1, 1982).
19. *Id.* at 251. Words in brackets added by the Robertsons in conversation with the authors (London, July 1, 1982).
20. *Id.* at 251–252. Words in brackets added by the Robertsons in conversation with the authors (London, July 1, 1982).
21. *Bennett v. Jeffreys* 387 N.Y.S.2d 821, 827 (1976).

Chapter 19. Crossing Professional Borders

1. Civil Action H-75-18, U.S. District Ct., District of Conn., February 2, 1982 (Zampano, J.). The children, then ages four and six, had been placed in another foster home.
2. The effect on a child is traditionally of secondary concern when courts use "specific performance"—enjoining or forbidding a certain action (in this context, ordering a change of custody)—as the remedy to right wrongs toward parents by agents of the state. In most other areas of the law, specific performance is treated as the exceptional remedy. "Historically, [money] damages have been regarded as the ordinary remedy for an invasion of personal interests in liberty." *Bivens v. Six Unknown Federal Narcotics Agents,* 403 U.S. 388, 395 (1970).
3. Memorandum in Opposition to Motion to Dismiss, *Rivera v. Marcus,* Civil Action H-75-18, U.S. District Ct., District of Conn., May 21, 1980.
4. *Ross v. Hoffman,* 364 A.2d 596, 598, 599 (Md. 1976).
5. *Id.* at 599–600 (emphasis supplied).
6. *Bennett v. Jeffreys,* 387 N.Y.S.2d 821, 829 (Fuchsberg, J. concurring) (1976). See *Petition of New England Home for Little Wanderers,* 328 N.E.2d 854, 861 (Mass. 1975):

> In invoking the "best interests of the child," the Legislature did not intend to disregard the ties between the child and its natural parent, or to threaten a satisfactory family with loss of children because by reason of temporary adversity they are placed in foster care. A parent cannot be deprived unless some affirmative reason is shown for doing so such as a finding . . . of a separation so long as to permit very strong bonds to develop between the child and the prospective adoptive parents.

7. *Ross v. Hoffman,* 364 A.2d 596, 599 (Md. 1976).

8. *Id.* at 600. See also Jane W. Ellis, "Evaluating the Expert: Judicial Expectation of Expert Opinion Evidence in Child Placement Adjudication," 5 Cardozo Law Review 587, n.61, 606–607 (1984).

9. See Book One, Chapter 7.

10. *Ross v. Hoffman* 372 A.2d 582, 593–94 (Md. 1977), citing *Bennett v. Jeffreys,* 387 N.Y.S.2d 821, 827, 356 N.E.2d 277, 283 (1976).

11. *Id.* at 593, 594 (1977).

And see *D. v. M.,* 3 All E.R. 897 (1982) in which Lord Justice Ormrod declared that generally accepted special knowledge from child development about continuity had by 1982 become a part of English custody law through precedent. Reversing a lower court's order to transfer a child from his mother to his long absent father, he stated:

> [It] is generally accepted by those who are professionally concerned with children that, particularly in the early years, continuity of care is the most important part of a child's sense of security and that disruption of established bonds is to be avoided whenever it is possible to do so. . . . This is not only the professional view, it is commonly accepted in all walks of life, and was the recommendation of the experienced welfare officer. [*Id.* at 902–903]

See also *Lehman v. Lycoming County Children's Services,* 458 U.S. 502, 513–14 (1982) in which the Supreme Court declined to permit the use of federal habeas corpus to give federal courts jurisdiction to hear reargument of final state court decisions to terminate parental rights. Justice Powell for the Court said:

> The State's interest in finality is unusually strong in child custody disputes. The grant of federal habeas would prolong uncertainty for children such as the Lehman sons, possibly lessening their chances of adoption. It is undisputed that children require secure, stable, longterm, continuous relationships with their parents or foster parents. There is little that can be as detrimental to a child's sound development as uncertainty over whether he is to remain in his current "home," under the care of his parents or foster parents, especially when such uncertainty is prolonged.

12. *Ross v. Hoffman,* 364 A.2d 596, 601–602 (Md. 1976). See Book Two on how time might be fixed for statutory purposes with special provision in certain cases for the use of expert testimony.

13. Or. Rev. Stat. §107.137 (1981). "None of these factors are to be considered in isolation or to the exclusion of the others" *(ibid.).* In 1987, the legislature added a fourth factor, "(d) The abuse of one parent by the other." Or. Rev. Stat. §107. 137(I)(d) (1994).

14. *Ibid.* (emphasis supplied).

15. *Derby v. Derby,* 571 P.2d 562, 564 (Or. App. 1977), modified on other grounds, 572 P.2d 1080 (Or. App. 1977). "No preference in custody shall be given to the mother over the father for the sole reason that she is the mother." Or. Rev. Stat. §107.137 (3) (1981). In 1987, the legislature added the words "nor shall any preference be given to the father over the mother for the sole reason that he is the father." Or. Rev. Stat. §107.137(4)(1994).

16. W. Va. Code §48-2-15 (1980). More recently, however, the West Virginia statute has been redrafted to give judges more detailed guidance in determining the best interests of a child in relation to custody or visitation. See W.Va. Code §20-124.3 (1994 Supp.).

17. *Garska v. McCoy,* 278 S.E.2d 357, 363 (W. Va. 1981). See also *Pikula v. Pikula,* 374 N.W.2d 705 (Minn. 1985): "We adopt the indicia of primary parenthood set forth in *Garska* to aid trial courts in determining which, if either, parent is the primary caretaker. . . . When the facts demonstrate that responsibility for and performance of child care was shared by both parents in an entirely equal way, then no preference arises and the court must limit its inquiry to other indicia of parental fitness. Once the preference does arise, however, the primary parent should be given custody unless it is shown that the child's physical or emotional health is likely to be endangered or impaired by being placed in the primary parent's custody." *Id.* at 713–714.

18. *Garska v. McCoy, supra* n. 17. at 364. The court recognized that "If the trial court is unable to establish that one parent has clearly taken primary responsibility for the caring and nurturing duties of a child neither party shall have the benefit of the primary caretaker presumption." *Id.* at 358. This may be especially the case in families where both parents are employed full-time outside the home. See also *Lewis v. Lewis,* 433 S.E.2d 536 (W.Va. 1993), reaffirming *Garska v. McCoy* and that the primary caretaker formula is not mechanical and the emotions of the parties must be taken into account as well.

19. A. B. Arons, "Achieving Wider Scientific Literacy," *Daedalus,* 91 (Spring 1983). Arons' argument that science should be taught in a historical and intellectual context rather than as "the mere assertion of end results" (*id.* at 105) led to our thinking about statutes and precedents in this fashion.

20. *Richard v. Collins,* 17 A.831, 832 (N.J. 1889).

21. *Ibid.*

22. *Id.* at 833.

23. *Chapsky v. Wood,* 26 Kan. Report 650, 654–655 (1881).

24. *Ragan v. Ragan,* 315 S.W.2d 142, 147 (Mo. App.1958).

25. *Ross v. Hoffman,* 372 A.2d 582, 594 (Md. 1977).

26. A pragmatic child advocate has suggested that Dr. Hague's report might be better received if it *began* by suggesting that daytime visits would be preferable to overnight visits, and *then* went on to explain why it would be better for Jane if there were no order of visitation.

27. Confronted with a dilemma similar to that of Dr. Burns, another child psychoanalyst tried to use his report to the court to "educate" the judge who had restricted the scope of inquiry in a way which precluded a professionally complete examination. The psychoanalyst abided by the judge's restrictions but prefaced his report with a paragraph chastising the judge. He wrote: "In all my years of working with the courts this is the first time I have ever seen such an order." The judge did not follow his recommendation.

28. *Report of the Committee of Inquiry into the Care and Supervision Provided in Relation to Maria Colwell, supra,* ch. 18, n. 15.

29. "[This] was *not* a moment which they [the social workers of the child care agency] would have chosen to hand Maria back" (*id.* at p. 159, par. 62; emphasis supplied).

30. *Id.* Presumably the social workers believed that they needed to be on good terms with Maria's mother and stepfather to continue serving Maria.

31. *Id.*
32. We question the appropriateness of allowing the same judge to preside at both the pretrial hearing where probable outcomes are discussed and the hearing on the case proper.
33. Letter from Hon. Frederica S. Breneman to Albert J. Solnit (November 24, 1982).

Chapter 20. Dual Role—Ambiguity and Ambivalence

1. Although dual roles may raise ethical and constitutional questions, we do not address these here. Rather, we address questions of function. See, e.g., American Bar Association, *Model Code of Professional Responsibility,* particularly Canon 7, pp. 36–46 (1979); *Model Rules of Professional Conduct* (adopted by ABA in August 1983); and see Guggenheim, "The Right to Be Represented But Not Heard: Reflections on Legal Representation for Children," 59 *New York University Law Review* 76 (1984).
2. See, e.g., Justice Blackmun's opinion for the court in *Wyman v. James,* 400 U.S. 309 (1971), in which he characterizes home visits under a program of Aid to Families with Dependent Children as "both rehabilitative and investigative" (*id.* at 317). Justice Blackmun observes:

> The visit is not one by police or uniformed authority. It is made by a caseworker of some training whose primary objective is, or should be, the welfare, not the prosecution, of the aid recipient for whom the worker has profound responsibility. As has already been stressed, the program concerns dependent children and the needy families of those children. It does not deal with crime or with the actual or suspected perpetrators of crime. The caseworker is not a sleuth but rather, we trust, is a friend to one in need. [*Id.* at 322–323]

> For a discussion of this romantic vision of the relationship between the social worker as authority and the welfare applicant as dependent, see Burt, "Forcing Protection on Children and Their Parents: The Impact of *Wyman v. James,*" 69 *Michigan Law Review* 1259 (1971).

3. We do not examine the dual role problem inherent in state laws requiring pediatricians, for instance, to report cases of suspected child abuse. However, these professionals ought, unrealistic as it may seem, to inform parents of their patients of the limits to confidentiality imposed by such laws.

    Also see A. J. Solnit, "Too Much Reporting, Too Little Service: Roots and Prevention of Child Abuse," *Child Abuse—An Agenda for Action,* ed. G. Gerbner, C. J. Ross, and E. Zigler (New York: Oxford University Press, 1980, pp. 135–146).

4. The therapeutic or working alliance refers to "the relatively nonneurotic, rational rapport which the patient has with the analyst. It is this reasonable and purposeful part of the feelings the patient has for the analyst which makes for the *working alliance.*" See Ralph R. Greenson, *The Technique and Practice of Psychoanalysis,* (New York: International Universities Press, 1967, Vol. 1, pp. 192–193). A clinician who carries out an evaluation in the context of a child placement conflict cannot establish a therapeutic or working alliance because of the lack of confidentiality and because the aim of the evaluation is to answer questions raised by the court and the parties to the dispute. Also see S. Freud, "The Dynamics of Transference," in *Standard Edition,* 12:97–108 (1912);

Hans W. Loewald, "On the Therapeutic Action of Psychoanalysis," *International Journal of Psychoanalysis,* 41:16–33 (1960); Leo Stone, *The Psychoanalytic Situation* (New York: International Universities Press, 1961).

5. *Report of Professor J. D. McClean Concerning Karen Spencer to the Derbyshire County Council and Derbyshire Area Health Authority,* ¶1.1 (1978).
6. *Ibid.*
7. *Id.* at ¶2.124.
8. Id. at ¶2.118–119.
9. Reproduced in *id.* at ¶2.120.
10. *Id.* at ¶2.122.
11. *Id.* at ¶2.123. Professor McClean added: ". . . I sense that a little optimism was thought to be essential if the Spencers were to be given a sense of purpose and direction."
12. *In the Matter of: Roy M. C., Jennifer C., Shannon C., and Jason C. and in the Matter of: The Child Welfare Act Part II* [1980] 14 R.F.L. 2d 21 (Provincial Dist. Ct. [Fam. Div.] of the Judicial District of York).
13. *Id.* at 2, 4 (slip opinion) (emphasis supplied).
14. *Re. W.,* 13 F.R.L. (2d) 381 (1979).
15. *Id.* at 382.
16. *Id.* at 384.
17. *Id.* at 383.
18. *Id.* at 385. See P. K. Milmed, "Due Process for Children: A Right to Counsel in Custody Proceedings," 4 *N.Y.U. Rev. of L. & Social Change* 177, 187–188 (Spring 1974):

> Regardless of whether the child or the attorney more correctly perceives what is in fact better for the child, the constitutional purpose of providing a person with representation is to enable him effectively to present *his* views to the court. The fourteenth amendment does not require the "best" result for the person whose interests are at stake; rather, it requires that a person be heard in proceedings which affect his interests. Since in custody proceedings the child's interests are at stake, due process requires that *his* preferences be expressed and considered.

> See also Guggenheim, "The Right to Be Represented But Not Heard: Reflections on Legal Representation for Children, 59 *N.Y.U. Law Rev.* 76, 117 *et seq.* (1984) and Guggenheim, "A Paradigm for Determining the Role of Counsel for Children," 64 *Fordham Law Review* 1399 (1996): "When lawyers advance a result they wrongly believe to be best for their client, the problem is that their advocacy may succeed" (at 1427). We agree with this view. See also the Connecticut statute mandating the appointment of a lawyer for the child in custody proceedings. Conn. Gen. Stat. §46b-136 (1995). It provides no clue as to whether a child's lawyer should advocate the child's wishes and/or the child's best interests.

19. *Re. W., supra* n. 14, at 385.
20. *Ibid.*
21. See Note, "Rehabilitation, Investigation and the Welfare Home Visit," 79 *Yale L. J.* 746, 759 (1970), which argues that because a welfare home visit combines both a

personal, rehabilitative function and an investigative one, "the only cure for welfare administration is the complete separation of services and investigation throughout the system."

Chapter 21. No License to Act as Parents

1. From their training and experience professional persons know that their care, guidance, and teaching of children should reflect an awareness that parents are the most important adults in the child's life. See Provence and Naylor, *Working with Disadvantaged Parents and Their Children* (New Haven, CT: Yale University Press, 1983), p. 4:

> We were influenced in our choice of both services and methods of study by the view that those closest to the child, his parents, exert the strongest influence on his development and that his development would be best followed, protected and promoted by the study staff through a continuing and close association with his parents—a partnership in behalf of the child.

2. See, e.g., *Beck v. Beck,* 86 N.J. 480, 432 A.2d 63, 71 (1981).
3. Professionals who teach, treat, or take care of children at the request of parents frequently become important adults to such children, especially the younger, more dependent ones. For example, a child in day care may become strongly attached to one of her teachers. Such attachments are secondary in strength to the primary relationship children normally have with "ordinary devoted parents." These secondary relationships continue into kindergarten and the first, second, and third grades, often with one teacher who is felt to be special. For the five- or six-year-old child, that teacher is the one who also may evoke the feelings and hopes that were directed toward the parents a year or two earlier. Such displacements are most clearly detectable when the child is seeing a therapist several times a week. Certain of these important adults become the persons to whom the child transfers part of her deeply felt wishes, affection, hopes, fears, and other attitudes and behaviors that originated within and are still part of the ongoing primary child-parent relationship. Such transferences are a vital aspect of psychoanalytic treatment, where they can be verbalized and played out, made explicit, clarified, and worked through:

> I now agree fully that during analytic treatment children regard their analyst not only as a new object for their affectionate or hostile, sexual or aggressive impulses, or as a helping person with whom they can establish a working alliance, but that, with therapy conducted within the correct limits, multitudes of transference phenomena appear, either additional to or instead of the same impulses and behavioral attitudes that the child displayed toward his original objects. [*The Writings of Anna Freud,* Vol. 1 (New York: International Universities Press, 1974, p. xii)]

4. See Anna Freud, "Termination of Treatment," in Joseph Sandler, Hansi Kennedy, and Robert L. Tyson, *The Technique of Child Psychoanalysis: Discussions with Anna Freud* (Cambridge, MA: Harvard University Press, 1980, p. 246); and John Bowlby, *The Making and Breaking of Affectional Bonds* (London: Tavistock, 1979). Experi-

ences of children being separated from a person who fulfills the parental role and whom they love, "especially if repeated, lead to a sense of being unloved, deserted, and rejected" (*id.,* at p. 10).

5. Justice Murray in *Emotional Needs of Infants and Young Children: Implications for Policy and Practice,* ed. Graham Martin (Adelaide, South Australia: AWCH, 1979 p. 251).

6. *In the Matter of Melissa M.,* 421 N.Y.S.2d 300, 101 Misc. 2d 407 (1979).

7. *Id.* at 304.

8. For a narrative account of a child welfare system that ignored the importance to a child of family integrity, see *The Autobiography of Malcolm X* (New York: Ballantine, 1942) pp. 20–26.

9. An analogous situation arises when a judge promises confidentiality. See *H v. H,* 1 All E. R. 1145, 1147 (1974) (Megaw, L. J.):

> It is of course often most desirable in [custody disputes] that the judge hearing the case should see the children and should see the children otherwise than in open court. One can well understand that in matters of this sort the children may be reluctant to express themselves freely and frankly when there is the possibility that what they say may be made known, and perhaps particularly made known to their parents. . . . Of course the concern of the court in these matters is the welfare of the children. It is certainly possible that when a judge sees the children in private, something may emerge which requires to be further investigated as a matter of necessity for the benefit of the children themselves; and that may involve the necessity of a judge disclosing that which he has heard. How can he do that if he has made a promise to the children at the outset that nothing they say will be disclosed to anyone? Further, there is the position of this court. There is an appeal as of right from the judge's decision. This court has to arrive at a conclusion affecting the welfare of the children and decide whether the judge was right or wrong. How can this court discharge the task if something which may have been important in the judge's decision is something of which this court cannot make itself aware without breaking a solemn promise given by a judge to the person who supplied the information?
>
> It seems to me that in this extraordinarily difficult situation, while the judge seeing the child privately must naturally do all he can to encourage the child to speak freely, frankly and without fear, he may not give the child a promise which would be such in its terms, or be understood by the child as meaning, that in no circumstances will anything that the child says be made known to anyone else.

10. In a custody visitation case, a trial judge's order that "all future proceedings . . . be brought before him personally and not before any other judge" was held to be beyond his power. In *Re Marriage of Matthews,* 101 Cal.App. 3d 811, 161 Cal. Rptr. 879, 881(1980), citing as controlling the California Supreme Court in *People v. Osslo,* 323 P.2d 397, 413 (Cal. 1958):

> An individual judge (as distinguished from a court) is not empowered to retain jurisdiction of a cause. The cause is before the court, not the individual judge of that court, and the jurisdiction which the judge exercises is the jurisdiction of the

court, not of the judge. Rules of court which provide that posttrial proceedings in a cause shall be heard by the judge who tried the matter are entirely proper, but the individual judge cannot order that such proceedings must be heard by him.

11. When a child has grown attached to "short-term" foster parents, separation from them is bound to cause her distress—a distress that will be repeated when the child has had multiple placements. In England during World War II the experience of the Hampstead Nurseries, which provided care for children whose parents could not look after them for a variety of war-related reasons, provides examples of the confusion and turmoil experienced by children under such circumstances:

Reggie had come to the Hampstead Nurseries as a baby of five months, went home to his mother when he was twenty months, and returned to the Nursery two months later. While he was at the Nursery:

[He] formed two passionate relationships to two young nurses who took care of him at different periods. The second attachment was suddenly broken at 2 years, 8 months when his "own" nurse married. He was completely lost and desperate after her departure, and refused to look at her when she visited him a fortnight later. He turned his head to the other side when she spoke to him, but stared at the door, which had closed behind her, after she had left the room. In the evening in bed he sat up and said: "My very own Mary Ann. But I don't like her!" [Anna Freud, "Infants Without Families: Reports on the Hampstead Nurseries 1939–1945," in *The Writings of Anna Freud*, Vol. 3 (New York: International Universities Press, 1973, p. 596)]

But the fact that such separations are bound to happen is not an argument against foster parents caring for children with warmth and love.

When choosing between the two evils of broken and interrupted attachments and an existence of emotional barrenness, the latter is the more harmful solution because . . . it offers less prospect for normal character development. [*Ibid.*]

12. J. Goldstein, "Why Foster Care—For Whom for How Long?" in *The Psychoanalytic Study of the Child*, 30:647, 658–660 (1975).
13. See also the *New York Times*, August 30, 1995, p. A12, reporting that in a Texas child-custody case the judge ordered the Spanish-speaking mother to start speaking English with her five-year-old daughter: "You get this straight. You start speaking English to this child because if she doesn't do good in school, then I can remove her because it's not in her best interest to be ignorant. The child will only hear English."

Outside of the child placement process, judges and lawyers more easily recognize when other professionals infringe upon parental choice. When, for example, a county jail banned visits from the children of inmates because "the jailer [believed] that it is not in the best interests of the children to visit their parents . . . in jail," the court declared the ban unrelated to any legitimate function of the jail (*Valentine v. Englehardt*, 474 F. Supp. 294, 301 [1979]). The court said that deciding the best interests of the inmates' children "simply does not lie with jail officials" (*id.* at 302).

14. It is not unusual for a psychiatric report to a court to contain a closing statement like:

> I strongly recommend further treatment *on a voluntary basis* for Richard, and for Richard and Mrs. Cross (his grandmother who has been taking care of him), and for Richard and his parents. Any insight obtained could improve the quality of their lives and subsequently Richard's.

The "on a voluntary basis" does not negate the intrusiveness of such statements. To suggest that the court join in giving such advice—which it sometimes does in a placement order—is likely to deprive *voluntary* of any real meaning.

15. Remarks of Richard Chilsom, in *The Emotional Needs of Infants and Young Children, supra* n. 5, at p. 252.

Chapter 22. Softhearted and Hardheaded

1. Wendell Berry, *The Unsettling of America: Culture and Agriculture* (New York: Avon, 1978, p. 31); Sigmund Freud, "On Beginning the Treatment," in *Standard Edition,* 12:121–144 (1958).
2. See, e.g., Stone, Tyler, and Mead, "Law Enforcement Officers as Investigators and Therapists in Child Sexual Abuse: A Training Model," *Child Abuse & Neglect,* 8:75 (1984):

> The police officer is frequently the first person to respond to a report of child sexual abuse and, therefore, bears a heavy responsibility. Sensitive treatment and understanding of the child by the first officer on the scene will affect the victim positively and may decrease the chances of long-term psychological damage. [*Id.* at 76]

Despite the suggestion of dual roles for the police in title and text of this article, the training program described seems primarily devoted to the need for the police to incorporate what we call humanness or softheartedness in fulfilling their investigative role when dealing with child victims of sexual abuse and their families.

> A training model for law enforcement personnel should take into consideration . . . (3) the importance of objective and sensitive interviewing techniques. A thoroughly trained police officer can lessen the traumatization of the child and family.
> The victim's physical and mental wellbeing must always be the police officer's first responsibility and concern. An officer who overreacts to the assault or acts in a punitive manner towards the offender [not only exceeds the limits of his authority, but also may] retraumatize the victim and add to the long-term psychological effects of the abuse. [*Ibid.*]

See also S. Marans and D. Cohen, "Children and Inner-City Violence: Strategies for Intervention," in L. Leavitt and N. Fox, *The Psychological Effects of War and Violence on Children* (Hillsdale, NJ: Lawrence Erlbaum Associates, 1993, pp. 281–301);

S. Marans et al; *The Police-Mental Health Partnership. A Community-Based Response to Urban Violence* (New Haven, CT: Yale University Press, 1995).

3. Reported in J. Goldstein, "Why Foster Care—For Whom for How Long?" in *The Psychoanalytic Study of the Child,* 30:647, 656 (1975).

4. Lewis, I. C., "Humanizing Pediatric Care," *Child Abuse & Neglect,* 7:413–414 (1983).

5. *Ibid.*

6. *Id.* at 417.

7. *Id.* at 415. See also James Robertson, *The Emotional Needs of Infants and Young Children: Implications for Policy and Practice,* ed. Graham Martin (Adelaide, South Australia: Association for the Welfare of Children in Hospital, 1979, p. 15) on hardhearted hospital policies:

> [As] societies become highly developed there is a constant tendency to push parents aside so that there may be no hindrance to the exercise of specialized skills— ignoring the fact that, whatever skills are available, there is a need to include parents within the system so that the family is sustained as a functioning entity.

8. Anna Freud, "Infants Without Families: Reports on the Hampstead Nurseries, 1939–1945," in *The Writings of Anna Freud,* Vol. 3 (New York: International Universities Press, 1973, p. 305).

Reflections

1. See Ann Landers, *New Haven Register,* February 26, 1996, p. C7:

> Dear Ann Landers:
> . . . The father died on the day he was to have sent Elisa [Izquierdo] to safety. The judge then overruled the objections of teachers and relatives and gave Elisa to her drug-addicted mother. According to police, the mother then rejected the scholarship, pulled Elisa out of school, tortured her in attempted exorcisms and finally killed her by smashing her head against a concrete wall. . . .

2. G. Gilmore, "The Storrs Lectures: The Age of Anxiety," 84 *Yale L.J.,* 1022, 1044 (1975).

INDEX

corollaries to, 97–98
Minnesota Supreme Court, 253
Mnookin, Robert H., 250–51, 262, 264, 282, 283
Moore v. City of East Cleveland, 243, 261, 263
Moving, custody rights and, 32–39
Mrazck, Patricia B., 272
Murder, 203–5
  Colwell case, 172–73, 196–97, 286–88, 289
Murphy, Judge, 130–31
Murphy, Tim, 218–19
Murray, Judge, 291–92

N

Nadel, Justice, 65–67, 70–77
Nadelson, C., 273
Natural parents; *see* Biological parents
Naylor, A., 292
Neglect, 6, 92
  Alsager case, 117
  denial of medical care as, 134–36
  difficulty of defining, 93
  emotional, 95, 113, 114, 119
  Infant Shay case, 114
  invocation and, 97
  legal representation and, 140
  physical, 94
  time, child's sense of and, 44–45
  Wambles case, 114, 116
Nemser, In re, 277
Neubauer, P., 266
Neurofibromatosis, case of child with, 135–37
New England Home for Little Wanderers, Petition for, 287
Newton v. Riley, 248
New York State Ass'n for Retarded Children, Inc. v. Rockefeller, 276
Nolan, 278
Nonexperimental medical treatment, 128, 131

O

Object constancy, 266
Olson, Tillie, 282
Oregon Supreme Court, 188–89
Organ transplants, 132–33, 136–38, 277, 278

P

Page, 265
Painter v. Bannister, 246
Palmore v. Sidoti, 272
Parens patriae, 27, 31, 91, 94, 134, 262
Parental autonomy, 81, 89, 90–91, 92, 223
  degrees of intrusion upon, 97
  denial of medical care and, 128, 129, 131, 132, 134
  disposition and, 96
  legal representation and, 139–40, 141, 142, 146
  professionals and, 151–52, 210, 214
Parental prerogatives, 207–14
  in direct and indirect contact with child, 213–14
  in direct contact with child, 207, 209–12
  in indirect contact with child, 207, 212–13
  notes on, 292–95
Parents; *see also* Child-parent relationships; Fathers; Maternal preference; Parental autonomy; Parental prerogatives
  biological; *see* Biological parents
  child placement requested by, 101–2, 264–65
  custody determination requested by, 101–2
  de facto, 256
  "divorced" by child, 144, 280
  failure to designate caretaker for children, 108–9

Parents (*cont.*)
    imprisonment of, 95, 110–11,
        197–99, 270
    legal representation for child re-
        quested by, 139, 141, 142–44,
        146
    psychological; *see* Psychological
        parents
    termination of parental status re-
        quested by, 100–101
Paulsen, M., 274
Peggy (case example), 195–96
Peller, Lilli, 273
Pelner, Dr., 75
People ex rel. Edwards v. Livingston,
    257
People v. Banks, 270
People v. Osslo, 293
Physical neglect, 95
Pierce v. Yerkovich, 27–32, 252
Pikula v. Pikula, 288–89
Plugh, Dane G., 259
Poe v. Ullman, 260
Pogue, In re, 130–31, 275
Police, 295
Posner, Richard A., 265
Poulin, John E., 245
Powell, Judge, 260–61, 278, 288
Power restraint, 98, 107, 263
    definition of concept, 93–94
    emancipation and, 147
Predictions
    long-range; *see* Long-range predic-
        tions
    short-term, 58
Pregnancy, in children, 147
Pressler, Judge, 32
Presumptions
    in favor of biological parents,
        185–88, 191–92
    in favor of fathers, 192, 288
    in favor of mothers, 188–89, 190,
        192, 288

Primary caretakers, 193, 289
    gender issue and, 189, 190–91
    other than biological parents, 187–88
Prince v. Massachusetts, 264
Privacy, 90, 92, 94, 97, 152–54
Probable cause, 95, 137
Professionals, 153–56, 225; *see also*
        specific types
    awareness of limitations in, 154
    boundaries of, 165–83, 284–86
    dual role of, 200–207, 290–91
    parental prerogatives assumed by;
        see Parental prerogatives
    professional versus personal beliefs
        of, 157–61, 283–84
Proffitt v. Evans, 246
Provence, Sally, 244, 261, 275, 292
Psychiatrists, 198
    dual role assumed by, 202–4
    knowledge of law used by, 195
    parental prerogatives assumed by,
        214–15
Psychoanalytic theory, 5–7
Psychological abandonment, 68–69
Psychological parents, 59, 81, 90, 213
    Baby Richard case, 59
    biological parents as, 11
    biological parents versus, 189
    foster parents as, 15, 21, 180
    "Judge Baltimore" on, 82
    long-term caregivers as, 104, 105
    misuse of concept, 185–86
    relationship with child, 11–13
    *Rothman v. Jewish Child Care As-
        sociation,* 67
Psychological tests, 184, 195–96
Psychologists
    judges acting as, 165–69
    knowledge of law used by, 195–96

R

Racial issues, 115, 272
Ragan v. Ragan, 289

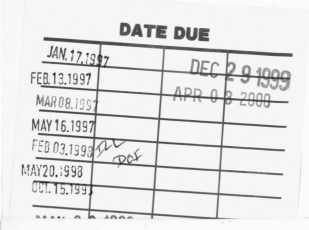